The Religious Other

Interreligious Reflections
Series Editor: Alon Goshen-Gottstein, director, Elijah Interfaith Institute

With the rise of interfaith relations comes the challenge of providing theory and deeper understanding for these relations and the trials that religions face together in an increasingly globalized world. Interreligious Reflections addresses these challenges by offering collaborative volumes that reflect cycles of work undertaken in dialogue between scholars of different religions. The series is dedicated to the academic and theological work of the Elijah Interfaith Institute, a multinational organization dedicated to fostering peace between the world's diverse faith communities through interfaith dialogue, education, research, and dissemination. In carrying out Elijah's principles, these volumes extend beyond the Abrahamic paradigm to include the dharmic traditions. As such, they promise to be a source of continuing inspiration and interest for religious leaders, academics, and community-oriented study groups that seek to deepen their interfaith engagement. All volumes in this series are edited by Elijah's director, Dr. Alon Goshen-Gottstein.

Titles in the Series

The Religious Other

Hostility, Hospitality, and the Hope of Human Flourishing

Edited by Alon Goshen-Gottstein

LEXINGTON BOOKS
Lanham • Boulder • New York • London

Published by Lexington Books
An imprint of The Rowman & Littlefield Publishing Group, Inc.
4501 Forbes Boulevard, Suite 200, Lanham, Maryland 20706
www.rowman.com

16 Carlisle Street, London W1D 3BT, United Kingdom

British Library Cataloguing in Publication Information Available

Library of Congress Cataloging-in-Publication Data

The religious other : hostility, hospitality, and the hope of human flourishing / [edited by] Alon
Goshen-Gottstein.
pages cm
Includes bibliographical references and index.
ISBN 978-0-7391-9256-6 (cloth : alk. paper)—ISBN 978-0-7391-9257-3 (electronic) 1. Religions—
Relations. I. Goshen-Gottstein, Alon, editor.
BL410.R437 2014
201'.5—dc23

                                        2014020793

♾™ The paper used in this publication meets the minimum requirements of American
National Standard for Information Sciences Permanence of Paper for Printed Library
Materials, ANSI/NISO Z39.48-1992.

Printed in the United States of America

Contents

Foreword

Alon Goshen-Gottstein

The chapters presented here have been prepared by an inter-religious think-tank, formed by the Elijah Interfaith Academy, the scholarly arm of the Elijah Interfaith Institute. This was the first research project undertaken by the Academy. Originally conceived as a pilot that would confirm the need for a permanent institution devoted to collaborative interfaith reflections, this first project has in fact been followed by several others. In all these projects, scholars of different world religions came together, in order to collaboratively address issues and challenges that arise from religion's encounter with contemporary society, as well as the present-day encounter between religions themselves. The present publication seeks to share with the public at large the work first presented to a gathering of world religious leaders in Seville, 2003. The chapters were prepared as background materials for the first meeting of the Elijah Board of World Religious Leaders. Bringing religious leaders into conversation against the background of well-prepared scholarly materials has proven a unique strength and one of the distinguishing features of the work of the Elijah Interfaith Institute. A series of successful initiatives has followed the one featured in this volume. It is with great pride that this first research project is being shared with the public at large as the first publication of Elijah's new series at Lexington Books, *Interreligious Reflections*.

Eight scholars participated in the first think-tank, representing five religions and five countries. Buddhism was represented through Richard Hayes, then Professor of Buddhism at McGill University and currently at the University of New Mexico; Christianity by Rt. Reverend Stephen Sykes, formerly Bishop of Ely in the Church of England and later principal of St. John's college at Durham University; Hinduism by Ashok Vohra, formerly Dean of Philosophy at the University of New Delhi; Islam by Vincent and Rkia

Cornell, then of the King Fahd Center for Middle Eastern Studies at the University of Arkansas and now at Emory University; Judaism by Alon Goshen-Gottstein of the Elijah Interfaith Institute and by Barry Levy, Dean of the Faculty of Religious Studies at McGill University.

The chapters of the think tank have been supplemented by several contributions, prepared for the present publication. Lord Jonathan Sacks, Chief Rabbi of the United Hebrew Congregations of Britain and the Commonwealth, composed biblical reflections on the theme of our conference. While his does not constitute a response to my presentation of a Jewish position, it does address the subject matter directly and indicates the kind of homiletical, educational, and reflective work that must be undertaken in order to overcome xenophobia. Accordingly, it closes our volume, with its educational outreach. Dharma Master Hsin Tao, Founder of Taipei's Museum of World Religions, authored a response to Richard Hayes's chapter. Hayes focused primarily on the Theravada tradition and the Dharma Master's response balances that perspective by offering a Mahayana view of the issues under discussion. Both have been consolidated into one chapter. Similarly, Ashok Vohra's chapter presented Hinduism in its philosophical ideal and did not engage some of the social realities that many contemporary Hindu thinkers struggle with. In that sense, it was also less self-critical than the chapters on Judaism, Christianity, and Islam. This led us to invite a second Hindu voice, representing another Hindu tradition and another scholarly perspective, to respond to Vohra's chapter. The response by Deepak Sarma of Case Western Reserve University has been integrated into the chapter on Hinduism.

The theme of the religious attitude to the other was chosen as a gateway to future conversations and research to be carried out in the framework of the Elijah Interfaith Academy. Xenophobia is a contemporary global problem of enormous proportions. The choice of this topic enabled us to address both a contemporary social ill and some issues that are fundamental to the very project of inter-religious dialogue and inter-religious collaboration. We hoped that reflection on this issue would contribute to improving relations among peoples and faith communities and simultaneously facilitate conversation and suggest subjects for continuing reflection at the Interfaith Academy. Later projects of the Interfaith Academy have indeed pursued some of the seeds planted through this first project.

The chapters prepared for the Seville meeting of world religious leaders were received with great enthusiasm. Regrettably, we did not try to capture the substance of the discussions in Seville and therefore are unable to report on the reception of the chapters and on complementary perspectives that may have emerged in the discussions. Elijah leaders did, however, issue a statement, based on their deliberations in Seville. The statement echoes the fundamental convictions suggested by the think tank and may be viewed on Elijah's website (www.elijah-interfaith.org).

The only way to characterize the involvement of everyone affiliated with the present project is as a labor of love. All scholars who joined the project lead extremely full professional and scholarly lives. Undertaking one more project was for all of them an expression of faith in the importance of this project and in the work of the Elijah Interfaith Academy. I acknowledge with profound gratitude the bonds of friendship, hospitality and love that have been formed through this process, along with genuine appreciation for the thoughtfulness and creativity that has taken shape through these chapters.

The contribution and hospitality extended to us by partner organizations and supporting bodies is what made this project possible. This is the moment to offer particular thanks to those institutions that facilitated the work of our group. The King Fahd Center at the University of Arkansas hosted the initial meeting of our think-tank in May 2002. The University of Durham hosted our meeting in March 2003. McGill University provided support along the way. Special personal thanks are due to Bishop Frank Griswold, then presiding Bishop of the Episcopal Church, who generously intervened in a moment of financial crisis, allowing our work to continue. Finally, we received a grant from the Carnegie Corporation to enable the think-tank to complete and publish its work and to present it at the Seville meeting. I am personally grateful to Vartan Gregorian, President of the Carnegie Corporation, for his understanding, support, and encouragement. His personal warmth means no less to me than the concrete assistance he has generously made available to our project.

Please allow me a moment to take stock of the achievements of our think-tank and to acknowledge areas that require future strengthening. Our activities have demonstrated the necessity and the viability of collaborative group work in which scholars from different religions come together to work on a common project. Our first attempt at working as a group revealed great disparity of perspective, methodology, and conceptualization. Our group process involved listening to each other, which in turn led to a clearer definition of the project, its theme, and the ways to approach it. We benefited from our critiques of each other's chapters and from the challenges posed by the different perspectives that each of us brought to the discussion. These are evident in the chapters, which individually and collectively address insights, queries, and objections that arose in the group discussions. Most significantly, we benefited from a reconsideration of each of the topics of our conversation, when viewed through the eyes of the other. Seeing the message of our traditions refracted through the eyes of the other catalyzed our own maturation and brought us to fuller self-awareness of our traditions and their significance. Our first attempt at finding common ground yielded a redefinition of our topic that allowed our chapters to start resonating with each other to greater and greater degrees. Opportunity to refine our work further could have yielded chapters that cohere and resonate with each other even more. Accordingly, the chapters are presented as hopeful and promising signs for future work, rather than as the final word on the topics under discussion. Disparities that still exist in conceptualization and in presentation should thus be taken as invitations to continuing study and dialogue. As we have moved from one project to the next over years of work at the Elijah Interfaith Academy, we have, in fact, learned how to work increasingly as an interreligious team, resonating ever more closely with each other.

Finally, I would like to offer my gratitude on an individual basis to the people who have made the present collection of chapters possible. First and foremost, I wish to once again thank the scholars whose labor of love we share herewith, as well as all those who partook of our deliberations, in person or long-distance. Special thanks go to Barry Levy, who accompanied this project from the very outset, helping shape it, conceptualize it, and support it in ways that are too numerous to specify. Barry also undertook the initial editing of this collection of chapters. Peta Pellach Jones, Director of Educational Activities at Elijah, completed the task of giving these chapters their present and final form. I am grateful for her continuing partnership. Maria Reis Habito was instrumental in moving the project along at key points. The manuscript was prepared for publication by Natalee Cohen, whose dedication and expertise seem to have no end. Finally, I am grateful to our partners at Lexington Books for providing Elijah with a platform through which to reach a broader public. This is the first volume in a series planned with Lexington Books, under the title *Interreligious Reflections*. May it be a good beginning and may all those who engage in the work of this series be inspired and grow as they share in our reflections, seeking to make the wisdom of our religious traditions speak to today's reality.

Chapter One

Overview

Themes and Problematics

Alon Goshen-Gottstein

The sequence in which chapters created in an interreligious think-tank are presented is always a touchy issue, as we seek to avoid the dominance of one tradition over another. The sequence that follows is intended to present a thematic unfoldment that allows us to best grasp the collective wisdom of this collection of chapters. Beginning with the so-called "Abrahamic faiths," presented in the sequence of their historical appearance, it moves on to the traditions of Hinduism and Buddhism. This introductory chapter will present the key ideas that emerge from the chapters in this collection; comparative reflections will be offered in the concluding chapter.

JUDAISM

"Judaism: The Battle for Survival, the Struggle for Compassion" struggles to locate the appropriate perspective from which to consider the themes of hostility, hospitality, and the hope of human flourishing as these are refracted through millennia of Jewish experience and expression. Hostility and hospitality are both by-products of the notion of an "other" and of the presence of an "other" in our midst. Awareness of self and otherness is fundamental to Israel's identity and thus constitutive of Jewish self-definition. Therefore an exploration of the attitude to the other is perforce an attempt to define the core of Judaism and to assess its various historical manifestations, its ultimate hopes, and its continued meaning and relevance. As is the case for all chapters, this implies a self-critical attitude toward tradition, or certain of its historical manifestations, and an attempt to offer a positive construction of

1

Judaism, emphasizing its continuing vision of hope for Israel and for the world.

One cannot approach the problem of the attitude to the other from a Jewish perspective without first taking stock of a fundamental issue involving the very definition of Judaism. Judaism is at one and the same time a religion, with a religious world view, a set of practices, and a universal message and way of life of one particular people. By its very definition, it is founded upon a fundamental duality, perhaps even tension, between an ethnic component—involving nationhood, territoriality, and a variety of expressions of particularity—and a religious component with universal ramifications that far transcend the boundaries of the original ethnic carriers of Judaism's vision. From the ethnic perspective, otherness is fundamental to the reality of Judaism that is constituted by the very creation of an "us" (Israel), in contradistinction to the rest of humanity, who thereby become an other. Issues of appropriate behavior and proper treatment of the other figure heavily in this perspective.

At the same time, Judaism is also a religious world view that is centered not only upon the constitution of one particular relationship with God, but also upon an understanding of the ultimate reality and person of God. This understanding is perforce relevant not only to Israel but to all of humanity. It includes not only an understanding of God, but also of the fullness of human potentiality, as this is ultimately achieved in relationship with God.

The relationship between these two components has been far from simple in the history of Judaism. In part, this is due to the natural human limitation of transcending one's immediate social group and its concerns. The human perspective tends naturally to narrow in on personal and group concerns and often fails to rise to the heights of a spiritual vision to which it aspires in its greatest depths. But something more has been at play in the history of the Jewish attitude to the other than the battle against natural human egoism and group interest. The evolution and expression of Judaism—the religion of the people of Israel—has been closely intertwined with the changes and vicissitudes in the life of the historical people of Israel. Israel's life has known different periods: exile, security in homeland, additional exile, persecution, attempts at annihilation, and more. Because Judaism is the religious expression of a particular people, it is heavily marked by that people's formative historical experience: the struggle for survival. For over two millennia the people of Israel have experienced the profound insecurity of life, not only as part of the universal existential human condition, but on account of the particular historical circumstances that are unique to them and that give expression to a mainly negative historical experience. Thus, any attempt to assess Judaism's attitude to the other must take into account Israel's painful historical reality as the context in which many of its attitudes were formed and much of its reflection concerning the other was formulated.

The first chapter in this collection is an attempt to strike a balance between these two perspectives. In so doing, it is cognizant of the fact that Judaism is, in some sense, in crisis. The relationship between the ethnic and the religious components, as lived in contemporary Judaism, fails to strike the appropriate balance between the two components. The ethnic-national component has to a large extent eclipsed the spiritual-religious one, or, in some cases, the reverse. Concomitantly, the scars from a long history of suffering have led to a kind of introversion that is negative and that may prevent Israel from fulfilling its broader spiritual mission to humanity. The chapter's thesis is thus that the balance between these two components of Judaism needs to be redressed. A kind of spiritual revival is necessary, placing God and the spiritual dimension at the center, in order for Judaism to rise to the ultimate heights defined by its own vision and self-understanding. A movement of return to its higher spiritual calling is also the key to more balanced attitudes to the other than those formed under the tribulations of Israel's history.

The tension between Israel's particular history and the broader perspective through which it reflects on the world is also expressed in the tension between creation and election or covenant. Both are formative moments in religious history and in Israel's self-understanding. The purpose of Israel's particularity must be understood in relation to the broader purpose of creation, a fact that is often overlooked in reflecting on the purpose of Israel's calling. Creation is also a significant moment in the shaping of the attitude to the other. The notion of the image of God, in which man was created, is central to a Jewish understanding of the human person, and hence of the other.

Nevertheless, this concept has not played as central a role in the shaping of attitudes to the other as might be imagined, perhaps precisely because it does not consider the "other" in his or her "otherness," but emphasizes the commonality of humanity.

It is significant that the most fundamental means of framing an attitude to the other is not divorced from historical memory. Repeatedly, the Torah offers admonitions of how one ought to treat the *ger*, foreigner, alien, sojourner. Repeatedly it implores us to respect, treat with kindness, and offer identical rights and obligations in relation to the law, but most of all to love him. This surprising command to love the other is grounded in the transformed memory of our exile in Egypt. As former slaves, we are expected to show sensitivity and understanding to the human condition of the *ger*. The historical memory of a pained exile is thus transformed into a commandment of justice and love. It is conceivable that the Torah is going against human nature in requiring us to react in this way toward the *ger*. Its repeated admonitions indicate how central this commandment is, and how much of Israelite virtue revolves around its fulfillment.

Because the history of the people extends beyond the liberation from Egyptian bondage and the attainment of freedom in the land, the powers of history and the ways it conditions human nature have time and again impacted upon Jewish attitudes to the other. From the perspective of a continued exile, Israel could no longer be the host extending hospitality unto others.

In a millennia-long struggle for survival against one oppressing force after another, some of the tenderness of heart that the Torah sought to cultivate was lost. The Jewish psyche has understandably become suspicious and xenophobic. Concern for survival still operates as the most central driving force in the life of the people of Israel and shapes most parts of Jewish reality, material as well as spiritual. Judaism thus possesses a profound teaching of hospitality that it has not been able to implement in the course of a bitter history.

The founding of the State of Israel has further exacerbated the situation. As recent studies indicate, the Israeli people maintain deeply ingrained xenophobic attitudes, though these change in relation to who the outsider, the other, is. Clearly, the marks of the Israeli-Arab conflict are visible here, with the Arabs constituting the group towards which the greatest degree of xenophobia applies. Furthermore, attitudes to the other, in particular the Arab, serve not only real or perceived security needs, but also the needs of identity formation. Significant aspects of Israeli collective identity are formed in contradistinction to and through tension with the otherness of surrounding societies.

If Judaism's vices are a product of history and human reaction to this history, its hope lies in the rediscovery of its spiritual resources, and above all of God. It is only by bringing God to the center of the institutions and life of the people and its religion that Judaism can retrieve a lost sense of purpose and the hallmark of its identity and particularity. This is also how the purpose of its calling and its continued relevance to the world can be best realized. Alongside the narrower legal perspective for the hope of human flourishing is found a broader more spiritual perspective. The narrower perspective sees Judaism's message as the dissemination of a basic code of morality, the Noachide commandments. The broader perspective sees God and His knowledge as Israel's ultimate contribution to humanity. Only by placing God at the center of religious structures and concepts can Judaism rise to the heights of its calling.

Following this historical analysis of the tensions that constitute Judaism, its self-understanding and its attitude to the other, the latter part of the chapter revisits many of the topics raised in the earlier part by attempting a new positive formulation of the purpose of Israel's calling and of its attitude to the other. Following the teachings of Rabbi Nachman of Breslav, the concept of compassion is explored through a series of associations, particularly with *da'at*, knowledge and consciousness. Judaism's task is to spread compassion, which is born of the knowledge of God. Compassion permits making space for the other. It also allows us to shift the consideration of religion and its workings from the intellectual and ideological realm to the fields of morality and being. The Torah's instructions to the *ger* are thus seen as the ultimate form of instruction to compassion. A theory of hospitality grounded in the notion of compassion is not blind to the threat of survival; it places limits on and directs the application of compassion in such a way as to not undermine survival. All of this leads to a great theological and spiritual challenge: Is it possible to have compassion upon one's enemies? Herein lies the ultimate challenge to a successful bridging of the ethnic and the religious, the historical and the spiritual. The challenge of compassion articulated in the latter part of the chapter may be one way of conceptualizing how such growth, necessarily based in a living recognition of God, may take shape.

CHRISTIANITY

Stephen Sykes's "Making Room for the Other: Hostility and Hospitality from a Christian Perspective" also begins with the constitutive tension between different moments—creation and salvation. The former appeals to the common creation in the image of God; the latter, to the rescue and restoration of humanity following its fall through the atonement brought about by Christ.

Unlike the tension between the universality of creation and the specificity of election characteristic of Judaism, the redeeming work of Christ reconciles the entire world to Christ. This poses a fundamental problem: What is the origin of hostility? In the light of Christian teaching, there is no room for hostility, yet Christian history has evidenced much of it. This problem provides the backbone for Sykes's challenging and self-critical analysis of the theological roots of intolerance and hostility in the history of Christianity. The chapter engages Christian history and theology in an open and daring way, exposing potential pitfalls of Christian thought. The assumption of this chapter is that only through proper identification of the theological faults or pitfalls contained in theology can we advance beyond past historical failures. Such advancement is necessary not only for the correction of past wrongdoing, but in order to allow Christianity to manifest its ultimate message, thereby offering the hope it holds for human flourishing.

Sykes's presentation has a dual focus: on the one hand, exposing the theological weaknesses that have led to past hostility, and, on the other, the construction of a new theory of hospitality grounded in a Christian context. Such hospitality is more than hospitality to individuals or collectives. It is hospitality to ideas—hospitality to the other in the fullest sense. Sykes's presentation is thus heavily theological, drawing primarily on New Testament texts, as these are studied both for the weaknesses, made manifest in the history of their interpretation, and for the positive constructive suggestions contained in them.

Sykes suggests that hostility is more than an expression of unreformed Christian behavior; it is an unfortunate by-product of essential Christian categories. The very distinction between old and new, untransformed and transformed behavior, as these identify respectively the non-Christian and Christian communities, sows the seeds for separation by suggesting a division not only between different actions, but between different people. This may give birth to a theologically based hostility. Theological language also resorts to metaphors that, taken out of context, may harbor hostility. Thus battle metaphors are deployed by Christian faith to signify the seriousness of the struggle with evil. The radicality of battle language may be deployed against people who are thought to constitute a threat to holiness. Historically, these could include groups and races whose customs were unfamiliar or misunderstood.

Thus, the notion might develop that it is a Christian duty to oppose the people who practice alternative forms of life, considered immoral, unholy, or undesirable. When the personification of evil coincides with political and social power, this can lead to the oppression or destruction of the other. In this context it should be noted that use of the concept "image of God" also can have unwanted effects in relation to the other. The concept did not guarantee the human dignity of the other. Biblical interpretation of such passages as the curse of Ham further strengthened the view that not all of humanity partook of the divine image, which in turn could support injustice, mistreatment and hostility.

Sykes's discussion of the concept of hospitality struggles with the fundamental problem of the relevance of the teaching of Christian hospitality to the non-Christian. This problem has several dimensions. A key passage in the discussion is 1 Corinthians, chapter 15, where it is stated that Christ died for us. But what does Paul mean by "us"? In saying that "as all die in Adam, so all will be made alive in Christ," does Paul suggest a broad universal understanding of the relevance of Christ's resurrection? Whether the consequences of Christ's resurrection are universal or limited to the community of believers is debated among Christian interpreters. Following this, one may recognize both more universalistic and more sectarian tendencies in Christian thought. This is important for the issue of xenophobia. If one is a stranger to the significance of Christ, this could, under certain circumstances, under the sectarian tendency, lead to segregation, fear or outright hostility, and persecution. This has been particularly vicious in relation to the Jewish people, coupled with charges of deicide.

The universalistic option provides a further possibility for how Christ is significant to an eradication of hostility. Christ's human nature, which he shares in common with all of humanity, opens the door to a unifying vision in which all humans are united in Christ. Thus, "there is no longer Jew or Greek, there is no longer slave or free, there is no longer male or female" (Galatians 3). A universal reconciliation of any reality estranged from God is the consequence of the coming of God into human life.

In struggling to come to terms with these universalistic and sectarian tendencies within Christianity, Sykes opts for a historical understanding of how the sectarian tendency was formed in the struggles of nascent Christianity that followed the expulsion of Christians from the synagogues. Thus, the sectarian tendencies are a means of identity-building. Despite Jesus's teaching of love of the enemy, the marks of such historical opposition between Christians and others have given and continue to give rise to exclusionary politics of hatred. This element of tradition must be kept in check by other elements of the tradition that offset it. If it has any justification, it is similar in kind to that discussed in the chapter on Judaism, namely resistance against attempts at annihilation and the quest for the community's survival. Nothing obliges any contemporary Christian community to view every form of opposition in this manner. A call for wisdom is issued, to discern what kinds of opposition are truly threatening to the community's survival, justifying, so to speak, the appeal to tradition's more violent face.

Christian resources for hospitality may be classified as theological or more specifically as Christological, and ethical. Alongside the notions suggested above, Sykes locates an ethical teaching of hospitality in the writings of the New Testament; to take one typical text, "Do not neglect to show hospitality to strangers, for by doing that some have entertained angels without knowing it" (Hebrews 13:2). While such an exhortation is directed to a group of believers, it is set within a universal context. The Christian tradition of hospitality is a direct outgrowth of the practice of hospitality that existed in ancient Israel. The uniqueness of the attitude of hospitality, described in my article in relation to the *ger*, may have filtered into Christian practice because many early Christians experienced this care as gentiles and strangers to God's people. Moreover, Jesus's ministry had hospitality at its core. He makes contact with Samaritans, outcasts, sinners, lepers, and unclean and foreign women. Following these precedents, we find hospitality as a fundamental practice for early Christians. Loving and welcoming the stranger is set side by side with the love of one's Christian family members. It is further important to note that hospitality is practiced not in isolation but in the context of a community that provides the strength and resources to carry its inherent burdens. Along with the notion of grace, these are important aids in the Christian realization of hospitality.

Throughout his chapter, Sykes has attempted to point not only to ways in which Christian theological understanding must be circumscribed and nuanced to eradicate hostility, but also to the ways in which the Christian teaching of hospitality is relevant to and can be extended beyond the specific Christian community. In the final part of the chapter, he returns to the question of whether the Christian tradition may be generalizable. It is here that the balance of factors raised in his presentation comes together: universal versus sectarian tendency, limiting the oppositional trend in Christianity to particular moments of historical conflict, and the quest for locating a broader message of hospitality that is universally valid. Because he is aware of the multiple voices of tradition and their different and conflicting tendencies, Sykes cannot simply opt for one particular option within the tradition. But the thrust of his argument clearly indicates a strong desire to offer hospitality as a broad category, whose significance extends well beyond the confines of the Christian community. It therefore leads him to the affirmation that what qualifies a person to Christian compassion and hospitality is her humanity, understood in light of the Christian teaching spelled out above.

The final part of Sykes's chapter is devoted to an exploration of the relevance of the concept of hospitality to ideas, as distinct from people. Here Sykes introduces the metaphor of "making space" for an idea. Human learning is only possible on the assumption that we carry with us a reservoir of unexplored ideas. Many remain dormant; some are revived by new encounters. Thus, room may be made for a new idea, which is so far unassimilated to the larger schemes through which we think. Sykes affirms that the idea of "making space" for an idea from a religion whose schema we do not hold is both possible and desirable. Such "making space" is a form of hospitality, a taking seriously of the Other as "other," an acceptance of the Other on his own terms, without assimilating him to an existing rejection or caricature.

ISLAM

Vincent Cornell's chapter "Islam: Epistemological Crisis, Theological Hostility, and the Problem of Difference" suggests the unique ways in which the problem of xenophobia is relevant to Islam in general and to the relationship of Islam and world religions, on the one hand, and the West, on the other. Islam's problem is not cultural xenophobia. As a world religion that has a sweeping vision of how different cultural differences can be maintained within the broader umbrella of a unifying religious system, Islam is comfortable with making space for the cultural Other. Hospitality, a classical virtue of Arab society, has a profound impact upon the practices of Islam. Therefore, Islam's problem is not that of the cultural Other. Rather, it is profoundly ill at ease with the theological Other. Cornell's chapter is therefore an exploration of the range of possibilities contained in Islam for a pluralistic world view that accepts the legitimacy of other religions. Hostility in this context is essentially a theological or ideological hostility that does not recognize the religious Other as fully legitimate.

Events of the early twenty-first century have demonstrated the far-reaching concrete hostility to which such theological hostility can give rise. Cornell's chapter is thus concerned primarily with the tension between theological hostility and hospitality. Underlying this concern is the realization that Islam is sitting on a time bomb that may explode to its own detriment and that of the world at large. Addressing the profound theological and ideological issues that shape most of contemporary Islam and recovering from within Islam the theological resources that will address Islam's present crisis are necessary precursors to fulfilling a view of human flourishing that allows all societies to coexist in peace.

Underlying Cornell's presentation is an acute sense of crisis that plagues contemporary Islam, of which the violent face of theologically hostile Islam is an expression. In order to tackle this crisis, one must understand its historical and theological roots. One must distinguish between particular historical forms of Islam, including the form of Islam that has come to dominate large parts of the contemporary Muslim world, on the one hand, and, on the other, the Islam that contains multiple possibilities for actualizing the Islamic reality—many of which were implemented in earlier historical periods, now mostly obliterated from collective Muslim memory. Cornell's insight offers a distinction between Islam, with a capital "I," expressing the spiritual ideal, contained in scripture—if we will, in God's mind—and the variety of historical islams (now lower-case), each of which is in some way historically contingent and imperfect. Cornell's thesis is a finely balanced statement. Based on historical precedent and the necessary understanding of the ideal (uppercase) Islam, it simultaneously offers a penetrating critique of Islam's present shape and shows how, through an insider's way of constructing and presenting Islam, it can be accepting of and hospitable toward other religious realities. Cornell therefore has first introduced the reader to the current Islamic crisis and to the ways in which large parts of contemporary Islamic reality distort the religion on which their spiritual lives are based. Cornell shares with the reader the pain he feels from the fact that significant parts of the historical Islamic spiritual reality have all but ceased to exist. These include open and creative hermeneutics and Scriptural interpretation and the pursuit of philosophy, accompanied by a loss of spirituality and the marginalization of Sufism. Instead, Islam has become for so many a program of social reformation, attempting to impose a uniform vision of society and a monolithic understanding of Islam upon Islamic society and ultimately upon the world. In so doing, Islam has in fact become an ideology rather than a religion. Instead of beginning with the transformation of the human person, through her relationship with God, Islam has become a program for the reshaping of society. Islam is thus measured in terms of power and political dominance.

All this is achieved at the heavy price of the thinning down of the texture of Islamic reasoning and spirituality. The nuances of hermeneutics and the historical riches of spirituality are sacrificed and lost while a monolithic, monochromatic, single-textured Islamic reality is constructed. While such construction has come to dominate much of contemporary Sunni Islam, where it is presented as the true, ideal, or pure Islam, Cornell suggests it is in fact a novelty itself, merely one construct and as such both historically contingent and fallible.

Exposing the historical contingency of this construct of Islam allows Cornell to point the way to the retrieval of earlier historical constructions of Islam that contain theological and hermeneutical riches that offer better ways to deal with the challenge of diffusing the bomb of hostility upon which it sits. Cornell performs the task of the "Muslim intellectual to look critically at Islamic history and to formulate a theology and moral philosophy that has its roots in the classical intellectual tradition of Islam rather than in a utopian golden age or in a modern ideological construct."

He begins his retrieval of Islamic riches by juxtaposing contemporary simplistic Islamic self-understanding with the classical recognition of Islam's sophisticated complexity. Such complexity begins with the hermeneutical process and the recognition of the multiple layers of Scripture and its interpretation. Cornell introduces Al Ghazali's five levels of Scriptural understanding as an illustration of such complexity and as a gateway to approaching classical Islamic texts in ways that appropriate contemporary needs. Based on Al Ghazali's principles, hermeneutical space is opened up for a variety of alternative interpretations, thereby undermining attempts to impose any monolithic and simplistic understanding of Islam. Cornell illustrates the usefulness of Al Ghazali's rules through Sufi interpretation. Abd al-Karim Al Jili, an important Sufi figure of the fifteenth century, may be understood to be applying these rules to specific Qur'anic verses when he develops a theory of the existence of all religions as expressions of God's will. While Islam is God's quintessential religion, all religions are valid, when considered from the perspective of God's will, as expressed in the Qur'an. A significant contribution to hermeneutics is made when, following Sufi precedent, it is undertaken with God on its horizon.

Cornell continues his exposition by juxtaposing two distinct commands of God, each carrying its own moral imperative. The one is God's creative command, the other is the command of obligation. The former is the perspective through which human beings share natural duties and responsibilities that result from the covenant contracted between God and humanity before the creation of Adam. The latter is the more specifically Muslim perspective, from which practical obligations arise. The former leads to the recognition of a universal commonality, which in turn leads to the acceptance of the other. The latter emphasizes the particularly Muslim obligations and leads to issues of difference and discrimination. From a moral and theological perspective, both commands must be balanced. The problem for so much of contemporary Islam is the almost exclusive privileging of the command of obligation, at the expense of God's creative command. But it is God's creative command that reminds us of the ultimate commonality of humanity. Objectifying the "other," to which the second perspective might lead, means to forget the common basis of all of humanity. It is only by striking the appropriate balance between these two commands that Islamic perspective on the other can open up to hospitality and advance beyond present hostility.

This balance is essential, because fundamental rights are grounded in God's creative command. These include the duty of mutual respect, the right of human dignity, the right to life, and the right of free choice. Furthermore, it is only by balancing the two divine commands that the ideal balance between justice and mercy can be established, with mercy being a derivative of the creative command. The appropriate understanding of the relationship between the two commands also involves the proper understanding of the relationship between moral duties and legal requirements. Cornell establishes the priority of the former, grounding it in the creative command. This moral priority allows him to allocate to the creative command its proper place in the broader economy of commands and thereby to redress prevailing imbalances. Only through such prioritizing can an Islamic perspective transcend the narrow constraints of individual experiences or those of particular societies.

Finally, Cornell appeals to the Qur'anic concept of the human being as vicegerent (*khalifa*) of God on earth. Taking this concept seriously implies taking into account the priority of the creative command and of moral duties that precede the particularities of religious obligations. Furthermore, it implies taking seriously the multi-dimensionality of humanity's existence, mirroring as it does the multi-dimensionality of God's creation and will. By his very nature the human person is a bridge builder, and such bridge building between conceptual worlds extends to the differences between diverse religious systems as well.

Ultimately, Cornell's construct brings to the fore the centrality of God's will. Seen from the perspective of the balance between both commands, it suggests a broader understanding of God's will, through which space is made for the other, grounded in God's very will that the Other, including the Other's alternative religious path, should exist. The will of God is not unidimensional. Following Ibn Arabi, we must be reminded that unless we adopt a multi-dimensional perspective, in which individual obligations are viewed in the context of the creativity of God's will, we risk the gravest of sins— namely the association of God and another being's, in this case, our own limited, narrow and egoistic understanding of God's will and design. In this way, our own egos are the ultimate cause of all theological hostility, making us lose sight of the ultimate point of our existence.

HINDUISM

Ashok Vohra's "Metaphysical Unity, Phenomenological Diversity, and the Approach to the Other: An Advaita Vedanta Position" tackles the very notion of other from an essentially philosophical perspective. His thesis is disarmingly simple: there is no room for a theory of the Other in Hinduism. Of course, Hindus have for generations recognized the religious differences between themselves and people of other lands or other religions. Yet, Vohra claims, this does not amount to the creation of a theoretical "other" but merely a practical other, an other *de facto* but not *de jure*. The concept of "the other" cannot be elevated to a formative status in a Hindu context, as many contemporary philosophers attempt to do, because all "otherness" is considered by the Hindu to be merely phenomenological. There is no metaphysical basis for a notion of the Other. The underlying metaphysical concept is that of unity of all life. All is Brahman, absolute being; all differences are thus contingent, phenomenological, possibly illusionary. Vohra introduces the reader to the notion of the human person, according to the Upanishads. The human person is ultimately that which is beyond sensate reality. While sensate reality divides people, based on considerations of class, race, and the like, the ultimate reality unites people, who are all manifestation of one ultimate metaphysical reality.

The implications of this world view to the theme of xenophobia are obvious. If there is no "other," there can be no xenophobia; there can be no hostility. All forms of hostility are ultimately expressions of a philosophical error, a wrong perception of reality. Clearly, on the phenomenological level hostility exists, but it is unfounded, the child of ignorance. Therefore, it is not religious teaching that needs to be modified in order to eradicate hostility but rather ignorance of the truth of religious teaching. Vohra does not tell the reader how violence and hostility actually come about. We do not know whether they are purely the effects of personal imperfections—ego, greed, and so on—or whether improper religious instruction plays some role in it. It would seem the fault lies exclusively with the human person, not with the teachings of religion. Therefore, the means for correction lie not in the transformation of religion, but in the transformation of the person. Hostility is a function of ignorance, and it is combated by combating ignorance. Thus, teaching and spiritual understanding are the ultimate weapons in the battle against hostility.

Vohra goes further to demonstrate that not only is hostility metaphysically unfounded, but hospitality is the natural state of the Hindu mentality, founded as it is upon a recognition of the metaphysical unity of all life. This point is made in two ways. The first is through examining the concept of *mleccha*, the other, the foreigner. This concept would seem to be the Hindu equivalent of our concept of "the other," and Vohra therefore analyzes it through the dual perspectives of hostility and hospitality. He finds no room for hostility toward the *mleccha*; at worst the attitude toward him is characterized by lack of interest. Such lack of interest will be explained in light of the phenomenological concerns of "religion on the ground" and its attempt to preserve its identity, integrity and purity. But unlike other cultures, these concerns will not lead to an active combat with the outsider. One assumes the basis for this is the underlying metaphysical unity, characteristic of the Hindu world view, presented by Vohra. Furthermore, he suggests that, in many ways, the *mleccha* is assimilated into prevailing culture. Laws and norms concerning the *mleccha* in many ways resemble those relating to the Hindu. Because the *mleccha* is assimilated unto Hindu culture, the classical Hindu other is either uninteresting or less of an outsider than originally imagined. Either way, the *mleccha* provides a very weak sense of "otherness," ultimately tempered by the recognition of metaphysical unity.

Hindu mentality is still more profoundly hospitable. Thanks to Hinduism's recognition of ultimate metaphysical unity, it teaches something profoundly hospitable that allows it to accept all religious forms as valid and as pointing to the same ultimate reality. In Vohra's description, Hinduism is far less interested in the particulars of life style, action, faith, and worship, than the three Abrahamic religions already discussed. Through a study of the history of the term "Hindu," Vohra arrives at the conclusion that the lack of a name for the religion suggests its inclusivity. It cannot be named because it cannot be narrowed down by juxtaposition with anything else. Because it is all-inclusive, it contains all forms and hence escapes definition and naming. While historically the term "Hindu" was coined by real historical religious others (Muslims), the self-application of the term intends to convey a broad inclusiveness that escapes definition. Such inclusiveness is a fundamental trait of the Hindu faith. Once again, we may recognize such inclusiveness as founded upon the ultimate metaphysical unity taught by Hinduism, a unity not threatened by the existence of others. Rather, it encompasses and contains them, making them a part of itself. Hindu writings even contain attempts to incorporate both Jesus and Mohammad in Hindu narrative and thus in the framework of the Hindu imagination.

Working from these metaphysical premises, it is easy for Vohra to point out how Hinduism is not only hospitable to the individual or the cultural and ethnic other, as he does with regard to the *mleccha*s, but how it also accommodates the religious and theological other. Thus a theory of the relations of Hinduism to other religions emerges. This theory is illustrated through the teachings of several of the great spiritual teachers of modern India—Ramakrishna, Vivekananda, Gandhi, and Radhakrishnan. It recognizes the equal validity of all religions and encourages a particular kind of borrowing and sharing of the finest of spiritual ideals found within the religions. Significantly, the goal is not one of conversion. Vohra takes great care to explain that conversion is impossible in Hinduism; one cannot convert to Hinduism. Perhaps, I might add, this is so because Hinduism, as presented by Vohra, is less of a specific religious path than it is a total orientation. Such orientation may positively influence other religious understandings, but it does not invite others to join its own confines. What India's modern teachers have taught is a fundamental respect for other religions and an openness to the sharing and transfer of the finest spiritual ideals between them.

Vohra presents Hinduism from the viewpoint of its ideal philosophical articulation. In so doing, he relies on a view of Hinduism that draws from the philosophical teachings of the eighth-century teacher Sankara and of the philosophical school associated with him, Advaita Vedanta. This school is often the public face of Hinduism, especially in the West. It is, however, only one of several philosophical schools. Deepak Sarma's response to Vohra is formulated from the perspective of one of the competing schools, founded by the thirteenth-century Madhvacarya. If Vohra's perspective highlights idealism, thereby rejecting alterity, Sarma tackles the topic from a realist perspective, suggesting that alterity is deeply rooted within Hindu thought. Not only is alterity recognized as normative within the discourse of competing philosophical systems, it also provides the backbone for intellectual activity that is relevant still today. Within the history of Indian philosophical study, debate occupies a place of great importance. Debate is a form of recognizing otherness and of channeling its potentially violent aspects in a more positive direction. Sarma recommends this culture of debate as particularly relevant for the contemporary interreligious context, wherein it may address differences constructively, rather than ignoring or downplaying them, in light of philosophical idealism. Finally, Sarma points out how contemporary Hindu identity politics are anything but the ideal recognition of otherness as sameness. In fact, much of contemporary Hindu identity, as developed by Hindu nationalists, is constructed in opposition to other religious groups, thereby making identity construction potentially (and often more than just potentially) violent. Recognizing alterity thus emerges as a more useful foundation for the construction of a modern society than its denial, based on ultimate metaphysical considerations.

BUDDHISM

Richard Hayes's chapter provides another perspective on our theme from a non-Abrahamic angle. Like Vohra, and unlike the three Abrahamic chapters, Hayes does not engage in a critique or a reconstruction of the tradition. Yet, his presentation of Buddhism is replete with novel suggestions and insights, touching on the relevance of Buddhism today, in particular to non-Buddhists, and on the engagement in inter-religious dialogue from a Buddhist perspective.

The Buddhist perspective sees the root of all hostility in an inappropriate understanding that must be corrected through discipline of the mind. The inappropriate perspective relates to the psychological processes that are characteristic of Buddhism. The personal, psychological emphasis typical of Buddhism leads Hayes to a discussion of various virtues, which introduces us into an arena that is a very fruitful meeting place for the religions. While their metaphysical backgrounds vary, there is room for significant exchange in the areas of virtues and morality. While these can never be divorced from the broader economy of religion, they do provide a meeting place worth pursuing. We are grateful to Hayes for bringing this emphasis into such clear focus.

Hayes departs slightly from the thematic focus of the other chapters. While he is consciously concerned with the issue of hostility and the methods of overcoming it, he does feel that hospitality is not the most useful category from a Buddhist perspective. He prefers universal friendship as a category that is truer to internal Buddhist orientation. As he suggests, hospitality is close to universal friendship and constitutes a related antithesis to hostility.

His analysis opens with a discussion of the source of hostility. Where for the Hindu it was ignorance of the ultimate metaphysical ground of being, the Buddhist perspective suggests an inward movement to discover the root of hostility within human psychology. Hayes quotes a poem in which the Buddha says that, as he looked into the hearts of human beings, he saw there a barely visible dart, a subtle and yet deep wound that makes human beings run around frantically and crazily, a wound that tragically undermines all human efforts to find peace. The dart that has wounded us so gravely is identified as the dart of arrogance and self-importance. It is our pathetic need to see ourselves as special that makes us set ourselves apart from others, to denigrate others and eventually to go to war with others. All conflict, whether in the form of quarrels among individuals or wars among peoples, ultimately stems from the universal tendency to measure oneself up against others. When we do this, either we feel inferior to others and then resent them, or we feel superior and then scorn them, or we feel equal and then compete with them until one gets an advantage over the other. But the wise person looks at all this competition and says "Let them contend with one another all they wish; they shall get no quarrel from me."

Complementing this analysis of the root of hostility as grounded in human psychology is the affirmation of the fundamental unity of humanity, itself the basis for the ultimate aspiration for universal friendship, or, if we prefer, hospitality to the other. Hayes demonstrates the Buddha's belief that the racial, ethnic, and cultural divisions among humans are purely conventional and unnatural. Although observable differences exist among humans, these differences were typically seen by Buddhists as trivial in the context of the overwhelming similarities in both the physical and psychological attributes that everyone shares. But while recognizing the fundamental unity of humanity, the Buddha also recognizes the moral diversity among people. This recognition led to the recommendation that his followers avoid too much contact with such people. In other words, while associating with like-minded people is the best way to cultivate all the recommended virtues, associating with other-minded people is the best way to undermine one's efforts to cultivate virtue. And so it appears that, after all the talk of the unity of the human species, we have the basis for a distinction between "self" and "other," between "us" (the good folks) and "them" (the bad ones) of just the sort that could undermine the project of seeing the unity of the human species. Thus, different kinds of behavior—virtuous and non-virtuous, moral and immoral—undermine a perceived unity of humanity, thereby posing a challenge to this unity and threatening it with hostility.

Hayes addresses this challenge by examining how, in Buddhism and in other Indian philosophical systems, the religious or theological Other is considered, in relation to one's own system. The Other is not regarded as other in the sense of belonging to an alien species or perhaps another race or social group, but rather as other in the sense that an adult is other than a child of the same species. The other, then, is just a being much like oneself in an earlier stage of development—someone to be nourished, protected, and helped along until maturity and refinement set in. The process of maturing is seen as a long and gradual continuum with more or less well-defined stages along the way. The transition from spiritual adolescence to adulthood, called the transition from being a foolish ordinary person to being a stream-entrant, is characterized as leaving behind the relatively self-centered preoccupation with following rules and reaping their rewards and moving into a more altruistic mood of cultivating kindness either for its own sake or because kindness makes life more pleasant for others.

What we find in Indian Buddhism is not much different from what we find in the religions of India in general. No matter which system of religious thought or practice one examines, the most commonly encountered pattern is that a school will see itself as the model of maturity and other religious systems as earlier stages of development through which it is natural to pass on the way to maturity. There may be a somewhat paternalistic attitude toward people following paths other than one's own, but hardly ever is the practitioner of another religion seen as a threat or even as an annoyance that must be tolerated. Such is the prevailing ethos in Indian religions.

Hayes's discussion of the roots of hostility understood from a Buddhist perspective leads him to a comparison with Kant's views on history and to an assessment of the West's ethos of war, contrasted with the Buddha's prognosis for the world and the appropriate reaction to the violence it contains.

Kant's views on history are brought into the discussion because many people in our times, and particularly a good many of those making war or preparing to do so, are acting as if they are convinced that an eventual end to war will somehow come about by making war on those who are perceived as enemies of the very idea of making peace. This conviction seems to be particularly prevalent among those who see something like Kant's Nature operating behind human history—that is, an intelligence with good intentions that has provided human beings with the means to rescue themselves collectively from the human condition, but only after making themselves very miserable. If Buddhism has anything to offer the world in its present condition, it is a critique of that conviction. The classical Buddhist view, presented in detail in Hayes's chapter, extends an invitation to reconsider the evidence of history.

While the Buddha's message may seem bleak, it does offer a kind of hope. The hope provided by the Buddha's vision is that it is possible for at least some people to attain to a state of maturity wherein they will be able to learn that dividing the naturally uniform species into unnatural divisions such as clans, tribes, races and nations leads only to xenophobia, that xenophobia leads only to conflict, and that conflict leads only to further conflict. These mature people will appreciate the words found in the opening chapter of what is probably the best known and most frequently quoted Buddhist text, the Dhammapada (1:3–6):

> He insulted me, he hurt me, he conquered me, he robbed me. The wrath of those who never think like that will end.
>
> For wrath is not conquered by wrath; wrath is conquered by leaving it behind. This is a universal principle.
>
> Others do not know that we can live here in harmony. Those who do know it leave fighting behind.

Hayes goes on to discuss the achievement of moral virtues. Specific attention is paid to a set of ten virtues that are suggested as a summary of Buddhist teachings. The ten factors discussed are wisdom, heroism, concentration, mindfulness, joy, flexibility, equanimity, faith, resolve and good moral habit.

Hayes concludes his chapter with reflections on religious pluralism and its relation to the fulfillment of human potential and to the achievement of human flourishing. He reminds us of the power of community as a means of achieving the virtues and hence as an instrument of human flourishing. Thus, the realization of human potential is one that requires the combined efforts of all people. Moreover, cooperation is something that requires mental and emotional flexibility and a willingness to learn not only from one's own experiences but also from the experiences of others. From these two considerations, Hayes suggests that it follows that the healthiest human community is one that encourages individuals to benefit from the entire collective wisdom and experience of humankind as a whole. This leads Hayes to the third observation, that when Buddhist principles are taken to their logical conclusion, they must embody a spirit of religious pluralism and can never be seen from the narrow perspective of the Buddhist tradition alone. He mentions figures such as the Dalai Lama, Thich Nhat Hanh, and Stephen Batchelor as contemporary Buddhists who hint at the most promising direction for humanity as a whole. That direction consists in seeking wisdom from whatever source it can be found.

A complementary view of Hayes's presentation is offered in Dharma Master Hsin Tao's addendum. Overall, the vision of life offered by the Mahāyāna tradition, claims Hsin Tao, is more optimistic and offers greater hope than the minimal hope that some individuals might learn that dividing humanity into groups will only lead to conflict. Rather, a more optimistic view is propounded that has social consequences as well. Overcoming the social boundaries of classical Indian society is itself a revolutionary message of hope.

The Buddha's message of hope provides the background against which historical and Buddhist societies may be critiqued. The application of Buddhist principles, once those become intertwined with the social and political order, falls short of the original ideals. The exclusion of women from ordination and the use of Buddhist identity to exclude others in Sri Lankan Buddhism are two examples of how Buddhist societies fail to live up to true Buddhist teaching. Hsin Tao's response seeks to bring to Buddhism the same self-critical gaze found in the chapters representing other traditions.

Ultimately, the Buddha's message asks for more than simply overcoming hostility and practicing hospitality. It asks to give our whole selves for the happiness of all sentient beings. This happiness is the hope that the Buddha offers the world.

AFTERWORD

In his response to the first chapter of the collection, Former Chief Rabbi of the United Kingdom Jonathan Sacks hones in on the core issue of the entire collection—the attitude to the other. He offers us a series of biblical reflections through which he seeks to formulate some fundamental principles that ought to guide attitudes to the other. He turns to Judaism's most fundamental Scripture, the Torah, in an attempt to draw guidelines or rules that would be of universal relevance concerning the attitude to the other. In Sack's hypotheses one might discover a definition of the purpose of the present project and, to no small extent, of the purpose of interfaith relations as a whole. "Until I know the Other, I do not know myself," is one such hypothesis that mandates knowledge of the other as a means of self-knowledge. The dual hypotheses that "conversation is the alternative to conflict" and that "God does not reject the Other" are in fact the foundations of this project's attempt to trace a path that would take us from hostility to hospitality. Rabbi Sacks provides us with an example of the kind of educational and hermeneutical work that must be undertaken if we are to be successful in this task and to bring a new vision of the other to our religious communities.

Chapter Two

Judaism

The Battle for Survival, the Struggle for Compassion

Alon Goshen-Gottstein

Judaism is the religion constituted by the story of one particular people and its relationship with God—the people of Israel and the story of its life under God's covenant. This story is told first and foremost in the Hebrew Bible, whose narrative shapes Jewish awareness. As the constitutive story, read and interpreted for thousands of years, it suggests the basic ways in which Israel understands and positions itself in the world and in relation to the rest of humanity. It is significant that, as a story concerned mostly with Israel's particular relationship with God, expressed through such notions as covenant and election, the Biblical narrative begins with the story of the creation of the world. While that which is unique in Israel's self-understanding occupies center stage in the Biblical story, the contextualization of Israel's particular story in the framework of creation forces our attention to revisit, time and again, the relationship between the particular and the universal. Israel's story cannot be read apart from the story of creation, the story of all of humanity. Ultimately, Israel's very particularity is an attempt to realize a potential that is grounded in creation. It therefore belongs properly to all of humanity and constitutes part of the ultimate hope and vision held by Judaism for all of humanity.

UNDERSTANDING JUDAISM—SELF-DEFINITION AND OTHERNESS

Locating Israel's Story: Creation and Covenant

Judaism's very formation implicates it in notions of "otherness" and in the attempt to find the appropriate relationship to the Other. Its story is a story of setting apart, of forming a particular individual relationship, at the exclusion of other relationships. Whether we locate the beginnings of Judaism at the covenant made with Abraham[1] or at the covenant made with the collectivity of Israel at Mt. Sinai,[2] Israel's story is one of relationship. The making of the covenant, much like the marriage relationship to which it is compared by the prophets,[3] is one of particularity that implies some kind of exclusion and the creation of otherness. A relationship has been formed with this particular one, not another, and the very formation of the relationship creates an Other, the Other who is not part of the particular relationship. As identity thickens, through association with God, land, peoplehood, and teaching, all identity markers become points of demarcation—our God versus theirs, our teaching versus theirs, and so on. This is particularly important to understanding the anti-pagan polemic that characterized much of biblical literature and helped differentiate biblical Israel from the religious cultures of its neighbors. Understanding otherness is thus the flip side of the identity of Judaism, constructed as it is on the fundamental separation involved in the establishment of a particular relationship.[4]

Because Israel's identity is so deeply intertwined with a sense of separation and particularity, one must recall time and again how its story is contextualized in relation to creation. Israel's story is intended to fulfill a goal that is ultimately shared by all of humanity. Its particularity is thus deeply universal. We may consider sin and failure as the factors leading to the formation of a particular relationship.[5] Or we may consider particularity and individuality as fundamental to the nature of humanity and therefore an essential component of the biblical teaching and world view, illustrated by one specific particularity—Israel's.[6] That which is particular is ultimately a pointer to that which is universal, suggesting that the lessons, paradigms and benefits of particularity are ultimately of universal significance. Judaism's liturgy, its yearly cycle as well as its theology and religious reflection, all give manifold expressions to the creative tension between two fundamental constitutive moments in Israel's life and theological self-understanding: creation and covenant, the universal and particular. Failure to strike an appropriate balance between these two perspectives will have deleterious consequences on Judaism's attitude to the Other and ultimately on its own self-understanding, and on its ability to fulfill its destiny, the purpose for which its particular relationship was forged.

The biblical creation story furnishes us with some important insights on humanity and its unity. Unlike all other forms of life that are created according to the diversity of species, humans alone are not created in species.[7] The Bible presents us with a vision of a single humanity, issuing from a single common ancestor. The Bible tells of creation according to the image and form of God, thus endowing humanity with qualities that allow it to share in God's reality; all of mankind shares in the divine image.[8] This affiliation with the divine is at the very least a source of respect for the life and dignity of others. It is also the basis of the biblical prohibition of bloodshed—man was created in God's image.[9] But the concept of man's creation in God's image does not seem to provide a firm enough basis for establishing an attitude to the Other. With the exception of the creation story and the just cited appeal to it, nowhere else in the Hebrew Bible does man's creation in God's image figure again.[10] The man created in God's image lacks the particularity that comes with identity, lacks all the specificity that allows us to distinguish between ourselves and others. The human person as organized through collectives, through competing means of establishing identity—social, national, religious, and such—cannot adequately be addressed through the notion of the image of God. Perhaps this is also why the concept has played a relatively minor role in shaping the attitude of Judaism to the Other.

Not all manifestations of Judaism have succeeded in maintaining the ideal balance between the two constitutive poles of creation and election. The vicissitudes of Jewish history, the sense of suffering and oppression that has endured for thousands of years of exile, have produced some forms of Judaism that are relatively withdrawn from the outside world and isolated from Israel's purpose in relation to it. In all likelihood, there exists a strong relationship between historical circumstances and the balance of extroverted and introverted Jewish self-understanding. The present chapter approaches the question of the attitude to the Other by trying to articulate an ideal balance, not by describing one or another model or precedent of historical Judaism.[11] But before we can embark on ideals, we must attempt a deeper understanding of what creates "otherness" in a Jewish context. Let us then turn our attention to a consideration of the very identity and definition of Judaism.

Peoplehood and Religion

Judaism is unique among the world's religions. Though it is considered a world religion, properly speaking it is the religious way of life of a particular people, the people of Israel. Membership in the religion is identical with membership in a people and vice versa. The relationship between these two components of Judaism's identity is not free of tension; indeed, membership in a people and adherence to a set of beliefs and practices can be competing claims. This is one of modern Judaism's fundamental existential issues, especially when Jewish identity is related to membership in a modern nation-state, the state of Israel. The tension between these key components of Jewish identity finds contemporary political expression. It is relevant also to a consideration of core religious and theological issues. The subject of the attitude to the Other is significantly affected by the dual perspectives of peoplehood and religious faith.

For thousands of years, Israel has suffered from adversarial relations with other nations. A bitter history of exile, suffering and antisemitism, culminating in the attempt to implement a "final solution" to the "Jewish problem," has left the Jewish psyche embittered, suspicious and inhospitable. Xenophobia is a natural consequence of such a painful history. Fear of the Other, caused by repeated suffering and persecution by the Other, has become second nature. Regardless of how favorable the present political climate may be, Jews are always anxious about unexpected changes that may threaten their security and survival. With the founding of the State of Israel, the survival instinct and the attendant fear of the other have been focused largely upon the future of the nation-state. The seemingly perpetual war with some or all of its neighbors, in which Israel has been engaged since its birth, continues to provide justification for the basic fear of survival that is endemic to the Jewish psyche. From the perspective of the Jewish people, xenophobia and the deeply rooted survival instinct are inseparable. Indeed, the Jewish people are deeply fearful about their collective survival. [12]

But Judaism is not identical with the Jewish people. Judaism is a teaching, a spiritual vision. And Judaism's spiritual vision of the Other is quite distinct from attitudes born of history and implanted in the psyche of the Jewish people. It is not always easy to draw a neat distinction between expressions of the victims' state of mind and the "higher" teachings of Judaism. These teachings, articulated in tomes of Scriptural commentaries, works of rabbinic erudition and a range of philosophical and theological reflections, often bear witness to the pained history of the Jewish people. Nevertheless, the present discussion will proceed from the distinction between these two fundamental components of Jewish identity—peoplehood and religious teaching. At the very least, this distinction bespeaks the complex nature of the task at hand, reflecting upon "Hostility, Hospitality and the Hope of Human Flourishing." Hostility and hospitality are attitudes of a people, even when reflected in religious teaching. By contrast, a vision for the flourishing of humanity is only a matter for religious teaching. History and religious vision must both be taken into account when suggesting an ideal view of the Other.

Due to the interdependence of historical perception and theological vision, fresh theological articulation of Judaism's vision of the Other must be attempted in a constantly renewable effort to disengage the attitude to the Other from the particularities of individual historical circumstances. Such fresh articulation will obviously best be carried out under historical conditions of security that allow the mind to be elevated beyond the concerns of continuing survival. Historically, we do indeed find periodic novel attempts to articulate Judaism's attitude to the Other as part of its spiritual concerns. Such articulations typically take place in Jewish societies that enjoy relative security and stability.[13] The second part of the present chapter will offer some thoughts in this direction.

Hostility and Identity—The Lesson of Abraham

It is likely that separation and the concomitant sense of "otherness" will lead to hostility. The Other, whether the unknown Other or the well-known Other from whom one seeks to separate, may be the object of hostile behavior. Such hostile behavior may further strengthen group identity, but such a possibility is far from the Torah's vision of how particularity should engage with the Other.

Separation in the forms of both wandering and exile are crucial to the founding moments of Israel as a people and a religiously covenanted community. The confession of faith and gratitude, pronounced in historical times at the Jerusalem Temple upon bringing the first fruits as an offering and repeated annually since the destruction of the Temple as the key text underlying the recitation of the Passover Haggadah, is found in Deuteronomy, chapter 26. The opening verse of this confession reads:

> A wandering Aramean was my ancestor; he went down to Egypt and lived there as an alien, few in number, and there he became a great nation, mighty and populous.[14]

The biblical story of Abraham commences with the command that Abraham leave his home and go to an unknown country; the wandering of our first ancestor relates to specific blessings.

> Now the Lord said to Abram, "Go from your country and your kin and your father's house to the land that I will show you. I will make of you a great nation, and I will bless you, and make your name great, so that you will be a blessing. I will bless those who bless you, and the one who curses you I will curse; and through you all the families of the earth shall be blessed."[15]

Abraham is promised progeny, a great nation. But his wanderings are also related to what may be considered the Other, in the widest possible sense—all families of the earth. The wanderer moving from place to place is a blessing to all. The attitude of heart and mind of the one on the move, seeking God's ultimate resting place, is one of openness and generosity. The story of Abraham's wanderings is one of such openness to the other.[16]

Exile is a less benign form of wandering. Abraham's children experience the first Jewish exile in Egypt. Israel as a people was born and shaped by this formative exilic experience. As the Zohar states: "When God wished to make them a unified people, a whole people, and to bring them close to Him, had they not first descended to Egypt and been cleansed there, they would have not become His single people."[17] The exile in Egypt has shaped Israel's historical experience, providing the archetypal experience that is to be repeated time and again ever since. Hence, the celebration of the exodus from Egypt is never only a commemoration of an event in the distant past. All later exiles are subsumed under this archetypal exilic experience. The Passover Haggadah, the liturgical text celebrating the memory of the exodus from Egypt, makes repeated reference to the continued relevance of the formative exilic experience in every generation: "In every generation, each person is required to see himself as if he left Egypt." Our survival is continually at stake, much like that of the Israelites in Egypt. Like them in former times, we too depend on God alone for our salvation.

What are the effects of such an exilic experience on the attitude to the Other? The victim of exile is naturally far less open than his ancestor who enjoyed the freedom of wandering, calling God's name in all places to all he encountered. The victim, by contrast, seeks his own liberation and the fall of his oppressor. His own freedom and wellbeing are uppermost in his mind, even at the expense of the oppressor. The natural reaction to the war of survival, to the experience of exile, is one of protective turning inwards. The Other cannot be part of one's spiritual purview when one's physical survival is at stake. However, natural reactions do not always convey the highest spiritual ideals; so it is too with the memory of exile. An experience that might have yielded a closed withdrawn attitude is recast in terms that evoke compassion, understanding and generosity toward the Other. Such recasting cannot take place while the people are imprisoned in Egypt. It requires the safety of homeland and the distance of time.

Hospitality in the Land—Implementing the Lessons of Exile

Israel's attitude to the Other is not limited to formative exilic moments. It is also a consequence of other historical times and conditions, in which Israel enjoyed freedom, sovereignty and independence. Under such conditions the Torah seems to transform the natural reaction to the historical oppressor, suggesting instead another lesson and another attitude that may be borne of the exilic moment.[18] In the security of homeland, the harshness of historical memory is transformed to a compassionate vision of the Other.

The moral lesson learned from the memory of suffering, perhaps even the transformation of that memory, is accomplished through the Torah's reference to the *ger* and through appeal to Israel's own similar status in Egypt.

Ninety-two times the Torah issues commands concerning how the *ger* should be treated. Who is this *ger*? Literally translated as "foreigner," "alien," or "sojourner," the *ger* is the outsider, one who dwells within the nation, but is not of it. Historically, it is not clear how, if at all, the formal status of the *ger* was defined. Most scholars would agree that the kind of formal conversion processes that developed in later Judaism were not yet in practice in biblical times. Hence, the *ger* would be any foreigner living in the midst of ancient Israelite society, even if he had not consciously taken up full membership in Israel and its faith.[19] When the Torah envisions Israelite society, it takes great care to address the status of the outsider, the foreigner.

Two key imperatives emerge from the Torah. The first is the absolute legal equality of the *ger*, who is to enjoy the same status as the Israelite in all matters, both legal and ritual.[20] The other is the loving attitude the Torah commands in relationship to this outsider. The same section of the Torah in which the classical command to love one's neighbor as oneself[21] includes also the express commandment to love the *ger*.

> When an alien (*ger*) resides with you in your land, you shall not oppress the alien. The alien who resides with you shall be to you as the citizen among you; you shall love the alien as yourself, for you were aliens in the land of Egypt: I am the Lord your God.[22]

Full equality and love of the stranger, the alien, are justified by appeal to the historical memory of Israel's exile in Egypt. The admonition and its reasoning are repeated time and again in all fundamental legal collections within the Torah.[23]

The Torah seems to make the following point: We are not to treat others as we ourselves have been treated. The formative exile in Egypt should sensitize us to the condition of the stranger and the alien, teaching us how not to inflict upon others the suffering that was inflicted on us.[24] The Torah's point is not only one of legislation; it is also one of human psychology and sensitivity. "You shall not oppress a resident alien; you know the heart of an alien, for you were aliens in the land of Egypt."[25] Israel's experience in Egypt sensitized them in a particular way, making them aware of the heart, or feeling, of the *ger*. Israel is to be permanently marked by this sensitivity, acquired through its own suffering.

These words of the Torah continue to resonate down to some of the most recent formulations of what it means to be Jewish in today's world. Thus, in the words of Emmanuel Levinas:

> The traumatism of my enslavement in Egypt constitutes my very humanity, that which draws me closer to the problems of the wretched of the earth, to all persecuted people. It is as if I were praying in my suffering as a slave, but with a pre-oratorial prayer; as if the love of the stranger were a response already

given to me in my actual heart. My very uniqueness lies in my responsibility for the other. [26]

The concept of hospitality encountered here goes beyond the power relations of the host making space for the guest. Power relations are dealt with through the insistence that all be equal before the law, thereby flattening differences of power. But the biblical concept of hospitality involves more; it involves love as fundamental to the practice of hospitality. We are thus commanded not only to treat the *ger* fairly, but to love him.

Significant as these teachings are, it would be wrong to assume that these key biblical teachings can provide us with an adequate description of Jewish society's attitudes to the Other. Historical circumstances have made these attitudes far more complex.

The Struggle for Survival — The Movement of Introversion

We may safely state that the Torah's teachings do not necessarily reflect the standard attitudes toward the foreigner in our midst found within various manifestations of Jewish society. Of course, the Torah's ideals never cease to inspire and to draw one to the height of their vision, but other forces that significantly constrict the vision of hospitality suggested by so much of biblical legislation have operated within Jewish history and continue to operate within Jewish society today.

Foremost among the influences that have determined that these biblical texts and teachings have not been the sole shapers of the Jewish attitude to the outsider is the fact that Jewish history continued where biblical legislation left off. The latter recalled the memory of a past exile under circumstances of present-day independence. But such independence was to be lost for thousands of years, with a harsh and enduring exile taking its place. The teaching of hospitality to the outsider could no longer set the tone of Jewish relations to the Other. To the extent that the Torah's legislation makes a statement concerning Israel's psychology and the sensitivity it acquired through suffering in Egypt, this sensitivity was to give way to a hardness born of continued suffering. Israel's lot had become a continued battle for survival. Antisemitism has been a formative force in Israel's history at least since Roman times. [27] The possibility of hospitality all but vanished in the face of a reality in which hostility was a basic mode of being. The victim could not show hospitality, and the victim without a land had no place in which to do it, even if so inclined.

Perhaps no other nation in the world is as concerned, even obsessed, as Israel with its own continuity and survival. The sense of threatened survival characterizes Jewish existence wherever it is. It takes on special weight in the context of the Jewish state, fighting an enduring physical war for its survival.

But concern for survival is also concern for the continuity of the Jewish people in spheres other than military and security. Demography and culture are no less the battlefields on which the war of Jewish survival is fought. Intermarriage, cultural assimilation, and loss of collective identity, both in the state of Israel and in the Diaspora, are concerns that continue to shape the public Jewish agenda.[28] These concerns focus public awareness inward. Despite over half a century of independence of the Jewish state, the frame of mind of its leaders, and of leaders of the Jewish world at large, is that the battle for survival is far from won. Such inwardness of concern perpetuates attitudes and priorities typical of Israel's long battle for survival, making the attitude to the Other less of a central concern than it seems to have been for biblical legislation.[29]

Conceptual development within Judaism plays an important role in undermining the biblical ideal of accepting the alien. We noted above that the identity of the alien, the *ger*, in biblical times may have been left vague, allowing various kinds of strangers and foreigners to be embraced by the overarching welcome offered to the *ger*. Later Judaism could not tolerate such lack of clarity. One of the hallmarks of rabbinic Judaism is its quest for clarity, definition and the establishment of clear boundaries. A subject as fundamental as membership in the community of Israel could not be left to vague definitions and would have to be strictly defined. The rabbinic approach to the law, the halakhah, insists on clear-cut boundaries that distinguish clearly between one considered a Jew and one who is not. One may conjecture as to the historical circumstances that led to the insistence on clearly demarcated boundaries; whatever the case, they are real and have become normative.[30] Regardless, one can also understand these developments independently of any historical circumstances.[31] Definitions and the clear demarcation of boundaries characterize the rabbinic approach to the Torah as a whole. The need to define membership in the community goes hand in hand with the formalization of the process of entry into the community and the fixing of clear rules and rituals for entry into the community of Israel by conversion.[32] Following these changes, the basic antinomy is no longer between Israel and the alien amongst them, but between the Jew and the non-Jew. A heightened sense of difference, otherness, and potential conflict characterizes the rabbinic attitude to the Other. The Other is now considered apart from the community and no longer as an outsider who becomes part and parcel of society, its norms and celebrations.[33]

What, then, of the biblical *ger*? For the rabbis, he is no longer the outsider, the alien, but the convert, the one who was outside the people and formally entered through conversion. The rabbis recognize two types of *gerim* (pl.)—one who has fully entered the people of Israel and one who has undertaken a minimal standard of religious observance without receiving full membership. It is easy to read the various biblical references to the *ger* in relation to either of these models. Still, even if the formal application of the term remained possible and the meaning of biblical Scripture could be upheld, a fundamental change occurred within Jewish society. Instead of society accepting an Other within it, now the Other had to become a part of it, forfeiting the sense of otherness and becoming part and parcel of the people. Seen from the eyes of later rabbinic tradition, one is hard pressed to account for why the Torah should go to such great lengths in addressing the rights and the status of the *ger*. After all, the *ger*, at least one type of *ger*, is a full-fledged member of Jewish society. Just as in present-day Judaism there is no need for a massive educational effort aimed at accepting such a convert as a full member of society, it seems unlikely that the Torah would have to expend such great energy toward the sole aim of accepting the convert as a full member of society.[34] Clearly, a major transformation has taken place. The upshot of this transformation is that conceptually there is no more room for the alien, for the Other.[35] The Other, the biblical *ger*, loses his otherness and becomes one of us. With this conceptual redefinition, perhaps the most important biblical resource for the present topic, hospitality to the stranger and the alien, loses much of its sway.[36]

We note with fascination how little of rabbinic literature is actually concerned with the *ger*, in comparison with the careful attention paid to him by the Torah and later books of the Bible. Outside of commentaries on biblical references to the *ger*, we have very little rabbinic concern, reflection, admonition or interest in his status. Liturgical evidence is also suggestive. An examination of the term *ger* in the Jewish prayer book indicates that almost all references are found in quotes from biblical texts, primarily the Psalms, where God's love for the *ger* and similar notions appear. In contrast, I have been able to locate only one reference to the *ger* in the entire corpus of rabbinically composed prayers—and these are the core prayers of Jewish liturgy.[37] One of the benedictions of the *Amidah*, the principle Jewish prayer, addresses the lot of the righteous who trust in God. In a list that mentions various righteous members of society, we come across mention of the *ger tzedek*, the righteous convert, who deserves God's reward. Such emphasis is very different from the central position the *ger* occupied in biblical literature. While for biblical literature, attention to the *ger* can be considered a major expression of ethics and morality, for the rabbis the individual *ger* is more succor and support for the people and religion under duress than a serious moral challenge facing society as a whole.

Rabbinic definition of the *ger* and how his status is attained is important to the consolidation and definition of Judaism, but it shapes and defines Judaism in more than one way. Beyond the legal definition of membership in the people and its religious identity, it shifts the definition of what constitutes the community and its primary moral and religious concerns. If concern for the alien could be suggested as a governing, if not definitive, concern of biblical religion, for rabbinic Judaism the clear establishment of the Torah's norms emerges as the defining religious force. Society is not defined by its treatment of its minority or its alien members. Rather, the individual alien is redefined in accordance with the norms and boundaries of the Torah that he or she consciously undertakes through conversion. Thus, Jewish society is defined as a society of the Torah, allowing Israel to proceed with the safety of structure provided by law through the course of its bitter history. The gain at this point in history outweighs the loss. As Israel once again enters exile, it is far more concerned with its own security and survival than with the status of the stranger in the stable majority Jewish society that is no more.

Amalek—Israel's Perpetual Enemy and the Struggle for Survival

A nation seeking to make sense of its continuing suffering, coping with the ubiquitous oppressor, finds in Scripture the lens through which reality is perceived. Along with the biblical teaching of hospitality there is a biblical teaching of hostility. This teaching is not directed to the alien within society but to a distinct and particular Other who dwells beyond the border of Israelite society. An encounter with Israel's primordial enemy took place in the first instance beyond the border of civilization, as Israel wondered from place to place in the desert. Exodus 17 narrates how Amalek attacked Israel in the desert.[38] Following the description of the battle with Amalek, we encounter the outstanding statement, according to which Amalek is not only Israel's enemy but God's enemy.

> Then the Lord said to Moses, "Write this as a reminder in a book and recite it in the ears of Joshua: I will utterly blot out the remembrance of Amalek from under heaven." And Moses built an altar and called it, The Lord is my banner. He said, "A hand upon the throne of the Lord! The Lord will have war with Amalek from generation to generation."[39]

The war with Amalek is perceived as an eternal continuing war, God's own war. Later in Scripture the Israelites are commanded to remember Amalek's attack on them in the desert, when they were faint and weary, and to wipe out his memory.[40]

The hostility shown to Amalek seems to draw on Israel's survival instinct. Amalek threatened Israel's survival in a fundamental way, without any due cause, as though hurting Israel was a goal in and of itself. It is conceivable that the commandment to wipe out Amalek's memory is itself based on the likelihood that such vicious antagonism is likely to emerge anew, thereby once again threatening Israel's existence.[41] The war with Amalek is thus part of Israel's wider battle for survival. Amalek threatens Israel's survival, drawing forth a hostile response, based on the instinct for self-protection.

In biblical times, Amalek was an identifiable people. Post-biblical Judaism recognizes that Amalek is no longer a distinct ethnic enemy, as indeed many of the biblical peoples are no longer recognizable. Yet, Scripture speaks of an eternal war with Amalek. If all biblical texts invite a hermeneutic of continuity and relevance, regardless of changed circumstances, this is especially true of a text that is self-consciously transgenerational. We can readily see how one would arrive at the understanding that Israel, along with God, has an eternal enemy. Because this enemy is no longer identified as a particular people, it can be elevated to the level of a principle. Consequently, all of Israel's concrete historical enemies that seek to annihilate Israel's existence can be seen as manifestations of the general principle of Amalek. A nation perpetually exposed to violence, hatred and attack could come to see its enemies as expressions of a higher principle of enmity; thus, all enemies are Amalek.

The above reconstruction is not in any way a universally acknowledged formal teaching of Judaism. It cannot be, since Amalek cannot be historically identified with all of Israel's enemies, and since Israel's classical religious foes, Christianity and Islam, were typologically identified with "other" biblical figures, Esau and Ishmael. Nevertheless, there exists a popular notion that is backed by understandings that are semi-halakhic, that any enemy at any time may be identified with Amalek, when it seeks to destroy Israel.[42] Beginning with the rabbis who read the story of Esther in light of the Amalek principle,[43] later generations of homileticists and popular thinkers would time and again identify the concrete enemy with the metaphysical principle of Amalek, as they did for example, with Nazism.[44]

In seeking to portray the complexity of the Jewish attitude to the Other, one must recognize that Judaism also contains a teaching of hostility to the Other. This teaching is deeply imbued in Jewish awareness, not because of its theological centrality but on account of the historical centrality of the experience of suffering and enmity. A hostile history extends the teaching of hostility from ancient memory to a present continuum that upholds a dualistic view of reality.[45] Reality is thus divided into two groups, we the victims and they the oppressors, perpetually and eternally caught in a battle that is ultimately God's own war.[46]

Xenophobia in Contemporary Israel

All strangers are not Amalek and all others are not out to destroy Jews or Israel. Yet, the impact of thousands of years of persecution on the psyche of the people of Israel seems to be measurable in terms of their attitude to the Other, and inhospitable attitudes to the Other seem to figure highly among them. Our discussion has long shifted from the teaching of Judaism to the attitudes of Jewish people. The centrality of the state of Israel to the people of

Israel suggests that attitudes that have been studied within the state of Israel are significant to any discussion of the Jewish attitude to the Other. Beyond that, it is likely that findings in other geographical locations may not be dissimilar.

One study on xenophobia in Israel[47] indicates that past suffering may have contributed to the diffusion of xenophobic attitudes. The Jews, who encountered so much suffering in the recent past, seek isolation and distance themselves from others. A vast majority of Israelis would like to close the state's gates and leave "others" outside its borders.[48]

I am struck by the extreme contrast between how past suffering is supposed to have sensitized us to the suffering of the Other, according to the Torah's instruction, and how in reality past suffering seems to have increased hostility to outsiders. In stating this, I do not criticize the pain of victims nor their feelings, nor do I despair of the possibility of the Torah's vision ultimately being implemented.[49] I only note the nearly impossible goal of the Torah to transform human nature through its teaching and commandments, enjoining love and acceptance of others, where natural human reactions would lead to closure and exclusion of others.

Some additional points of interest emerge from the above mentioned study, which measured attitudes toward three distinct groups of "others": Ethiopian Jews, foreign workers and Arabs. Such nuancing is significant. Even though hatred toward Arabs far exceeded hatred toward the other two groups, various degrees of inhospitality and hostility were present in relation to Ethiopian Jews and even more so in relation to foreign workers. Israeli attitudes to foreign workers are far from perfect. Many are treated in ways that are anything but a direct expression of the biblical commandment to love the stranger.[50] Even as this volume is prepared for final publication this is a pressing public issue, relating to Israeli treatment of thousands of African asylum seekers, in relation to whom the range of historical attitudes to the stranger, especially negative attitudes, are applied. Though distinct, each group triggers some aspect of hostility and suspicion, derivative of Israel's continuing battle for survival.

Hate is an illness that cannot easily be compartmentalized. Hate of the outsider manifests an attitude of being that is bound to find expression within as well. In thinking of inhospitable attitudes to the Other in contemporary Israel, one must therefore recall that the Other is not always the Other without but is often the Other within. The authors of the study here cited noted instances of xenophobic attitudes towards Ethiopian Jews, a visible Other within. Yet, exclusionary, inhospitable, and at times outright hostile attitudes have been part of internal social group relations since Israel's establishment. Tensions between Jews from Western countries and those from Arab countries, broken down at times by more specific geographic places of origin, are the darker side of the magnificent job of absorption and integration of millions of Jews from different social and geographical backgrounds in the effort to shape Israeli society and establish its identity.

The Role of the Other in Constructing Israeli Identity

Authors of the study on xenophobia in Israel point to one factor that I find both comforting and alarming. Unlike xenophobia in other countries, which is often motivated by economic concerns such as the competition for employment or housing, Israeli xenophobia is motivated by ideological and principled concerns. Israeli xenophobia is thus not of a piece with the type of xenophobia usually encountered in the Western world. Rather, the negative attitude to the Other grows out of the attempt to establish one's own identity; in the process of identity establishment, the Other plays a crucial role. Cultural incompatibility, accentuating differences from the Other, is a natural source of hostility. This is, some suggest, the root of antisemitism.[51] There is, however, a profounder sense in which the Other is significant for the construction of identity.[52] It has become a commonplace of contemporary philosophy that one needs the Other in order to construct one's own identity. In a dialogical context such a perspective means one thing; in an antagonistic context it means quite another.

Israeli antagonism to Arabs seems to be based, at least to some extent, on the role that Arabs as an Other play in the shaping of Israeli identity. Especially where there is an identity crisis, as there is indeed in modern-day Israel, "the calm self-certainty that might facilitate unproblematic relations with the minorities gets lost. Then society turns to historic myths promising to solve the crisis of identity; on the other hand, this very search for origins breeds exclusion of the others."[53] Israel thus needs the Arab as an Other, to help determine the human limits in relation to which Israeli identity can be constructed.[54] One expression of this process is the way in which Israeli and Arab identities are created and sustained in an effort to establish Israeli collective identity.[55] A more extreme form of the same process is how group identity can be sustained through hate of the other. Hateful attitudes to Arabs far exceed "security needs," nor can they be justified as merely reactions to Arab hostility. Rather, a far more complex process of "othering" the Arab takes place, as part of modern popular Israeli society's own construction of its identity. Politics of hate play a significant part in such "othering."[56]

As a matter of principle, constructing one's identity only in reaction to an Other may betray a deeper sense of loss of self and identity. A famous Hassidic dictum, attributed to Rabbi Menachem Mendel of Kotzk states: "If I am I because you are you, and you are you because I am I, then neither you nor I truly is; but if I am I, because I am I, and you are you because you are you, then both I and you truly are." Self may be constructed in dialogue with the Other, but it cannot be defined exclusively in reaction to the Other.

Modern Israel's identity crisis will obviously not be solved through the projection of an Other, let alone a hated Other, any more than the reality of a common enemy provides sufficient grounds for the existence of Israel itself. It is striking to note how a slogan that once defined Israel's purpose has all but ceased to be heard in the public arena. Israel's early years were accompanied by a vision of an Israel that is to be a "light unto the nations," consciously echoing a prophetic phrase.[57] The slogan conveyed a sense of purpose and a vision of Israeli identity. This vision certainly stood in relation to others, yet it was based on a sense of self and purpose, finding expression in a calling and an example to the world. Such slogans are no longer heard. Israeli society's grapplings for its identity have forced it to turn inward in search of its identity rather than outward in fulfillment of a mission.

The Hope of Human Flourishing—Judaism's Need for the Rediscovery of God

We have seen how Jewish history, the life of the people, and the teachings of Judaism mirror one another, reflecting a complex dynamic. On the one hand, Judaism's teachings are closely indebted to social and historical processes affecting the people of Israel. On the other, religious teachings can help elevate the lived experience of history to spiritual heights, providing meaning and direction, and raise the people of Israel beyond the vicissitudes of history and their natural reactions to them. How then does Judaism as a religious system stand in relation to the processes just described?

In the most obvious sense, Judaism could be construed as the alternative to natural human reactions, to the spread of hate, and even to the various complex attempts to construct contemporary human identity, both personal and collective, through human machinations. But portraying the relation only as one of a contrast or a corrective oversimplifies matters. Judaism too is trapped, to some extent, in the same introvertive dynamics that characterize the psyche of Israel. Just as the fledgling state of Israel over the course of its short history has moved from a sense of self-awareness and mission that reached out to others to a more self-involved, enclosed mode of being, so Judaism too has undergone similar transformation. The ongoing battle for survival and the attempt to flourish under hostile circumstances may account for both. Thus, Judaism itself is in need of spiritual revival.

This revival may emerge from the picture I attempted to paint in the first part of this chapter, highlighting the tension between the national/ethnic component of Judaism and its religious/spiritual dimension. One cannot overstate the effects of history on attitudes of the Jewish people, affecting in turn the teachings of Judaism. But it is not enough to excuse the Jewish people's failure to live up to the highest biblical ideals by appeal to the suffering of Jewish history. The key to transformation may lie in our ability to address the imbalance between spiritual teaching and collective history. The covenantal reality in which Judaism is grounded brings together two parties—God and Israel, in a vision that ultimately must serve as a blessing for humanity. If due to the circumstances of history, Judaism has come to place too great an emphasis on the human component of the covenant—upon the life of Israel itself, surely to repair this imbalance we must seek the rediscovery of God as the central orientating principle of our religious lives. Judaism is in need of more and more teaching of God, as a balance to its own engagement in the life of the people. It is in need of a spiritual revival.

The rediscovery of the living God as the ultimate heart of Judaism may allow Judaism to consider its own contribution to humanity from a vantage point significantly broader than that informed by its history and suffering. Awareness of God as the conscious center of the entire religious system may allow Judaism to discover its deepest commonalities with humanity. One interesting way of illustrating this idea is by appeal to some of the later biblical developments that concern the notion of the *ger*. In the book of Chronicles, we find appeal to our status as aliens, *gerim*, not on account of the exile in Egypt, but because being alien is fundamental to human existence. "For we are aliens and transients before You, as were all our ancestors; our days on the earth are like a shadow, and there is no hope."[58] We are not aliens because of a particular historical event, but because of the very nature of what it means to be human, living forever in the shadow of death, a vision all humanity shares. Death provides the deepest bond of brotherhood for humanity. Yet, the status of *gerim* is one that is lived "before You," in God's presence. Thus, it is God who is the ultimate host, while we are all aliens in His sight. In God's sight, all humans are *gerim*.[59] Shifting perspective from human society to the presence of God allows us to reconsider relations between peoples and to find the deepest bond of brotherhood.[60] The present chapter opened with a consideration of creation (importantly: in the image of God) as the basis of common humanity. It continued with the commonality of human experience, evoking the memory of Israel's status as *gerim* in Egypt. We now come to what may be the most significant perspective based upon which human unity may be recognized—our common existence in God's presence and the transience of that existence.

Bringing God back to the center of the religious conversation allows us to embark upon the third part of our theme: The hope of human flourishing. In this context we shall seek to address Judaism's vision for the flourishing of humanity. What vision does Judaism hold out for all who are not part of its own religious system? Perhaps it is better to speak of visions, rather than of a single united vision. In any event, what shall interest us most is the attempt to construct such a vision with God at its center.

The Flourishing of the Other—Visions of Judaism

Judaism's vision of human flourishing and its contribution to such flourishing is determined, to a large extent, by the breadth of the lens through which Judaism examines the world at large, which in turn hinges on the dual nature of Judaism, suggested above. From one perspective, Judaism is the life of a covenanted community and the story of its particular covenantal relationship with God. Covenant, like marriage, is a personal relationship that does not perforce carry wider implications for others, beyond the establishment of the relationship itself within the wider societal context. On the other hand, Judaism as a system of religious teaching relates to a universal God. When God, rather than Israel or its covenanted way of life, is placed at the center of the religion's economy, obvious ramifications for Israel's mission to and vision for humanity emerge: Judaism's knowledge of God should be translated and transported to all people. Various forms of Judaism have historically placed greater emphasis on one pole or the other, thereby producing Judaisms that emphasize to greater or lesser degrees the religion's mission to humanity. Accordingly, one can suggest two visions of what Judaism's message for humanity, its view of human flourishing, might be.

The narrower, more introverted vision is typical of the greater part of Judaism since rabbinic times. This vision for humanity is captured in legal terms, aiming at the regulation of the moral life of humanity. According to this vision, Judaism's teaching for the world revolves around the spreading of what are known as the seven Noachide commandments. These are basic moral obligations that Judaism considers indispensable to what it means to be human and that must serve as the basic fabric of all society. These commandments are, for the most part, a series of prohibitions: idolatry, blasphemy, murder, forbidden sexual relations, theft, and eating the flesh of a living animal; the seventh commandment entails the establishment of a judiciary system. There exists a standard understanding of Judaism, according to which Jews are commanded to observe 613 commandments, while non-Jews are required to observe only seven. This spiritual vision for non-Jews does not extend beyond the fulfillment of these obligations. Non-Jews who seek further spiritual advancement may join the ranks of Judaism and undertake the full religious life it offers. Thus, the reply to the question of what Judaism has to offer to humanity would be an ordered moral life.[61] However, such a moral life seems to fall short of the kind of concerns that religion, taken in its fullest sense, has. Significantly, no relationship with God is developed through the Noachide commandments. God is acknowledged through the prohibition of idolatry, but such acknowledgement is not tantamount to a full relationship.[62]

The alternative vision for humanity grows from an understanding of God, rather than from an extension of the notion of commandment to include the non-Jew. Knowledge of God and the possibility of establishing a Divine-human relationship are uppermost here. Not surprisingly, this vision is echoed primarily in Biblical prophetic texts. Despite changes in Jewish relig-ion in the rabbinic period, this vision finds continuing expressions, as the biblical texts are echoed time and again by later writers. Human knowledge of God, leading to a personal relationship can be understood in terms of conversion to Judaism but also independently of conversion, affirming hu-manity's potential to come to know God in a variety of ways. The prayers of the high holy days, themselves a biblically infused creation of the rabbinic period, offer a vision of humanity, considered from the perspective of the universal knowledge of God.

> God and God of our fathers, reign over all the universe in Your glory, and be exalted over all the earth in Your grandeur. Shine forth in the brilliance of Your majestic might over all inhabitants of the world, Your earth, so that every creature may recognize that You have made it, and so that whatsoever You have made may see that You have formed it, and that everything that has breath in its nostrils may say, "God, the God of Israel, is King and His king-dom rules over all things."

The deepest Jewish vision for human well-being is thus the knowledge of God. This vision, of course, does not conflict with the moral vision of the seven Noachide commandments, but complements and expands it.

Both visions of what Judaism has to offer the world are largely a matter of theory, of prayer at best. There is very little by way of a program of action for the spreading of God's knowledge among non-Jews. Judaism is a bruised religion, far too vulnerable to undertake an active program of mission or teaching to the nations.[63] Also the seven Noachide commandments are more of an internal concept than a concrete educational program for the nations.[64] Judaism has thus more of a vision for the well-being and the flourishing of humanity than it does a concrete path or program, that it actively implements.

COMPASSION AS THE BASIS OF A NEW JEWISH THEOLOGY OF THE OTHER

It would be presumptuous to assume that what follows is my "contribution" to the spiritual revival of Judaism. It does, however, flow from my under-standing of the necessity of such revival and from my awareness that any such revival must be based on new theological and spiritual articulations of Judaism's teachings. It is thus my way of stating the need rather than a presumptuous attempt to fulfill it.

My own presentation of how Judaism can be seen and understood may be read as a theological response to the difficulties and complexities that characterize it, as described above. This response is dialogical in a number of ways. It is a theological dialogue with history and with the current form of Judaism; it is also a dialogue with particular voices within tradition. What follows may be considered a dialogue with the teachings of a Hassidic thinker who has had a profound influence on my own thinking, Rabbi Nachman of Breslav (1772–1810).[65] Based upon various historical data presented in the first part of the chapter, as well as a conceptual framework drawn from Rabbi Nachman's teachings, what follows constitutes an attempt at a fresh statement of Judaism's vision of the Other, as well as its ultimate goal and message, though this dialogue may take his ideas beyond the scope and context initially intended by him.

It is also a dialogue with other world religions. It is my personal conviction that part of Judaism's spiritual revival must come through its rediscovery of the meaning of being religious in a sense other than the historical/national sense that conditions so much of Judaism or the behavioristic focus on ritual that dominates so much of contemporary "religious" life. Interreligious dialogue thus has a great theological contribution to make to Judaism. In this context, I cannot ignore the possibility that the theological statement I shall attempt below is also dialogically informed, in relation to other religions. My own theological statement of Judaism and its message is based on the concept of Compassion, first and foremost through several of the teachings of Rabbi Nachman. While I believe the intuitions that follow grew from my own reflections in a Jewish context, I am also aware of ways in which my thinking may have been influenced by the thought of other religions, primarily Buddhism. But if this is indeed the case, it provides still further proof for the usefulness of dialogue with other religions for stimulating one's own theological reflection and creativity.[66]

Compassion in the Thought of Rabbi Nachman of Breslav[67]

Rabbi Nachman's teachings are contained in a work called "Likutey Moharan." Section 64 in this work is one of Rabbi Nachman's most famous and commented upon teachings.[68] The opening statement reads as follows:

> God created the world because of His compassion, because He wanted to reveal His compassion, and if the world had not been created, to whom would He show His compassion? Therefore He created all of creation, from the beginning of the emanation to the final center point of the physical world, in order to show His compassion.

This statement leads to a discourse in which Rabbi Nachman discusses various metaphysical issues, including the problem of theodicy. Placing compassion as the goal and ground of creation will color one's view of all that takes place within the created order. Even those instances of suffering and cruelty that challenge faith are to be recognized ultimately as expressions of divine compassion.

In other contexts, Rabbi Nachman affirms compassion as fundamental to the nature of creation. Commenting on Deuteronomy 30:11–12, where an unspecified "commandment" is said to be close to the heart and present, Rabbi Nachman describes compassion as omnipresent or as visible to all.[69] Similarly, the world is described by Rabbi Nachman as full of compassion, just as God is all-compassionate.[70] The association of compassion and creation is thus well established in the thought of Rabbi Nachman. That divine compassion is the purpose of all of creation allows us to consider the relevance of compassion to an all-encompassing view of the goal of Judaism and the purpose of life.

Compassion is not a spiritual quality that is cultivated independently of other aspects of the spiritual life.[71] Rabbi Nachman relates compassion to *Da'at*. *Da'at* can be understood as knowledge, understanding, awareness or consciousness. In other words, there is a relationship between a person's degree of evolution of consciousness and his or her capacity to show compassion. As *Da'at* grows, so does compassion.[72] In a telling and painful admission, Rabbi Nachman discusses our ability to draw forth God's compassion upon us. He states: "There is no one who is able to pray in such a way as to draw forth divine compassion, because no one recognizes sufficiently the greatness of God."[73] Peace and compassion grow to the extent that *Da'at* grows.[74]

Compassion is also an expression of faith, a concept closely related to the concept of *Da'at*; only one who has true faith in God can have full compassion.[75] Compassion is thus related to the movement away from self into the presence of God, and it is grounded in the existential perspective that relies upon God alone in fullness of faith. The true leader must be motivated by compassion alone and not by any desire to rule. Until faith has been perfected, true compassion is not available, and one should not undertake leadership positions.[76] Faith stands in opposition to idolatry, Judaism's classical enemy. Hence, compassion emerges as the attitude of being that is the opposite of what an idolatrous attitude would engender.[77] If Israel is understood as a people whose task and message are to combat idolatry, this can be recast in terms of compassion—the people whose task it is to spread compassion. Rabbi Nachman offers the following acronym for the name of Israel: *El Shaday Yiten Lachem Rachamim*—The Lord Shaddai will give you compassion.[78] Compassion may thus be said to be fundamental to Israel's character.

God is the source of compassion, so in having compassion we emulate God. Such emulation is conscious, and it allows the drawing forth of divine compassion in reaction to the human practice of compassion. Israel is called to act in accordance with the thirteen attributes of divine compassion.[79] The notion of emulating God is, in and of itself, an important source for various forms of supererogatory behavior. Spiritual ideals that cannot be exhausted through legislation can be cultivated through the aspiration to emulate God. [80] Compassion is received through giving to others. [81] Life may thus be seen as a school for compassion, providing opportunities to give and thereby to receive and to grow in compassion. Anger and cruelty are constantly overcome and transformed to produce compassion. The spiritual path is thus one of transformation of natural tendencies to their opposite, producing compassion as its fruit. This process of transformation will be realized only in the messianic future. It is only with the ultimate expansion of *Da'at* in the eschaton that compassion shall prevail, putting an end to human cruelty and anger, and ushering in the messianic peace. [82]

Compassion finds practical expressions. One of them is the ability to judge favorably, seeking virtue rather than fault. This theme is significant in Rabbi Nachman's teaching. The attempt to view both self and other in a favorable light, seeking virtue, is transformative, growing in a person those positive qualities that have been found and advancing his or her progress. [83] However, compassion must not be naive. The recipient of compassion must be worthy of it. Having compassion on the wicked can have adverse effects. Self-defense calls for care in the exercise of compassion, which must not be shown to one who instead of growing compassion in himself will take the power of compassion and apply it to cruelty. [84]

Judaism and the Teaching of Compassion

Following the teaching of compassion, as it emerges from the writings of Rabbi Nachman, I would like to offer an overview of the various topics of the present chapter, seen through the lens of compassion. I believe the following summary statement allows us to address Judaism's call and mission, the purpose of the spiritual life and the attitude to the Other, both in the concrete ways occasioned by common living and through a consideration of Israel's ultimate message and contribution to others.

The identification of Israel and compassion allows us to put forth the notion that compassion is constitutive of Israel's identity. Various rabbinic dicta speak of compassion as one of the fundamental traits of the Jewish people, Abraham's descendants. [85] Indeed, Israel's history of suffering has produced extraordinary qualities of charity and communal support within the people. I believe one is not exaggerating in seeing loving-kindness, charity and compassion as traits of Jewish society, throughout history, down to present times. However, much of this compassion and loving-kindness is directed inward, toward members of the Jewish community. If compassion is constitutive of Israel's identity, we should also consider its role in Israel's relations with other peoples.

Such compassion might find expression in the battle against idolatry. For Rabbi Nachman, the greatest form of compassion is the removal of ignorance. Israel's battle against idolatry should therefore not be construed as a triumphalist move of one particular truth over another, but as an expression of compassion in eradicating false perception and spreading *Da'at*. But more interestingly, compassion can also serve as the yardstick for distinguishing between various forms of religious life. If idolatry is associated with cruelty and compassion with faith, the religious life can be measured not only by doctrinal claims but also by the quality of life it engenders in its believers. Where compassion is found, there God is found, and vice versa. The boundaries between higher and lower forms of religious life may thus not overlap the group identities of the religious communities. Each religion may contain both idolatrous and compassionate forms. Judaism's role is to uproot idolatry, first within itself,[86] and later from the world. Whatever Judaism may have to contribute to the world should therefore be judged by the yardstick of compassion—does it enhance and grow compassion? Is it born of a compassionate movement of heart, or is it merely an expression of national self-aggrandizement?

As we have seen, compassion is not natural and may necessitate the transformation of natural reactions and tendencies. Having presented the adverse effects of Israel's painful history on its attitudes to the Other, we must raise a highly challenging question for contemporary Jewish spirituality. Can Judaism rise above its role and reaction as victim? Can the continuing battle for collective survival make space for a vision that does not cast the Other only in the role of persecutor and aggressor? If Jewish history is understood as a spiritual training through suffering, provided by God for His chosen people, we must ask how Israel's suffering can be integrated and transformed as part of a wider vision of Israel's spiritual growth and its contribution to the world. One answer that presents itself for our examination is the teaching of compassion, suggested here.

Can Judaism adopt an attitude of compassion toward its enemies? This is one of the most challenging questions one can place before it, and it is doubly hard when the battle for survival continues. Compassion does not mean giving in to an enemy that seeks to destroy us. We have already seen the limits placed on the showing of compassion in situations of cruelty. But a deeper existential attitude of compassion, grounded in the fullness of the *Da'at* of God, may serve as a corrective to the excessive inwardness that so marks the Jewish people. Judaism has long resisted the idea of loving the enemy, partly because the idea is so strongly identified as Christian. Addressing the enemy, addressing the Other, and addressing life through the compassion that is already ubiquitous in God's creation may not have the same objectionable ring. If compassion and loving-kindness are extended from within Jewish society to the Other, Judaism may find itself close to the fulfillment of the prophetic vision with which it was entrusted and able to handle the pains of history in a transformative manner.

Compassion can serve as a helpful category through which to understand Judaism's attitude to the Other, as developed in the earlier part of this chapter. Perhaps it would be truer to the intention of the Torah to consider the various commandments to love the *ger* as, in reality, commanding a compassionate attitude toward such a person. Compassion can be awoken through the evocation of the memory of our own exile in Egypt. Though the Torah legislates it, love can not be commanded; but recollection and reflection may awaken an attitude of compassion toward the Other. Compassion is certainly the appropriate reaction to the memory of the common human fate of death and the transience of life, making all humans *gerim*. If the suffering of later Jewish history has wiped away the tenderness of heart that the recollection of our bondage in Egypt was to produce, surely a deeper reflection on the meaning of all of human life, in the presence of God and death, may draw forth a compassionate response.

Reflection is a key to the awakening of compassion. It is only the unreflective self that can perpetuate attitudes of hate and hostility. Much of biblical life and Jewish history can provide us with reflective resources through which an attitude of compassion to other people can be developed. Thus, exile as a phenomenon relevant to all human beings may emerge already from the opening human story of the Bible, the exile from Eden.[87] From another perspective, recognizing that we are in God's presence and on God's earth is also a necessary corrective to some of the harmful spiritual consequences of a protracted existential battle, focusing on people and on land. Almost from the very start, Israel's present-day attempt to establish a homeland has been accompanied by confrontation, with the inevitable ensuing hardening of attitude toward the aggressor. We do well to recollect a third biblical context in which we are called *gerim*. "The land shall not be sold in perpetuity, for the land is mine; with me you are but aliens and tenants."[88] Facing God Himself and trying to live by the laws set by Him for living on the land evokes a deep tension between the sense of possession and owning that characterize the narrative of the conquest and the humble recognition of our own alien nature.[89] This dual perspective must be kept in mind. Affirmation of rights for homeland must be tempered by an awareness of the transience of all of human life and of how, even in our own homeland, we are but aliens and strangers. One of the greatest prices we pay for our continuing war is that it makes us forget some of our most fundamental religious perceptions.

The teaching of compassion may also serve us as a way of approaching anew Judaism's message and teaching for others. We noted above the insufficiency of the seven Noachide commandments as a spiritual path for people who are not part of the Israelite covenant. I suggest the seven Noachide commandments be considered as expressions of Judaism's teaching of compassion. Such compassion must be based on a minimal recognition of God, the source of all compassion, hence the prohibition against idolatry, itself associated with cruelty, as Rabbi Nachman suggests. Following the establishment of that minimal attitude to God, the seven Noachide commandments ensure a minimum of compassion, in human relations to other humans as well as to animals. Thus, the prohibitions against murder and theft, the obligation to set up judiciary structures and, last but not least, the prohibition of showing certain kinds of cruelty to animals, are all expressions of this wider ethic of compassion, he;e translated into a fundamental legal code. Such legal expression falls short of the fuller dissemination of the spiritual teaching of compassion. Such teaching is accomplished through Judaism's teachings about God's being and presence. As Rabbi Nachman has taught us, the measure of knowledge of God is also the measure of compassion. [90]

Judaism may thus affect the world on two levels—through the teaching of compassion and through the law of compassion. Law provides the basic guarantee for compassionate behavior. This is true of the laws governing Israel's behavior toward the alien and is offered by Israel to others as a fundamental way of living. But beyond law lie the spiritual vision, the understanding and the quality of compassion as a mode of being that cannot be contained within the confines of law. The people of Israel may not always be able to ascend to the heights of the vision of Judaism, because the pains of history may not allow them to transcend their own suffering. It is then that law, Jewish law as well as the law of the Noachide commandments, provides a minimal harbor, anchoring the ideals of Judaism in practice. Ultimately, as all law must be subsumed as part of the spiritual reality that gave birth to it, so too Judaism's law of compassion must be subsumed in a higher teaching of the knowledge of God and of human compassion that Judaism has to share with the world.

When we consider what teachings Judaism has to share with the world, we do well to recall some of Judaism's special treasures. The entire range of Judaism's extra-legal spiritual teaching—including its teachings about God—is not usually considered by Jews as part of what they have to share with others. Hence, exquisite teachings regarding attitude to the other, care for proper speech, control of the passions, ways of approaching God and so much more are usually considered in-house treasures that do not fall within the purview of Judaism's contribution to humanity. I would argue that, if Judaism is to be true to its ultimate calling, it must spread the teaching of how it has come to know God and to live in His presence beyond the confines of Judaism. I suggest neither conversion of all people to Judaism nor extending the range of the halahhah to include others. Simply, the expansion of awareness and consciousness that has been achieved within some parts of

Jewish society must be made available to others as part of Judaism's mission to the world, a mission of *Da'at* and of compassion.

Some words are in order, in this context, also concerning Israel's archetypal enemy, Amalek. Why is Amalek such a terrible enemy? Most traditional answers emphasize the threat he poses to Israel's existence. However, another answer emerges from the sources as well. Amalek is the epitome of cruelty.[91] His was an unnecessary war; it did not serve the needs of his own survival. His cruel attitude to the wandering weak people places him as the antithesis of what Israel is to represent in the world. One cannot show compassion to one who is cruel. The ramifications of that would be self-destructive. Amalek is to be seen as part of the continuing threat for Israel's survival. But not every enemy is Amalek. The threat Amalek poses is unique inasmuch as it threatens the fundamental moral fabric of Israelite society— compassion.[92]

CONCLUDING REFLECTION

Historical circumstances provide opportunities for the growth and transformation of religion. Israel's history of pain and persecution provides an opportunity for the development of a teaching of compassion, even if this teaching awaits such times as when Israel is dwelling in safety on its land. But history may offer other kinds of opportunities as well. Rabbinic Judaism established boundaries between self and other in ways that are probably stricter than biblical literature had envisaged. These boundaries are now once again slipping away as the certainty of the distinction between self and other is gradually undermined; as contact increases, boundaries become more permeable and new identities are constructed and sought. This change also provides us with an opportunity to return to biblical teachings that have all but fallen into oblivion through history and through the reinterpretation of tradition. Along with them comes an opportunity to reawaken the spiritual resources of Judaism in an attempt to address contemporary crises, advancing beyond the common and predictable human reaction to history. Through these opportunities Jews and Judaism, and others along with them, can grow.

Yet Judaism is not alone in facing such challenges and opportunities; it is not alone in its need to grow. If Judaism has lost sight of fundamental elements of its calling, it may need the help of others to realize and regain them. The loss of sense of mission, "a light unto nations" is not only a consequence of undue introversion; it also expresses a genuine perplexity as to the nature of this light. What can Judaism actually teach and share about God, beyond the most formal and rudimentary truths? As part of its own spiritual revival, Judaism must seek answers to such questions. One path through which the answer may be discovered is conversations with others:

those who have God, those who don't, and those who have God in a different form. Part of the contemporary context that challenges Judaism to rediscover its ultimate calling involves an openness to the Other, in a movement that is profounder than the one-way transmission of inherited knowledge. If Judaism is in crisis, one dimension, perhaps ever so small, through which it may be helped to rediscover its ultimate mission is the mutual exchange that inter-religious dialogue offers. It is my humble conviction that the importance of the dialogue is not only as a means for Judaism to share its own wisdom and knowledge of God but also as a means to rediscover its own identity and calling. Through contact, challenge and a genuine openness to other sojourners on God's earth, Judaism may be helped to rediscover its ultimate teaching for itself and for humanity. If through history so much of what is essential to Judaism was eclipsed, the new emerging historical paradigms, offered by dialogue at its best, may hold the promise of the rediscovery of self, in conjunction with the Other.

NOTES

1. See Genesis, chapters 15 and 17.
2. See Exodus, chapter 19.
3. See Hosea, chapter 2 and Ezekiel, chapter 16.
4. For present purposes, it is sufficient to recognize that the establishment of relationship and identity involve exclusion and otherness. The present chapter will not engage the other way in which identity and otherness are related, namely how identity is constructed through adversarial relations to the other. The recognition of this dimension of identity construction is significant for a critical assessment of historical positions taken within Judaism to other religions.
5. This is a fair reading of the sequence of the biblical narrative, leading from creation, through the respective sins of the generations of the flood and the tower of Babel, to the formation of a particular relationship with Abraham, in Genesis 12. See Afterword of this volume.
6. This understanding was suggested by Jonathan Sacks, *The Dignity of Difference: How to Avoid the Clash of Civilizations* (London: Continuum, 2002) p. 50 ff.
7. Contrast Genesis 1:11 and 21:24 with verse 26.
8. Throughout the generations, a variety of understandings of the image of God have been offered. Some classical options are analyzed in Yair Lorberbaum, *The Image of God: Halakha and Aggada*, Jerusalem, Schoken, 2004 (Hebrew). For the parallel view in Christianity, see page 54; for the observation in Islam that God Created all humanity from a single soul, see page 85; for the Buddhist view of unity in the human species, see page 126.
9. Genesis 9:6.
10. Goshen-Gottstein "The Body as Image of God in Rabbinic Literature," *Harvard Theological Review* (87:2), 1994, pp. 171–95. Lorberbaum, *Imago Dei* , suggests that the concept is of greater significance than it seems at first sight.
11. Nevertheless, one cannot avoid the recognition that there is no ideal vantage point, fully divorced from the particularity of historical context. I must therefore state that my own formative perspective is conditioned by my living in the modern-day state of Israel, and to a large extent it is colored by some forms of religious-Zionist theology. It is conceivable that some of the ways in which Jewish history is presented in this chapter might be different were the chapter written from the perspective and ideology of the Jewish diaspora. I seriously doubt, however, that the ultimate attempt to strike a balance between the formative poles of creation

and covenant would yield different results if approached from a different historical Jewish perspective.

12. This encapsulation of Jewish history ignores many moments of positive coexistence and good relations between Jews and others in their host countries. Here, more than anywhere else in this chapter, I may be expressing my Israeli vantage point. Still, it seems to me this sense of permanent anxiety is relevant even to societies where Jews have found a home and become full members in all walks of life. Little has changed in the collective psyche over the past forty years, since the analysis of Jon Groner, "Beyond Xenophobia, Jewish Fears and American Realities," *Response 24*, 1974–1975, pp. 7–14. Nevertheless, the counter-testimony of many positive instances of excellent inter-group relations throughout Jewish history is most relevant to the present discussion. Such moments may suggest alternatives to ingrained attitudes, and writings produced in such societies (such as medieval Al-Andalus) will often present attitudes that can serve as a corrective to attitudes formed under hostile historical conditions.

13. Examples that come to mind include the works of Elijah ben Amozag and Rabbi Abraham Isaac Kook.

14. Deuteronomy 26:5.

15. Genesis 12:1–3.

16. One notes with interest that Abraham enjoys peaceful relations with his neighbors. The only instance of war involving Abraham, in Genesis 14, is fought on behalf of Lot, and it does not reflect his own normal pattern of relations. Furthermore, as many scholars have noted, the book of Genesis does not portray the Patriarchs in struggle with idolatry. See Robert Cohn, "Before Israel: the Canaanites as Other in Biblical Tradition," *The Other in Jewish Thought and History: Constructions of Jewish Culture and Identity*, ed. Laurence J. Silberstein and Robert L. Cohn (New York: New York University Press, 1994), pp. 74–88.

17. Zohar I, 83a.

18. Jonathan Magonet, "Guest and Hosts," *Heythrop Journal* 36, 4 1995, p. 415, makes the very fine point that the frequent repetition of the admonition concerning the foreigner suggests that it is not simply an affirmation of the natural state of Israelite generosity but an awareness that a different psychology must be created, even imposed, on the newly emergent nation. Once we consider the Torah's laws as combating and transforming natural human tendencies, we may go further and reflect on the depth of instinctual xenophobia. The papers collected in *The Sociobiology of Ethnocentrism*, ed. V. Reynolds, V. Falger and I. Vine (University of Georgia Press, 1986) suggest that the roots of xenophobia can be traced biologically to other species. Xenophobia is thus not exclusively a human social phenomenon. Just as the Torah addresses various animal components of the human person and of human behavior, it may address this one as well. The tension between Jews and Judaism, that underlies my presentation, can thus be seen in the framework of a wider theory of how the Torah's commandments address human nature and seek to transform it.

19. Magonet, p. 416.

20. See for example Exodus 12:48–49.

21. Leviticus. 19:18.

22. Leviticus 19:33–34.

23. The Book of the Covenant in Exodus 22, the Holiness Code in Leviticus 19, and the covenantal blessings and curses in Deuteronomy 27, Deuteronomy 10:19. I would not go as far as Magonet, p. 416, in claiming that how one treats the outsider is the ultimate measure of the nature and quality of the new society in the making, but it is an important component thereof.

24. In the context of this formulation, it is interesting to recall the golden rule (in its negative formulation: Do not do unto others etc.), as articulated in the famous story of Hillel and the convert, in the Babylonian Talmud, Shabbat 31a, according to which this is the key rule from which the entire Torah can be derived. The Torah's injunctions in relation to the *ger* may be the earliest expression of this golden rule.

25. Exodus 23:9.

26. Emannuel Levinas, "Difficult Freedom," in Sean Hand ed., *The Levinas Reader*, Cambridge, 1989, p. 252; cf. also p. 202.

27. See Daniel Schwartz, "Antisemitism and Other Ism's in the Greco Roman World," in ed. Robert Wistrich, *Demonizing the Other: Antisemitism, Racism and Xenophobia* (Harwood,

1999), pp. 73–87. Some scholars date antisemitism still earlier; see Yehezkel Kaufmann, *A History of Israelite Faith* (Jerusalem-Tel Aviv, 1920) vol. 8, pp. 440–443 (Hebrew).

28. In the modern world, questions of identity are inseparable from the very definition of nation-states, particularly as they are challenged through the existence of multiple ethnic identities. See *Identity and Intolerance: Nationalism, Racism and Xenophobia in Germany and the United States*, ed. Norbert Finzsch and Dietmar Schirmer (Cambridge: Cambridge University Press, 1998). In this sense, the problem the state of Israel faces has commonalities with issues faced by other modern Western nations. But the particular history of the Jewish people and the uniqueness of Israel as the only Jewish state provide an important perspective on what is also a wider problem.

29. To the outside observer, concern with the alien may be as essential to Israel's faithfulness to its identity, expressed through its covenantal obligations, as concern with perpetuating the people and their spiritual heritage. Thus, Gary M. Burge, *Who Are God's People in the Middle East?* (Grand Rapids, 1993) pp. 74–75, points to the biblical obligations toward the alien, as fundamental to the covenant, and hence to Israel's faithfulness to its spiritual calling. That such a perspective comes from the outside is, in part, testimony to the introverted quality of Jewish awareness. It also reveals differences in understanding who is the biblical *ger*, as these differentiate biblical and post-biblical Judaism, as I shall presently suggest.

30. Such insistence may be historically related to heightened tensions between Jews and non-Jews and the beginning of the introvertive movement within Judaism. It may also be related to increased Torah observance among gentiles, creating the need to establish clear boundaries. Ultimately, we are unable to pinpoint the precise historical circumstances that led to the development of the laws of conversion as found in rabbinic literature. See also the next note.

31. See Shaye J. D. Cohen, *The Beginnings of Jewishness: Boundaries, Varieties, Uncertainties* (University of California Press, 1999), pp. 198–237. Probably because he dates the ceremony to the second century, Cohen sees the ceremony as a "vehicle by which the rabbis attempted to regulate and formalize what until then had been an entirely personal and chaotic process" (p. 236). It is significant that this understanding, highlighting the internal processes of tradition, makes no attempt to offer a broader inter-group perspective, against which the conversion ceremony should be understood. Lawrence Schiffman, *Who Was a Jew?* (Ktav, Hoboken, 1985), suggests an earlier, pre-Christian date for the conversion process. While Schiffman is concerned with inter-group relations, these focus only upon how the definition of identity functioned in a Jewish-Christian context, after the categories had come into being. Schiffman does not suggest what historical forces gave rise during second Temple times to new definitions of group identity.

32. See Gary Porton, *The Stranger within Your Gates* (Chicago: 1994), p. 7.

33. Such redefinition obviously has far-reaching legal consequences. We have seen the biblical insistence on one law applying to Israel and to the *ger*. Once the *ger* is understood as the full-fledged member of the community of Israel, the question of the nomic status of the outsider, now the non-Jew, emerges with full force. The morally problematic distinctions between Jews and non-Jews in the context of financial rulings are, as Steven Fraade has shown, an almost inevitable consequence of the logical application of certain premises, central among which is the association of the Torah and its nomic status to Israel. See Steven Fraade, Navigating the Anomalous: Non-Jews at the Intersection of Early Rabbinic Law and Narrative, *The Other in Jewish Thought and History*, p. 145 ff.

34. It is conceivable that a nation that is tribally structured would indeed have a harder time integrating elements that do not fit into patriarchal family structures. But if that were the issue, something should have been said concerning *gerim*, family, and tribe structures. Despite hundreds of references to the *ger*, nothing is known of their relationship to Israeli tribal structure, and this suggests the place of the *ger* in biblical society should not be construed in light of how later converts were absorbed into Jewish society.

35. The famous "God-fearers" who crowded the synagogues of late antiquity are apparently not to be found in rabbinic literature. It seems the rabbis, operating through a series of legal definitions, could not accommodate them within their world view. They are, perhaps, the closest we can get to an Other, who is not in opposition or antagonistic to the continued well-

being of the Jewish people. Their absence from rabbinic literature underscores the radical conceptual transformation characteristic of rabbinic literature. The question of the historical existence of the God-fearers is, however, a more complex question, and my suggestion is only one of several ways of making sense of the historical data. Issue 12,5 of *Biblical Archaeology Review* (1986), devoted to the question of "The God-fearers—Did they Exist?" still offers a good overview of this complex issue and various perspectives on it.

36. One could, of course, attempt to uphold the biblical message in relation to the *ger toshav*, the second type of *ger*, who has not become a full member of the people of Israel and who therefore continues to maintain some sense of otherness within society. However, as spelled out in the body of the chapter, interest in the subject of the *ger* decreases so markedly in rabbinic literature that one cannot ignore this radical shift, even if the biblical texts can be read in light of this later categorization. In any event, the category of *ger toshav* is more of a theoretical construct than it is a concrete reality, affecting the life of Jewish society in late Second Temple and Talmudic times. Later authorities, in fact, make it a purely theoretical category, that cannot even be applied, due to various secondary considerations. See Maimonides, *Laws of Idolatry* 10, 6.

37. I am unable to locate additional references to the *ger* in liturgies or in textual traditions composed in communities that were able to freely accept converts to Judaism. Thus, the possibly negative attitude of host nations to Jewish conversions does not seem to account for the paucity of reference to *gerim*.

38. For the Christian view on Amalek, see page 60.

39. Exodus 17:14-16.

40. Deuteronomy 25:18.

41. Many halakhic authorities have understood the biblical story in this way. See the discussion of Yakov Medan, "The Story of Amalek, God's Command and Morality—Are They Compatible?" *The Other: Between Man, Himself and the Other* (Tel Aviv, 2001), pp. 367–401 (Hebrew).

42. For a discussion of whether or not the commandment to wipe out Amalek is halakhically applicable at present, see Medan. In referring to a semi-halakhic understanding, I refer to the position of Rabbi J. D. Soloveitchik, who, in a distinction typical of his brand of talmudic scholasticism, distinguishes between the person and the ideology of Amalek. See J. D. Soloveitchik, *In Aloneness, In Togetherness: A Selection of Hebrew Writings*, ed. P. Peli (Jerusalem, 1976), pp. 392–93 (Hebrew). While the rhetoric appeals to halakhic categories and distinctions, the homiletical context of the passage is significant and leads me to classify this position as semi-halakhic.

43. Haman is an Aggagite, Esther 3:1. This is understood by the rabbis as indicating descent from Amalek's King Agag (1 Samuel, chapter 15). Thus, even though the historical enemy is Persian, the conceptual or archetypal enemy is Amalek. The fact is highlighted by the readings of the Torah before and during the feast of Purim, Exodus, chapter 7, and Deuteronomy, chapter 25, the two Amalek texts.

44. See also J. D. Soloveitchik in Abraham Besdin, *Perakim Bemachshevet Harav* (Jerusalem: 1984), p. 136 (Hebrew).

45. The outsider may legitimately pose the question: why not let go of all past memories, for the sake of the quality of future life. A response to such a challenge is twofold. On the one hand, we recognize that memory does play a constitutive role in the formation of the Jewish psyche. See Yosef Hayim Yerushalmi, *Zakhor: Jewish History and Jewish Memory* (Seattle and London: University of Washington Press, 1982), especially chapter 1. Forgetting does not seem to be one of the available educational options in handling the pain of historical memory. Rather, as we saw in an earlier section of this paper, memory may be transformed and recaptured in appropriate ways. Thus, the choice is not between remembering and forgetting but between ways in which historical memory may be channeled and applied constructively in the present. This leads to the second, and more crucial consideration—forgetting, as well as the transformation of memory, are only possible when hostility is a matter of the past. From the perspective of Jewish experience, such a point in time has not yet come. Thus, present enmity draws upon ancient paradigms in trying to make sense of a hostile reality. Such reality cannot be ignored; it must be transformed.

46. Before concluding the discussion of mandated hostility and the struggle for survival, one must at least acknowledge one major topic left untreated by the present chapter. The biblical battle against idolatry takes shape both as an anti-pagan polemic and as the commandment to conquer and destroy others. The biblical world view is thus inhospitable to paganism, and Israelite society is commanded to be equally inhospitable. The battle against idolatry lies at the heart of Jewish self-understanding and is considered crucial for Judaism's survival. It is so fundamental that it continues to influence present-day attitudes to other religions in the modern state of Israel, forcing the question of whether some contemporary world religions should or should not be considered idolatrous. Israel's first Chief Rabbi, Isaac Herzog, took the conscious ideological stance that all forms of Christianity, as well as most forms of world religions, do not fall under these biblical, and later halakhic, categories. See Rabbi Isaac Herzog, "Minority Rights According to the Halakhah," *Tehumin* 2, 1981, pp. 169–179 (Hebrew). Nevertheless, biblical precedent and latter day halakhic discussion force upon us the realization that the present discussion of the status of the "Other" addresses the Other primarily as a person, devoid of specific, let alone competing, religious identity. The question of Judaism's attitude to other religions is too broad and too complex to be engaged in the present context; the entire subject is in need of careful reconsideration and redefinition from a contemporary Jewish perspective. Important steps toward a fresh consideration of this issue are found in Alon Goshen-Gottstein and Eugene Korn (eds), *Jewish Theology and World Religions*, Oxford, the Littman Library, 2012.

47. The following discussion is based on Ami Pedahzur and Yael Yishai, "Hatred by Hated People: Xenophobia in Israel," *Studies in Conflict and Terrorism 22*, 2 1999, pp. 101–117.

48. Ibid., p. 115.

49. Is the tension between a religion's ideals and the ways these are lived by believers not universal to all religions? In any event, much of what is surveyed in this section are not attitudes of believers but attitudes of a national entity that is composed of believers and non-believers, with a strong preponderance of the latter.

50. Without unduly belaboring the point, one cannot help but reflect upon the fact that the non-profit organization devoted to helping foreign workers in Israel is the same organization that handles the cases of hundreds of women who are imported, at times kidnapped, to Israel, as part of a prospering modern sex-slave trade. Israel was until recently one of the world's leaders in this domain. It is only in the recent past that the complicity of wide sectors of Israeli society and officialdom has been broken. Still, the silence of official religious voices regarding this modern Israeli abomination must derive to some degree from the ills spelled out in the body of this paragraph.

51. See Michael Marrus, "Antisemitism and Xenophobia in Historical Perspective," in *Patterns of Prejudice* 28.3 1994, pp. 77–81. In this context Marrus offers the comforting thought that in today's world, in which difference is an increasing attribute of the Other, antisemitism is on the decline.

52. See Shalom Rosenberg, "The One and the Other—The Ontological Roots of Politics," *The Other*, p. 53 (Hebrew).

53. Pedahzur and Yishai, p. 105, citing Imhof 1993, quoted in Wimmer 1997.

54. See Silverstein's introduction to *The Other in Jewish Thought*, p. 5, where the work of Virginia Dominguez is cited. At times Silverstein's reformulation of Dominguez's theory is more convincing than the argument provided by Dominguez herself.

55. This is the thesis of Virginia Dominguez, *People as Subject, People as Object: Selfhood and Peoplehood in Contemporary Israel* (University of Wisconsin Press, 1989).

56. Establishing the validity of some of the parallels that readily come to mind to situations in which Jews have been on the receiving end of other people's hostility, lies beyond my own field of expertise.

57. Isaiah 42:6 and 49:6. In the absence of clear religious content, the phrase has also undergone significant secularization—for example, applied to the contributions of Jews to science and medicine.

58. 1 Chronicles 29:15.

59. I am reminded of Bishop Krister Stendahl's wonderful maxim: "In God's eyes we are all minorities."

60. Might this shift in perspective also create more space for hearing each other's stories, wandering as sojourners in an alien world?

61. The obvious drawbacks of this vision have led to broadened understandings of the Noachide commandments that incorporate more spiritual dimensions, either by increasing their number or by expanding the significance of the seven. Perhaps the most significant expansion is the demand, made by Maimonides, that the seven Noachide commandments be practiced on the grounds of belief in mosaic revelation. See Maimonides, *Laws of Kings and their Wars* 8,11. Significantly, for Maimonides, observance of the Noachide commandments is also salvific, ensuring a place in the world to come, since it is based on some relationship with, or knowledge of, God. This in turn opens the gate for additional religious components to enter the Noachide relationship. I discuss this dynamic in my *Israel in God's Presence*, (forthcoming). For other dimensions of a spiritual understanding of the Noachide commandments, consider the contemporary statement by Yirmeyahu Bindman, *The Seven Colors of the Rainbow* (San Jose: Resource Publications, 1995).

62. The vision of an ordered moral life is obviously not unique to Judaism. Thus, considered from the perspective of other world religions, the common view of the Noachide commandments as Judaism's vision for humanity offers nothing unique, a fact made graphically plain in recent work by Hans Kung on global ethics as expressing universal religious moral teachings. While this may be considered a weakness, in turn leading to the broadening of the religious significance of the Noachide commandments, from another perspective the universality of the teaching of the Noachide commandments is also a strength, because the category possesses great interpretive potential. It has allowed later rabbinic authorities to interpret the religions of Christianity and Islam and to validate them in Jewish terms. Rabbi Yakov Emden provides a good example for how the Noachide commandments offer a hermeneutical category for interpreting other religions. See Blu Greenberg, "Rabbi Jacob Emden: The Views of an Enlightened Traditionalist on Christianity," *Judaism* 27, 1978, pp. 351–368. See also David Novak, *The Image of the Non Jew in Judaism: An Historical and Constructive Study of the Noachide Laws* (New York: Mellen Press, 1983).

63. I leave aside the complicated question of the meaning of these biblical prophecies concerning the knowledge of God in a world in which two other religions that preach belief in the one God have sprung forth from Judaism.

64. One notes with great interest that Judaism's greatest missionary teacher of the past century, the late Rabbi Menachem Mendel Schneerson of Lubavitch, not only engaged in an extensive program to bring Jews back to Judaism, but also engaged in an aggressive public campaign to spread knowledge of the seven Noachide commandments.

65. While the following section is conceived as a contemporary reflection in light of Rabbi Nachman's teachings, much of what follows is by no means exclusive to him. Some of the key concepts presented below may be grounded in various biblical and rabbinic dicta. Rabbi Nachman provides the conceptual framework that brings these ideas together as part of a unified, broad understanding that can be translated to a contemporary theological reflection. One could arrive at many of the following reflections based upon earlier sources and concepts, such as "ways of peace" and other concepts that have governed Jewish attitudes to others over the generations. However, a broad application of such precedents would be more homiletical and at times more apologetic. Applying the integrated thought structure of a later thinker, such as Rabbi Nachman, permits a theological expose that is free of some of the awkwardness of broad application of traditional maxims.

66. Since authoring the present chapter, the Dalai Lama has put forth his own reading of all world religions, Judaism included, in light of the governing notion of compassion. *Toward a True Kinship of Faiths*, Doubleday, 2010. See note 1 on page 224.

67. For additional reflections on compassion in R. Nachman's thought see my "Compassion—The Teachings of R. Nachman of Breslav" in *Compassion in the World's Religions: Envisioning Human Solidarity*, Lit Press, Berlin, 2010, pp. 73–88.

68. I have discussed this teaching in great detail in my "Speech, Silence, Song—Epistemology and Theodicy in a Teaching of R. Nachman of Breslav," *Philosophia*, 30, 2003, pp. 143–187.

69. Teaching, 105.

70. Part 2, 49.
71. Compare to Buddhist views on compassion, p. 144.
72. This association is repeated numerous times in Rabbi Nachman's teachings. See Teaching 119; Part 2, Teaching 7.
73. Teaching, 105.
74. Teaching 56, 6.
75. Teaching 18, 3.
76. See Teaching 18, 3 and part 2, Teaching 7.
77. 18, 3 and part 2, 62.
78. Part 2, 62. Rabbi Nachman's own application of this acronym is less concerned with the identity of Israel and its presentation in terms of compassion. Rather, he emphasizes the fact that compassion is given into Israel's hands and should therefore be understood in human terms as well, not only in terms of a divine goodness that might manifest as harshness on the human plane. The conceptual potential of this acronym exceeds the application made of it in context.
79. See *Sichot Haran*, 89. The idea of emulating divine compassion underlies the classic kabbalistic moralistic work of Rabbi Moses Cordovero, *The Palm Tree of Deborah*. Rabbi Nachman does, however, acknowledge our inability to adequately awaken divine compassion through emulation of this divine quality.
80. The possibility of compassion to others being grounded in the emulation of God may be related biblically to the notion of the stranger. If we were strangers to whom God showed His compassion, we may be called to show similar compassion to other strangers. Emulating God's compassionate attitude to the stranger may serve as an alternative path to the recollection of our own alien status in Egypt. See Deut. 32:10, Ezekiel, chapter 16, and Meir Malul, "The Origins of the Israelite People in its Self-Perception—the Motif of the Other and the Foundling," *Zion* 47,1, 2002, pp. 5–18 (Hebrew).
81. Teaching 119. See also part 2, 4, 9.
82. See Teaching 56, 6.
83. Part 2, 1, 14 associates compassion with finding virtue. This association is found also in *Sefer Hamidot*, s.v. *Rachmanut*. A classical formulation of Rabbi Nachman's teaching on finding virtue is Teaching 282.
84. See part 2, Teaching 7.
85. See, for example, Babylonian Talmud, *Yevamot* 79a; Deuteronomy Rabbah (Lieberman), Ekev 4, etc.
86. Idolatry is used by Rabbi Nachman as an internal category, and not only as a category by means of which other religions are assessed. See, for example, part 2, 62.
87. Compare Magonet, p. 410.
88. Leviticus 25:23.
89. For continuation of this concept into Christianity, see page 63.
90. See Deuteronomy 10:8, where the attitude to the *ger* is grounded in the knowledge of God's greatness.
91. See Mishnah, Kiddushin 4, 14.
92. Rabbi Yehonatan Eibeschutz in his *Ya'arot Devash*, part 2, homily 9, poses the following question: Why do we not forgive Amalek? After all, forgiveness is a noble religious virtue. According to Eibeschutz, the natural reaction should indeed be one of forgiving. The Torah must go against the natural kindness of Israelites in commanding a war against Amalek. The justification for this war is that there is no compassion in Amalek. Similar reasoning may also be offered for the Torah's prohibition for receiving Ammonites and Moabites into Israeli society (Deuteronomy 23:4). The teaching of hospitality to the Other cannot extend to the cruel Other.

Chapter Three

Making Room for the Other

*Hostility and Hospitality from
a Christian Perspective*

Stephen W. Sykes

In this chapter I seek to identify two perspectives which bear upon the problem of xenophobia, the fear of strangers, from a Christian perspective. These
may be entitled respectively the "christological" and the "ethical" and form
the body of the chapter. They are preceded by a brief section in which a
general orientation upon Christian faith is offered. This offers a perspective
upon the phenomenon of hostility to the "Other" or "stranger," which un-
doubtedly has featured, and continues to feature in Christian history.[1] It
could be argued that hostility is a problem to which the christological and
ethical traditions provide the solution. But, as we shall see, embedded within
both christology and Christian ethics is a further question, namely whether
the Christian teaching embodying hospitality is intended to be applied to
inner Christian relations or whether it is generalizable to all social relationships (section 5). I argue that in order to understand the history of Christianity, especially in its encounters with what is strange or threatening, it is
essential to acknowledge the doctrinal sources from which policies of hostility to the other have derived. But both its christological and ethical strands of
teaching can justify a generous inclusiveness without loss of identity.

THE CHRISTIAN FAITH

The Christian faith is a teaching which intends to bring about a community,
society or church in which, together, women, men and children offer themselves to God. "I appeal to you, therefore, brothers and sisters, by the mercies

53

of God, to present your bodies as a living sacrifice, holy and acceptable to God, which is your spiritual worship" (Paul, Letter to the Romans 12:1). The church is itself an agent and a sign of something greater than the church, namely the doing of God's will upon earth. The church's prayer taught it by Jesus, includes the words, "Your kingdom come your will be done on earth as it is in heaven" (Matthew 6:10). God's will embraces all humanity, indeed the whole creation, in the realization of peace; the church, therefore, is open to all human beings without exception.

The teaching is both about God, who God is and what God has done, and also about the way in which, individually and collectively, the "living sacrifice" should be presented. It is a "sacrifice of praise and thanksgiving" offered in gratitude to God, the giver of the possibility of life. It is, therefore, as Paul says, the "worship" of God, and is characteristically celebrated in the sacraments of the Church, especially in baptism and eucharist. Both sacraments focus the believer upon Jesus Christ, and what God has done for humanity in his death and resurrection. The pattern of life which derives from them is said to be new, transformed, or abundant. This life is to be offered as "holy and acceptable to God," in a lifeservice embracing every aspect of human community and being.

Both themes of this teaching, the doctrine of God and the doctrine of sacrifice, imply an understanding of humankind, a theological anthropology. Human beings are said to have been made "in the image and likeness of God," a doctrine developed on the basis of the creation narratives in Genesis 1 and 2 (beginning with Genesis 1:26); human beings are thus designed for fellowship with God.[2] But the actual human situation is characterized by sin and evil, precipitated, it is taught, by the "fall" of Adam, and the expulsion of Adam and Eve from the Garden of Eden. "Sin came into the world through one man," asserts Paul in Romans 5, "and death came through sin." An analogy is drawn between the old head of creation (Adam) and the new (Christ). It is left ambiguous to what extent the image of God in humankind has been defaced, or even destroyed; Christian theological history debated the question vigorously. But the important point for our purposes is to see that Christian teaching presents what God has done for humanity as an act of rescue and restoration. It is an atonement (literally, "at-one-ment"), a bringing together of God and humankind. "In Christ God was reconciling the world to himself," says Paul (1 Corinthians 5:19).

Hostility

How then, in the light of such teaching, could hostility to strangers arise in the history of Christianity, as it plainly has done and does? One explanation can readily be offered by the content of Christian teaching itself. It is openly admitted that human beings frequently manifest the signs of the old, untransformed life. Hostility to strangers, that is, unreformed behavior, is evidence that the hoped for change has not occurred to the degree that it should.

But this explanation does not get to the heart of the matter. The fact is that the very distinction between old and new, untransformed and transformed behavior, creates and endorses a separation not merely between different action, but also between people. Paul, for example, frequently cites conventional lists of vices to avoid; but on at least one occasion the list is personal—"fornicators, idolaters, adulterers, male prostitutes, sodomites, thieves, the greedy, drunkards, revilers, robbers—none of these will inherit the Kingdom of God" (1 Corinthians 6:9–10; see also Ephesians 5:5; 1 Timothy 1:9). It is plain that it is easier to avoid certain forms of behavior if one avoids the company of those who carry them out. A chain of citations from the Old Testament is used by Paul as a warrant in an argument for not being "mismatched with unbelievers." He concludes: "Since we have these promises, beloved, let us cleanse ourselves from every defilement of body and spirit, making holiness perfect in the fear of God" (1 Corinthians 7:1).

Consistent with and supporting the social pursuit of holiness of life are the battle metaphors which are deployed by Christian faith, to signify the seriousness of the struggle with evil entailed by the new way of life (Ephesians 6:12). It is understood that in baptism a person has renounced sin, evil and the devil, and in this way has mystically participated in Christ's crucifixion and resurrection (Romans 6:6). The radicality of the conversion of life is signified by the language of "putting to death the old self." The reference is internal; but the same radicality is available for deployment against people who are thought, for whatever reason, to embody a threat to holiness. That these could include groups or even races whose customs were unfamiliar, or misunderstood, or easily misrepresented, was not surprising, however tragic.

In this way it could be regarded as a Christian duty, part of the active defense of God's will for human life, that one should oppose *the people* who practice things thought to be immoral, unholy or undesirable.[3] It must be said that in the second century Roman Empire, Christian Eucharists were thought to involve the murder of infants; and, of course, failure to offer sacrifice to the gods protecting the Empire was widely assumed to be a seditious omission. But in due course Christians in power were to make exactly the same assumption, in the medieval period about Jews, and after the Reformation about "heretics" belonging to minority groups. Witches were victims of the same modes of thought, where the personification of evil fatally coincided with the political and social power to oppress or destroy the "other." There were often, thank God, those who understood and defended the obligation to seek the truth from the distortion of propagandist hysteria. But at the very least, it is important for Christians to understand how the conflict metaphors which lie embedded within their tradition can be deployed against the "other," especially in a context of unusual corporate pressure and anxiety.

A further feature of Christian teaching needs to be acknowledged. The ambiguity noted above about the degree to which the fall defaced or obliterated the created image of God in humanity left open the possibility of regarding whole groups or races as a threat to holiness. The story told in Genesis of Noah's son Ham who "saw the nakedness of his father" (Genesis 9:22) and whose son, Canaan, was consequently cursed ("lowest of slaves shall he be to his brothers," 9:25), was deployed against black races in Southern Africa to justify apartheid and white dominance. At an earlier period, because it was not uncommon to identify the "image" of God with human rationality, mentally sick or handicapped people came to be regarded as no better than animals (that is, devoid of God's image), and even as late as the eighteenth century asylums in Europe might be visited as an amusing excursion, much as one would visit a zoo. Such examples are possible because the biblical sources lack explicit detail about the consequences of the fall, except in so far as it identifies death as the outcome. The use of the "curse of Ham" is a particularly gross example of finding biblical texts to justify injustice. The mistreatment of mentally ill people, which has no conceivable basis in the Genesis narrative of creation, illustrates the dangers of speculative interpretation fuelled by ignorance or anxiety.

Hospitality: Christological Doctrine

As has already been mentioned above, christology has from the days of the apostle Paul been an element in the way in which human beings have understood themselves in the Christian tradition. "Christological doctrine," that is, teachings about the narrative and the nature and significance of Jesus Christ, began in the very early communities of the Jesus movement of the first century CE. They were embraced by converts to Christianity, and taught by its leading authorities. The relationship of these teachings to what Jesus may have taught about himself is a complex matter of the reconstruction of evidence and lies beyond our scope. What is not in doubt is the fact that in the oldest book of the New Testament, 1 Thessalonians, Paul speaks of the "gospel" (good news), that it was held to be not a matter merely of report or word, but also of "power and the Holy Spirit and full conviction" (1:5), and that it could be summarized in the following way: "How you turned to God from idols, to serve a living and true God, and to wait for his Son from heaven, whom he raised from the dead—Jesus, who rescues us from the wrath that is coming" (1: 9–10).

Belief that Jesus had really died and had been raised by God from death is, thus, the specific form which belief in God takes in Christianity. It changes the view of who God is, to believe that God raised Jesus from the dead. Of course those who came to that belief already believed in God, but in a somewhat different way. Paul was a convert himself, and describes his conversion as a matter of God being "pleased to reveal his Son to me" (Galatians 1:15; where the Greek reads "in me," which has multiple layers of meaning). This christological shaping of belief in God is spoken of as "the gospel," which is precisely "good news" because it involves victory over death.

In a very extraordinary chapter of one of his letters Paul vigorously defends resurrection belief as a tradition of "first importance," which he himself had received from others. He speaks of it as follows:

> That Christ died for our sins in accordance with the Scriptures, and that he was buried, and that he was raised on the third day in accordance with the Scriptures, and that he appeared to Cephas [Peter] and then to the twelve (1 Corinthians 15:4–5).

It is evident from the way in which Paul speaks of Christ's resurrection that not everyone believes this, and consequently has no belief in the resurrection of the dead. But this, he argues, is tantamount to misrepresenting God. If the dead are not raised, then Christ has not been raised; and if Christ has not been raised, then we are left, miserably, in our sins.

But who, in this argument, does Paul mean by "us"? The disagreement of historical commentators at this point is instructive. They are based in the fact that Paul offers an analogy between the first man of biblical history, Adam, and Christ, both here and more extensively in his letter to the Romans. These two people are, he holds, individuals whose actions have decisive consequences for humanity as a whole, and stand therefore at the head of two "creations." Sin came into the world through Adam, and because of his sin death spread unavoidably to all humankind (Romans 5:12, where the Greek reads "so death spread to everyone because all have sinned"; the Latin version translated this text as "in whom all have sinned," and was taken to imply the transmission of "original sin" from Adam to all of Adam's descendants). Thus the consequence of Adam's sin is universal. But, "as all die in Adam, so all will be made alive in Christ" (1 Corinthians 15:22). It could be that the second "all" is as universal as the first. There are interpreters who hold that the consequence of Christ's resurrection is the resurrection of all humanity; not necessarily to eternal life, but at least to final judgement, when God finally discriminates between good and evil. But there are also those who hold that the "all" is not to be taken in the same way as the phrase "all die in Adam"; that there is a limit on the number of the finally saved, which is expressed in the words "those who belong to Christ" (1 Corinthians 15:23), which immediately follow.

The disagreement of interpreters at this point reproduces itself, and is reflected in the history of the tradition. It may be characterised as a more universalistic and a more sectarian tendency, according to whether the benefit of Christ's resurrection is thought to be shared by all humanity, or simply by those explicitly believing in Christ. This is a matter of some importance for the issue of the xenophobia, since the sectarian tendency lends itself to deployment where separation from the stranger is a socially attractive option. To be thought to be a stranger to the significance of Christ, whether through ignorance or rejection of christological beliefs, may under particular conditions of stress or anxiety, offer justification for segregation, fear or outright hostility and persecution. Allied to the charge against Jewish people of deicide (putting the Son of God to death) this became a particularly vicious option.

The universalist interpretation, however, remains in at least one form, even within the sectarian option—that is, in the belief in the requirement of universal evangelism. With comparatively rare exceptions it was held that the meaning of the words, "Christ died for our sins" (1 Corinthians 15:3) applied to all humanity, and that as a result this good news should be universally shared by preaching. Of course a missionary faith explicitly hoping for conversions is open to large temptations, and there is an important discussion to be held about the nature of improper influences. But in principle it must be asked whether the objections sometimes alleged against evangelism apply to any form of intellectual persuasion resulting in public behavior. Is it intrinsically worse to attempt to convince people of the resurrection of Christ than to convince them of the benefits of justice or democracy? The fact that it is possible to believe otherwise about any of these matters is not in itself a reason for failing to make the attempt. It could be argued that it is more honoring to human dignity to believe that persons are capable of rational convictions in the matter of religion as of politics than to treat their current views as inviolable prejudices.

The universalist option also reproduces itself in christological doctrine by means of further refinement of thought related to the humanity of Christ. Christian teaching insisted that Jesus Christ was genuinely human. A series of disputes in the fourth and fifth centuries CE led to a definition, agreed upon at a Church Council of Chalcedon (451 CE), which codified a certain type of language. In the one person of Christ there are said to be two "natures," a divine and a human nature, inseparably and unconfusedly united. But a direct consequence of the doctrine is that the risen Christ still bears his human nature—that is, our nature, but perfected.

This doctrine of Christ's common human nature is of vital significance for the issue of xenophobia, since it entails the unity of Gentiles and Jews in Christ. In the New Testament it is most explicitly taught by Paul in the Letter to the Galatians where he reflects upon his experience of conversion from the Judaism in which he was reared. The law, he holds, was a necessary but temporary expedient, which acted as custodian and disciplinarian of sinful humanity. But faith in Christ has changed this situation. Now all may be children of God:

> As many of you as were baptized into Christ have clothed yourself with Christ. There is no longer Jew or Greek, there is no longer slave or free, there is no longer male or female; for all of you are one in Christ Jesus (Galatians 3:27–28).

Social distinctions have been replaced by unity. All are in fact the offspring of Abraham, to whom was given the promise that all the Gentiles would be blessed in him. This promise Paul understands to be, in fact, the eternal gospel. Similarly, in the Letter to the Ephesians, attributed to, but not certainly by Paul, Gentiles are specifically addressed as once "aliens from the commonwealth of Israel and strangers to the covenant of promise" (2:12). But now Christ has broken down the wall of hostility making "one new humanity in place of the two, thus making peace" (Ephesians 2:15). This new humanity, later Christian orthodoxy was to teach, is permanent and united to God in the very being of the Holy Trinity.

The range of consequences of this thought for Christian doctrine was massive, especially in the devotional and spiritual life of Christians and in the understanding of the sacraments of baptism and eucharist. In the latter lay the point of intimate contact with Christ in his death and resurrection, a union available to any person, Jew or Gentile, who confessed their faith in Christ. Though only some may become converts, the plan of God for reconciliation has universal, indeed cosmic intentions. For, as the letter to the Colossians (similar to that to the Ephesians) declared:

> In him [Christ] all the fullness of God was pleased to dwell, and through him God was pleased to dwell, to reconcile himself all things, whether on earth or in heaven, by making peace through the blood of his cross (Colossians1:20).

A universal reconciliation of any reality estranged from God, human or natural, is the aim and consequence of the coming of God into human life in the person of Jesus Christ. Its eventual achievement is guaranteed by the permanent presence of the human nature of Christ within the Godhead.

It would, perhaps, be right at this point for me to clarify my own understanding of the universalistic and sectarian tendencies within this inheritance. In my view, the New Testament documents are strongly marked by a preoccupation with the forging of a new community identity. After the expulsion of Christians from the synagogues, which happened widely but not universally in the Graeco-Roman world after 80 CE, there took place in the new communities an intensifying of emphasis upon internal relationships with a strong sectarian character. This is particularly evident in the Gospel and Letters of St. John, which speak with great feeling about the importance of love to the life of the community. But they do so in a way that strengthens the boundaries between insiders and outsiders, particularly outsiders who represent a threat to the doctrinal integrity of the community. In the Gospel of St. John "the Jews," meaning the authorities responsible for opposition to Christians, are seen as hostile to Jesus and his disciples; in the Letters of St. John it is false teachers (antichrists) who are considered to be the source of danger.

This feature of the New Testament has unmistakably given rise, and still gives rise in Christianity, to the exclusionary politics of hostility and (even) hatred, despite Jesus's teaching about the love of the enemy. But this is only one element of the tradition, which has other impulses and imperatives. If it is to have a justification of any kind, that is, if it is not simply to be rejected out of hand (which would pose other problems of interpretation), then it lies in the sheer necessity of making discriminatory judgements. If the judgement upon Amalek is that it is bent on the cruel politics of annihilation and must therefore be resisted, it may have been once the case that the existence of Christian communities was subject to annihilating threats.[4] But nothing obliges any subsequent Christian community to assume that every form of opposition is of the same kind. The politics of retrenchment and withdrawal are not the only option in all circumstances. It requires an exercise of wise discernment to know truly the situation one is in.

So far I have considered only the issue of the sectarian tendency within the Christian tradition; but there is also the opposite, namely the universalistic. This is a less marked feature of the New Testament documents, but it remains the case that "universalism" has been a recurrent feature of Christian history. By "universalism" it is here meant the view that there is no form of hostility or opposition, not even the demonic, which ultimately escapes the supreme power of God's reconciling love. This view, which has its roots in a certain kind of philosophical theodicy, was expressed classically in early Christian thought by Origen of Alexandria (185–253/54) and was, even at the time, regarded as unorthodox.

But as a tendency within Christian thinking it has a very proper motive, namely resistance to a form of ultimate dualism. At the same time it has its own concomitant disadvantage. Rabbi Jonathan Sacks has recently identified this as the philosophical danger of abstraction, and termed it "Plato's Ghost." On the contrary, in his view, "our particularity is our window upon universality . . . we serve God, author of diversity by respecting diversity."[5] What saves the idea of Christ's perpetual humanity from being abstract, we might add, is the sheer particularity of his life and death. We are united to Christ's humanity not in virtue of some abstract principle, but by the concrete fact of suffering. The eschatological conviction according to which suffering is finally transcended does not make it unreal.

I conclude, therefore, that both of the tendencies in the Christian tradition that I have described have their merits and dangers. The historic Christian community uses the Scriptures to illuminate its own circumstances. But the application of past examples to contemporary events requires wisdom. Wisdom is attentive to particularities and differences. Each human being is the bearer of a humanity loved by God. If circumstances require the political act of disengagement, withdrawal or separation from particular persons, that should never be seen as more than a penultimate necessity. The primary instinct is that of reconciliation.

Ethical Doctrine[6]

There is a close relationship between this christological teaching about reconciliation with God and ethical instruction concerning love. For the author of 1 John, indeed, "God is love and those who abide in love abide in God, and God abides in them" (1John 4:16). The New Testament is full of instruction to believers to love one another. In an anonymous writing now known as the Letter to the Hebrews, a late first century CE author explicitly and closely associates such love with hospitality to strangers:

> Let mutual love continue. Do not neglect to show hospitality to strangers, for by doing that some have entertained angels without knowing it. (13:1–2)

These exhortations are set within the context of the letter's closing remarks. The author wishes to remind this fellowship of believers of the behavior that God desires: "Do not neglect to do good and to share what you have, for such sacrifices are pleasing to God" (13:16). While the exhortations are directed toward the group of believers, it is also set within a universal context. The preceding chapter encourages them to "pursue peace with everyone (*pantōn*) and the holiness, without which no one (*oudeis*) will see the Lord" (12:14). Thus, the author prompts these believers to focus on those outside of the community as well as those inside.

Both of these dimensions are brought out in the first two verses of Hebrews. It is difficult to convey the full impact of Hebrews 13:1–2 in the English translation. Above, the New Revised Standard Version (NRSV) has translated *philadelphia* as "mutual love." This has been done, no doubt, to avoid the gender exclusivity of the more common translation, "brotherly love." However, "mutual love" does not capture the familial sense that this word includes. The fellowship of believers is called upon to love one another as though they are siblings.

In another example, Romans 12:10, *philadelphia* is found with *philostorgos*, a pairing which highlights another dimension of family life, namely that of the love of parent for child. The verse in Romans reads, "love [*philostorgoi*] one another with brotherly love [*philadelphia*]." It is particularly striking that here Paul instructs the Roman believers, composed of both Jews and

Gentiles, to redefine their notions of family in order to be inclusive to members of their fellowship. Here, it is "the redefinition of boundaries in which Paul engages—a sense of family belongingness which transcended immediate family ties and did not depend on natural or ethnic bonds. The organic imagery of the interrelatedness of the body [Romans 12:4–5] requires to be supplemented for the emotional bond of family affection."[7]

The second verse in Hebrews 13 is equally striking. Here the audience is urged to extend hospitality to strangers (*philoxenias*) because, in so doing, some people have entertained (*xenisantes*) angels unawares. The root word xenos had the literal meaning in Greek of "foreigner," "stranger," and even "enemy." This meaning, however, evolved until it came to encompass guest and host alike. This is the sense picked up by the New Testament and the Septuagint, where extending hospitality is called *xenizein*.[8]

Furthermore the word "some" (*tautēs*) in Hebrews 13:2 surely includes a reference to Abraham's gracious hospitality to the three divine strangers at the oaks of Mamre (Genesis 18:1–8). In that episode, Abraham rushes to meet three unknown men and entreats them to sit in the shade of the oaks while he provides them with water for washing and a little bread. However, Abraham produces a feast for them of a slain calf, along with milk and curds. This type of hospitality is paradigmatic[9] and for the author of Hebrews, it is the way in which the believers are to welcome the stranger.

Jesus also entreats his followers to hospitality. In Matthew 25, he declares himself to be the *xenos* whom the believers are to feed, refresh, welcome, clothe, nurse, and visit (vv. 35, 36). Those who have shown hospitality to the *xenos* will be reckoned as sheep and welcomed into the kingdom of heaven (v. 34); those who were not hospitable will depart from the presence of the Lord into everlasting fire (v. 41). This is because Jesus considers the stranger to be his family member (*adelphos*, v. 40) and someone indelibly connected to him: "just as you did for the least of these who are my brothers, you did for me" (Matthew 25:40). Carmen Bernabé Ubieta notes,

> The distinction between "insiders" and "outsiders," between natives and foreigners which was made in a city by virtue of bloodline and ethnic group, was irrelevant for those who conceived their existence according to the Christian message. In Jesus, "in his blood," all human beings—recognized as brethren—have become sons, members and heirs to the House of God.[10]

Ubieta's reference (Ephesians 2) is significant. As we have seen, there Paul discusses the power of the cross, which created a new humanity. There are no more strangers and aliens, but citizens with the saints and members of God's household (v. 19).

The vision offered in Ephesians picks up on the theme that the people of God are the guests of God. In fact, being aliens and sojourners are aspects fundamental to Israel's identity. In Genesis 15:13, Abraham was told that his descendants would be sojourners in a land not theirs, where "they will be oppressed for four hundred years." As slaves within Egypt, God heard their cry and remembered his promises to the patriarchs (Exodus 2:24). God took notice of the Israelites and delivered them from slavery. It is with this status as descendants of a "wandering Aramean" and as slaves that the Lord called them out of Egypt and with which these people entered the land of promise (Deuteronomy 26:5–9). Within the context of the covenant between God and the chosen people, the Israelites were to acknowledge that the land belonged to God and "with me you are strangers and sojourners" (Leviticus 25:23).

As guests in God's land and with the memory of being slaves in a foreign country, the people of Israel were to extend graciousness to the strangers who lived in their midst: "The alien who resides with you shall be to you as the citizen among you; you shall love the alien as yourself, for you were aliens in the land of Egypt: I am the Lord your God" (Leviticus 19:34; see also Exodus 23:9).[11] As Christine Pohl says, "Israel's historical experience and spiritual identity as chosen-yet-alien was a continual reminder of their dependence on God. Israel's status as a guest in God's land was the basis for gratitude and obedience."[12] The practical expression of this was the care of the alien, along with other powerless people like the widow and the orphan (Deuteronomy 14:29).

This sort of care for *xenoi* was not common in the ancient world. Rather than concern for the welfare of others,

> animistic fear seems in many cases to have provided the first impulse for the noble custom of hospitality found among many primitive peoples. But then it came to be realized that the basic feeling was reciprocal, and that it was more deeply seated in aliens in a strange land than in natives of the land who encountered aliens. Hence the stranger came to be granted the fellowship of table and protection, and instead of being an outlaw, he became a ward of law and religion.[13]

The people of Israel, as the guests of God, extended protection and care to aliens in their midst.[14] Christians adopted this attitude of hospitality from their spiritual ancestors, doubtless because many of them experienced this care as Gentiles and strangers to the people of God.

Furthermore, Jesus's ministry had hospitality at its very core. When asked to sum up the whole of the law, Jesus quoted Deuteronomy 6:5 and Leviticus 19:18 (Matthew 22:37–40; see also Mark 12:29, 30, 33; Luke 10:27; Paul also made this statement in Romans 13:9–10). Love, complete love of God and love of neighbor, is the way of eternal life (Luke 10:25). The parable that Jesus tells here in response to the question "who is my neighbor?" is one in which a Samaritan, someone who is an outsider, is upheld as the exemplary neighbor (Luke 10:30–37). Through this parable and by his association of himself with outcasts (Matthew 25:31–46), Jesus blurs the boundaries of insider and outsider. The followers of Jesus are to live their lives according to new ideas of kinship and humanity, thus welcoming those who would have been previously unapproachable.

The gospels include numerous illustrations of how Jesus often came near people who were ostracized and allowed them to approach him. These people included sinners, lepers, tax collectors, unclean and foreign women, as well as those possessed by demons. His closest companions were people from the margins—manual laborers such as fishermen, tax collectors, and women. And it is these people from undesirable backgrounds whom Jesus taught and with whom he shared table fellowship, the most powerful symbol of hospitality.

John Koenig notes how Acts continues this line of ministry:

> For its part, Acts may be read as a collection of guest and host stories depicting missionary ventures that have originated in circles associated with the earliest churches. Luke's special concern is to show how itinerant residential believers can support one another in the worldwide mission of the Church. Through this mutuality, he believes the Holy Spirit will bring about rich exchanges of spiritual and material gifts; and the Church will grow. [15]

Philoxenia and *philadelphia* are fundamental practices for early Christians. It is significant that loving and welcoming the stranger is set side by side with the love of our Christian family members (Hebrews 13:1–2 and Romans 12:10, 13). It is within the context of communal relationships that humans are best equipped to support and care for those who are living in the margins. This is because actively extending hospitality is difficult. It requires time and energy, not to mention the qualities of compassion and empathy. Mutual support, then, within the community is necessary to sustain this ministry to which we are called. Indeed,

> to do hospitality well, we need models for whom it is part of a way of life. We must learn from those who have found ways to practice hospitality within the distinct tensions and arrangements of contemporary society. We also need a community with whom to share the demands and burdens of welcoming strangers. [16]

Finally, the concept of grace is an important motivation for acts of hospitality. Speaking from a Baptist tradition, but also for all who profess the mercy of God, Scott H. Moore says,

> hospitality is a sign of our commitment to a culture of life. Hospitality is the means by which we in the middle take care of the vulnerable ones at the edges. . . . Cultivating hospitality is what we Baptists used to call "growing in

grace." It is the means by which we treat others, not as the way they "deserve" to be treated, but in the way God has treated us. [17]

Generalizing the Tradition

As I have already indicated, there is a serious question to ask, which already has its roots in Christian history—whether the tradition of hospitality to the stranger is generalizable, or whether the only access to it is by conversion to Christianity. The latter view would be an example of what I have called the "sectarian" tendency, and it has large numbers of ancient and contemporary exponents. It has to be admitted that there is New Testament support for supposing that *philadelphia* is recommended as an internal Christian virtue, and is not the same as universal benevolence. On the other hand, as we have suggested there are social reasons why the protection and nurture of a particular identity was of importance at a particular moment of Christian history; and, in any case, there is a continuous need for wise discrimination between opposition of different kinds. "Universal benevolence" is neither wise nor appropriate in all circumstances. Furthermore there is, as we have just suggested, a connection between the fostering of an intensively supportive community of love, and the capacity to sustain the arduous task of the support of the marginal. The two should not be seen as competitive with, or alternative to each other. In other words it is Christian teaching that hospitality can and should be extended to strangers, whether or not they are part of the Christian community. What qualifies a person as someone with a claim on Christian compassion is their humanity, which is part of the humanity of Christ. To love them is to love Christ in them. As the Rule of St. Benedict memorably taught, *Hospites tamquam Christus suscipiantur*/guests are to be received as Christ (chapter 53).

Such a view might be expected to commend itself within Christianity, however much it has been contradicted in Christian history. The question is, however, whether it is dependent upon the christological reference. If so, it could only be expected to be of interest to Christians. To commend it to others would, in effect, be an invitation to conversion.

A double response to this challenge seems appropriate. On the one hand, I should like to be generally positive, rather than embarrassed about evangelism, which simply seems implicit in Christianity. It is true that the practices inspired by missionary zeal have included gross and wholly improper forms of constraint, manipulation and persuasion. But Christianity is rooted in an ineradicable desire for God, which it derives from the Hebrew Scriptures. It seems impossible for a person to enjoy the vision of God and not to long to share it with others. The heart of evangelism is this desire to share, which exists long before particular modes or policies of sharing have been formulated. Friedrich Schleiermacher (1768–1834) wrote of the longing to communicate which lies at the heart of all Christian experience, making it impossible for the phenomenon of Christian faith to be a solitary experience. The social character of the faith, above all participation in a community of praise, is of its essence. To hold this view of evangelism is a far cry from the psychological pressure and duplicity of which certain evangelistic practices are plainly guilty.

The great advantage of being positive about evangelism is that it enables Christians to speak of the relationship between love, suffering and repentance that is contained in the narrative of Christ's crucifixion. However difficult it may be for consistent theological formulation, it is at the crucifixion that God and the world's evil is brought into the closest relationship at least from the point of view of classical Christian theology. To abandon that crux is to run the danger of embracing Plato's ghost, and of opting for an abstract deity.

Given then that a Christian cannot reasonably be required to abandon a desire that others may share a view which has so enriched his or her own life, is there a way of formulating these thoughts about the significance of hospitality which make them accessible to people of other religious traditions? At this point I want to invoke a metaphor for a common psychological process that may assist the discussion, the metaphor of "making space" for an idea. Human learning is only possible on the assumption that we carry about with us a large reservoir of unexplored ideas and associations that we have picked up from a vast array of resources. Many of these simply remain dormant. Some are revived by new encounters; saying "I didn't know that I knew that" makes perfectly good sense. Equally sensible is the idea that room or space can be made for a new idea, which is so far unassimilated to the larger schemes we use for organizing our ways of thinking. We can discriminate between different kinds of new ideas, holding that some—for example, sci-fi fantasies—are too fantastic to be given serious thought, whereas others which may even include ideas which originated in science fiction have some serious points of contact with things we know or experience about the way the world is.

My suggestion is that the act of "making space" for an idea from a religion whose schema we do not hold is both possible and desirable. Moreover that idea will have more or less significance for us, the more we can relate it to things that we have already experienced. My suggestion is that to "make space" is itself a form of hospitality, a taking seriously of the other as other, a willingness to let the others be what they are on their own account, not to assimilate them to an existing rejection or caricature.

The difficulty for the conversation of religious traditions is that they work in a field already littered with caricature. Indeed so prevalent is this phenomenon that, rather like ubiquitous kitsch in religious art, it seems only practical to work with a theory that embraces, rather than one which excludes caricature. It might be possible to proceed in the following way. An unfamiliar thought from another religious tradition will bear a relation of some kind to an existing caricature in the mind, which itself will suggest certain allegedly negative features of that tradition. Rather than attempt to reject the latter out of hand, an internal argument needs to be set up between the caricature and the new idea. If this is articulated publicly, it can offer opportunities for a continuing dialogue with people of other religious traditions, who are in this way brought into, not excluded from, the processes of refining understanding by escaping from caricature.

Recently Miroslav Volf, reflecting upon the searing experience of the Balkan crisis (he is a Croatian who taught in a seminary at the outbreak of War in 1991), has written suggestively of the need for a proper distance from one's own culture, drawing upon the migration of Abraham as a "stepping out of enmeshment in the network of inherited cultural relations as a correlate of faith in the one God."[18] But departure is not to be understood as absence or flight; it is also a way of living in a culture, a creating of space within oneself to receive the other. The metaphor of "making space" is adopted to avoid inhabiting a self-enclosed world that shuns others, or only admits them on already preformulated terms.

The same book has a profound exploration of the complexity of establishing non-exclusionary identities. Exclusion involves either insisting on sharp separation without interrelationships, or a policy of subjugation and assimilation. In neither case is the other taken seriously as other. But to be human means both to take in, and to keep out; the spatial metaphor implies the making of space for the other. My suggestion is, here, that hospitality to ideas from other religions involves a non-exclusionary judgement, which discerns them in their difference, neither excluding nor assimilating them, but providing them with space. In that space lies the possibility for the correction of caricature, for the enrichment of the imagination, for the relating of new ideas to more familiar experiences, and—should it not be openly admitted?—for conversion. The fear that one may be laying oneself open to conversion needs to be honestly examined. Is not such a reaction unworthy of the love of God that casts out all fear? Does it not, from a Christian point of view, imply a curious narrowness in God's dealings with humanity to suppose that He has nothing to teach us through other ways of faiths? The anxiety that one is abandoning all forms of evaluation is groundless. To make space is explicitly to retain the possibility of a subsequent judgement or discrimination. The argument is in favor of a non-exclusionary judgement, which is well represented in the metaphor of "making space."

I write a final personal paragraph. Never in my life have I experienced anything remotely like persecution or oppression, especially not for my religious convictions. In this sense I may be uniquely disqualified from adding what a Christian is bound to add about repentance and forgiveness. Judgement about oppression may lead to anger against injustice, and anger is a human necessity. Without it we would have no way of resourcing our reactions to wrongdoing. But there is a difference between the immediate response to anger, and what a great English moral philosopher, Bishop Joseph Butler (1692–1752) called "settled anger." The latter can be, and has been in the history of human relations a great disaster for humanity. Unless humanity learns a way of making space for the other who has committed wrongdoing, violence will escalate to an intolerable degree. The mobilization and institutionalization of settled anger in politics is a threat to humanity, which the religions have no business to fuel.

NOTES

1. It is accurately controversial in Christian theology what this evidence signifies about the state of the Christian, and whether failure is inevitable. But *that* such unreformed behavior occurs is universally admitted and regretted.

2. For the Jewish view on the creation of humans in the image of God, see page 23; for the Muslim parallel, see page 85; for the Buddhist idea of the unity of humanity, see page 126.

3. For the Buddhist view on the importance of being with like-minded people, see page 128.

4. For a Jewish discussion on Amalek, see pages 31 ff.

5. Jonathan Sachs, *The Dignity of Difference* (London; New York: Continuum, 2002), 56.

6. I acknowledge the substantial assistance of Laura L. Brenneman, my research assistant, in the preparation and formulation of this text.

7. James D. G. Dunn, *Romans 9–16*, Word Biblical Commentary vol. 38b (Dallas: Word Books, 1988), 741.

8. Sir. 29:25; Acts 10:6, 18, 23, 32; 21:16; 28:7; Heb. 13:2; from John Koenig, "Hospitality" in *The Anchor Bible Dictionary* vol. 3 (New York: Doubleday, 1992), 299.

9. See Philo, *On Abraham* 107, 113; Josephus, *Antiquities* 1.11.2 196; *b. Sota* 1ba (Babylonian Talmud).

10. Carmen Bernabé Ubieta, *"Neither Xenoi nor Parakoi, Sympolitai and Oikeioi tou Theou* (Eph 2.19)," in *Social Scientific Models for Interpreting the Bible*, 276.

11. For the discussion of these concepts in Judaism, see page 43.

12. Christine D. Pohl, "Hospitality from the Edge," *The Annual of the Society of Christian Ethics* (1995), 125.

13. Gustav Stählin, *"xenos, xenia, xenizō, xenodocheō, philoxenia, philoxenos,"* in *The Theological Dictionary of the New Testament*, vol. V, ed. Gerhard Friedrich (Grand Rapids: Eerdmans, 1967), 3–4.

14. Indeed, when they did not, it was numbered as one of the reasons for punishment and exile from the land. See Jer. 7:5–7; 22:3–4, 15–16; Exod. 22:21–25; Deut. 24:17; 27:19; Job 31:13–22; Zech. 7:9–12; Mal. 3:5; cf. James 1:27.

15. Koenig, "Hospitality," ABD, 301.

16. Pohl, "Welcoming the Stranger," *Sojourners* 28 (1999), 14.

17. Scott H. Moore, "Hospitality as an Alternative to Tolerance," *Communio* 27 (2000), 608.

18. Miroslav Volf, *Exclusion and Embrace*: A Theological Exploration of Identity, Otherness and Reconciliation (Nashville: Abingdon, 1996), 39.

Chapter Four

Islam

Epistemological Crisis, Theological Hostility,
and the Problem of Difference

Vincent J. Cornell

In the Introduction to his chapter, "Judaism: The Battle for Survival, the Struggle for Compassion," Alon Goshen-Gottstein discusses the complementary roles of the historian of religion and the theologian in the critical study of religious thought and practice. In his view, the task of the historian of religion is to provide a descriptive analysis of religion, whereas the task of the theologian is to construct (or reconstruct) religion as a system of thought. Often, however, the task of the historian of religion may replicate that of the theologian. As Goshen-Gottstein stated in an earlier draft, the theologian's "success lies in his ability to recast the various historical data [of the religious tradition] into new structures of understanding, through which a vision of religion will emerge that will be faithful to tradition's history, which provides a fresh articulation and vision of tradition."[1] However, as Steven Wasserstrom has demonstrated about the works of Mircea Eliade, Gershom Scholem, and Henry Corbin, the historian of religion may also be involved in a reconstructive enterprise with important theological implications.[2]

HISTORY AND THE CRITICAL STUDY OF TRADITION

The historical analysis of a religious tradition often challenges the theological and moral ideals of the tradition by juxtaposing such ideals against the realities of the tradition as it is practiced and understood through time. Furthermore, since every work of history necessarily examines the past from the perspective of the present, all historical projects, including those of religious history, are interpretive and thus reconstructive in nature. A work of religious history either reconfirms tradition by memorializing it or helps to redefine tradition by critically examining the relationship between theory and practice. This dialogue with the past helps create new theological and moral perspectives, by which a religious tradition responds to cultural, political, or epistemological challenges. No tradition is static and every tradition is open to multiple histories. To paraphrase Hans-Georg Gadamer, a tradition— whether religious or otherwise—is always in a process of transformation.[3] Like the "Transformer" robots made by Japanese toymakers, a religious tradition may take on a different form in different contexts. Its overall structure remains the same, but the contours of interpretation may change according to the exigencies of time, space, and culture.

Unfortunately, this constructive view of the relationship between theology and history, which seems self-evident to comparative theologians and historians of religion, has been far from universally accepted outside of the academy. Histories of theology may be written for each religious tradition, but when history helps create new theologies, they are often resisted. Part of the problem is that the tradition-as-process perspective described above has often been construed as a Trojan horse for historical or genealogical critiques of religion. Such critiques are seen as antithetical to both religion and tradition because they challenge the reification of "authentic" tradition as primordial or unchanging (Tradition with a capital "T") and because they regard much of religion, including theology, as a human construct. In the study of Islam, these perspectives may be exemplified by the "sectarian milieu" critique of the Qur'an inspired by the work of John Wansborough[4] or by critical works on early Islamic history written from Marxist or Weberian perspectives.[5] Some studies, such as those of Wansborough and Crone and Cook, have been used polemically to deny the historicity of the Qur'an and hence the legitimacy of Islam as an independent religion.[6] In other cases, radical Muslim modernists have used historical revisionism to create theologies that have rightly been criticized for denuding Islam of either its tradition or its social meaning.[7]

The historical and genealogical perspectives have themselves been criticized by Western defenders of tradition such as Alasdair MacIntyre, who sees them as fostering a philosophically incoherent perspectivism that undermines any common foundation for the virtues.[8] However, as MacIntyre's own career demonstrates, it is possible to be a critical historian or a philosopher of religion without being a positivist, and it is equally possible to acknowledge the insights of genealogists such as Friedrich Nietzsche and Michel Foucault without accepting the full implications of their epistemologies. As MacIntyre reminds us, the genealogical perspective is not as self-critical as it appears to be and its epistemology is subject to the same critiques that its practitioners have applied to others.[9] If the worldwide religious revival of the past fifty years has proved anything, it is that God still exists, despite the efforts of both historical positivists and Nietzscheans to kill him. Even today, at the start of the twenty-first century, most adherents of the so-called Abrahamic faiths would agree with the sentiment once expressed by a bumper sticker sold by the Campus Crusade for Christ: "'God is dead': Nietzsche. 'Nietzsche is dead': God."

What critical studies of religion do most effectively is not question the existence of God or the legitimacy of a religious tradition, but question people's understandings of God and the structures of power that mediate how people think about God. Epistemologically, historical and genealogical critiques of religion challenge notions of ultimate truth by demonstrating, first, the wide variety of truth-claims held by human beings, and second, how notions of the truth have been mediated politically and socially through time. By embracing relativistic or pluralistic notions of truth, they contest the inalterability of religious laws and the primordial nature of tradition, thus posing a challenge to religious tradition that may at times be as significant as the threat of rival theologies. This is particularly a problem for Islam and Christianity, where creedal agreement as to the nature of the truth is a precondition for both salvation and religious identity. The fundamentalist revival in both religions reveals a crisis of cognitive dissonance: previous regimes of power and authority no longer dominate religious discourse, and the spatial and conceptual juxtaposition of alternatives to traditionally held world views provide moral and theological challenges that neither Islam nor Christianity has yet been able to meet adequately. This is especially acute for Islam, for unlike in Christianity, where both liberals and fundamentalists have largely accepted the premises of political liberalism and modernism, most Muslims have turned away from active philosophical engagement with modernity and have instead sought refuge in tradition and in questions of morality and political ethics.

OTHERNESS AND RELIGIOUS AUTHENTICITY

It is at this point that the epistemological crisis of contemporary Islam bears most directly on the subject of "Hostility, Hospitality, and the Hope of Human Flourishing." Shortly after the terrorist attacks of September 11, 2001, two corollaries of the historical and genealogical critiques of religious tradition—the acceptance of religious and cultural pluralism and the critique of unitary notions of morality—were cited by a Saudi al Qaeda activist as the theological and ethical consequences of liberal democracy. In an essay composed shortly before his death at the hands of Saudi security forces in 2003, Yusuf al-Ayyeri (the reputed head of Al Qaeda in the Arabian Peninsula) portrayed democracy as a grave ideological threat to Islam. According to

Ayyeri, this is because democracy "seductively" leads Muslims to believe that they can shape their own destinies and that by using their own reasoning, they can alter the laws that govern them. Democracy's reliance on public reason, Ayyeri asserts, will lead believers to accept moral relativism and cultural difference, ignore the laws promulgated by God for humankind, undermine the *Shari'ah* as the codification of God's will, and "make Muslims love this world, forget the next world, and abandon jihad."[10] The gendered tone of Ayyeri's argument is unmistakable: Eve, in the guise of a feminized Western democracy, seduces the Islamic Adam into accepting the forbidden fruits of personal autonomy and free will. According to Ayyeri's pessimistic moral calculus, theological and moral relativism are the inevitable consequences of individualism, and individualism is the ideological mask worn by egoism, the quintessential sin of humanity in Islam.

Although Ayyeri was an extremist, the issues he raises are not very different from the questions posed by less radical Muslim thinkers. For many Muslims, the entire problematic of "Religion and the Other: Hostility, Hospitality, and the Hope of Human Flourishing," is framed from the standpoint of Western liberalism. Most never consider that hospitality in a religious context means anything more than inviting non-Muslim guests to one's home or treating them in a civil manner. If by "hospitality" one means etiquette, then Islam, which long ago assimilated Arab traditions of hospitality and sociability, is one of the most hospitable of religions. Responding to the current lack of hospitality between Muslims and non-Muslims in many parts of the world, Muslims would most likely point out that the Qur'an and the Sunnah of the Prophet Muhammad are full of exhortations that call on believers to practice hospitality. The hostility between Israelis and Palestinians, or for that matter, between Afghanis and American troops, are due, they would say, to the effects of occupation and imperialist or neo-colonialist domination, not to the teachings of Islam.

If this problematic were posed from the standpoint of xenophobia, many Muslims would assert that "true" or "authentic" Islam has solved the problem of xenophobia by uniting humanity in a single brotherhood, the Islamic *Ummah*. According to Muslim idealists, who include a wide range of believers from political Islamists to ordinary Muslims who are active in mosques and Islamic centers, the fears and prejudices that have divided human beings throughout history can best be overcome by the conversion of everyone to Islam. What, after all, could be more hospitable than to welcome all nations into the great tent of God's love and justice? Christian fundamentalists would probably assert the same. For such idealists, the few cultural differences that might remain between people after conversion to Islam would be overcome through the systematic application of *tawhid* (oneness) to all aspects of life.[11] Practically speaking, this would involve subsuming all human relations under the Islamic legal category of *mu'amalat*, the aspect of the Shari'ah that covers public acts. Similarly, the concept of *tawhid*, which was formerly understood as the theological notion of divine unity, has become in the hands of Muslim idealists an alternative epistemology in which divine unity is replicated by Islamized versions of everything from politics, to economics, to the "Islamization of knowledge."[12]

To such partisans of the *Tawhidic* perspective, all reconstructions of Islamic theology and history that seek to transcend creedal boundaries are, by their very nature, inauthentic. According to this view, Muslim contributions to the present "Religion and the Other" project lack authenticity because this project seeks to transcend mere religious tolerance and asks fundamental questions of religious boundary maintenance, such as why theological differences produce hostility or how hospitality and human flourishing might be promoted in a pluralistic and multi-religious world. Even more, this project might suggest a covert political agenda, in which religious understanding is attained through a de facto world theology where theological pluralism is the norm rather than the exception. In this perspective, the problem of "Religion and the Other" is acute for every exoteric Muslim, because the concept of *tawhid* has historically militated against pluralistic world views. As a theology, *tawhid* rules out any religious perspective that cannot be construed as monotheistic. Medieval Islamic states actively suppressed theologies of dualism and polytheism, and non-theistic belief systems, such as Buddhism, were virtually beyond discussion. Even the Islamic juridical notion of religious toleration, expressed through the concept of "Religions of the Book," cannot accurately be understood as implying pluralism in the modern, liberal sense of the term. Although monotheists of other religions, such as Jews and Christians, often coexisted peacefully with Muslims, from the standpoint of Islamic law all such coexistence had to take place either within the boundaries of an Islamic state or in an international context where hostility was the normal state of affairs. The reason for this was as much epistemological as it was political: Only through the divinely bestowed laws of the Shari'ah could truth and justice be assured for all human beings. Seen in this light, the Islamist utopias envisioned by integrist organizations such as Hamas and Hizbollah are not so different from the political theories of mainstream scholars of the pre-modern period. For most medieval and modern Muslim activists alike, the only "real" civilization is Islamic civilization and the only "real" justice is Islamic justice.

THEOLOGY, MORALITY, AND DIFFERENCE

As an institutionalized religion, Islam has always had a problem with difference, and hostility toward non-Muslims has usually been accompanied by hostility against Muslim dissidents as well. Throughout much of Islamic history, meaningful debates about theology or epistemology were discouraged, whether inside or outside of the creedal boundaries of Islam. Adoption of epistemologies deemed alien to Islam, such as those of Hellenistic philosophy, brought charges of *bid'ah* (unwarranted innovation of tradition) or *zandaqah* (heresy), which could lead to imprisonment or worse. For the Muslim freethinker, heresy was more dangerous than apostasy (*riddah*), because the apostate could always repent and return to Islam, whereas the heretic had no such recourse. For Muslim jurists and theologians, it was not fear of the other as an individual that was seen as a threat, but fear of the other's ideas and values. Alien epistemologies posed the danger of ideological infection, which, it was feared, sowed doubt in the minds of Muslims, compromised belief in *tawhid*, and threatened the Muslim Ummah with social and religious discord (*fitnah*). Cultural xenophobia was less of a problem in premodern Islam than epistemological hostility or "ideophobia," a fear of alien concepts and world views. This attitude continues to exist today, not only in the doctrines of extremist groups such as al-Qaeda and the Taliban, but also in the beliefs of many mainstream Muslims who have been influenced by Wahhabism, Salafism, and other purist ideologies. Few of today's Muslims, beset as they are by ideological approaches to religion and postcolonial fears of Western imperialism, display the confident attitude of the Abbasid-era scholar Ibn Qutayba (d. 889), who wrote in *Uyun al-Akhbar* (The Sources of Knowledge):

> Knowledge is the stray camel of the believer; it benefits one regardless from where one takes it. It will not lessen the truth if you hear it from pagans, nor can those who harbor hatred derive any advice from it. Shabby clothes do no injustice to a beautiful woman, nor do shells to pearls, nor does gold's origin from dust. Whoever neglects to take the good from the place where it is found misses an opportunity, and opportunities are as fleeting as the clouds . . . Ibn 'Abbas (the cousin of the Prophet Muhammad) said: "Take wisdom from whomever you hear it, for the fool may utter a wise saying and a target may be hit by a beginner."[13]

Ibn Qutayba lived in an era when the Abbasid Caliphate dominated much of the known world and its intellectuals assumed that Islamic civilization was on the cutting-edge of historical progress. At that time, foreign epistemologies posed little danger; however, only a century later, the North African jurist Muhammad ibn Abi Zayd al-Qayrawani (d. 998), who was strongly opposed to the Abbasids and their project of translating Greek philosophical works into Arabic, concocted a myth that blamed the Byzantine emperor for the influence of Greek philosophy on Islamic thought. According to this story, the ruler of Byzantium was afraid that, if his own people took up the study of philosophy, they would abandon Christianity. Therefore, he collected all of the Greek philosophical works in his empire and locked them up in a secret building. When the vizier of the Abbasid Caliph heard about these books, he asked the emperor if he could have them. The emperor was delighted to comply with this request. He informed the Orthodox bishops that the works of Greek philosophy, which were a threat to Christianity, could now be sent to Baghdad, where they would undermine the religion of Islam.[14] Unfortunately, it is Ibn Abi Zayd, and not Ibn Qutayba, whose opinions are more common in today's climate of ideophobia and theological hostility in Islam.

In Muslim culture, theological correctness is related to morality in a way that is analogous to the culture of Catholicism during the Inquisition. For many of today's Muslims, bad theology leads to bad morals, especially when the offenders are Western liberals or long-time historical antagonists such as Jews or Hindus. This attitude promotes inter-religious hostility by compounding epistemological hostility with the fear of moral pollution. The conflation of theology and morality, which largely died out in Christianity (except in fundamentalism) during the Enlightenment, has been reinforced in Islam by the spread of anti-Enlightenment and narrowly scriptural doctrines of religious and moral perfectionism in the colonial and post-colonial eras. Islamic integrists such as Sayyid Qutb (d. 1966) and Abu al-Ala Mawdudi (d. 1979) have ascribed the political and social failures of secular regimes in the Muslim world to a new form of spiritual and moral infidelity (*jahiliyyah*) caused by the adoption of "un-Islamic" values and epistemologies. Qutb's view of *jahiliyyah* echoes the earlier ideas of Muhammad ibn 'Abd al-Wahhab (d. 1791), the founder of the Wahhabi sect of Arabia. In his influential book *Ma'alim fi al-Tariq* (Signs on the Way), Qutb asserts, "Any society that is not Muslim is *jahiliyyah* . . . as is any society in which something other than God alone is worshipped . . . Thus, we must include in this category all the societies that now exist on earth."[15] Qutb's concept of *jahiliyyah* remains central to the epistemological perspective of the Muslim Brotherhood, as well as to those of its successors, including Hamas, Islamic Jihad, and Tunisia's al-Nahda party. Al-Qaeda and its sister organizations from the Arab world to Indonesia also base their ideology on Qutb's concept of *jahiliyyah*.

Among Sunni Muslims not affiliated with these organizations, the concept of ideological *jahiliyyah* has led to a widespread distrust of Western systems of thought, particularly with regard to the humanities and social sciences, which are often seen as sources of epistemological infection.[16] Until quite recently, the intellectual tools that are provided by these disciplines have been acquired inadequately, if at all. The result in Sunni Islam has been the creation of a self-righteous and politically active cadre of applied technologists—engineers, doctors, and computer scientists—who view religion as a mathematical equation in which theology and virtue must balance on either side of a purified Islamic identity, and who also view the world as completely malleable to the human will. No doctrine of Islamic integrism is less justifiable from a Qur'anic perspective than the idea that human beings can make the world fully perfect through political or social action. Even if all of the world were Muslim, a perfectly just society would still not exist. It is hard to imagine a doctrine more religiously misguided and philosophically confused than this contradictory attempt to mix (a) scientific empiricism with regard to the physical world, (b) totalitarian perfectionism with regard to the sociopolitical world, and (c) fundamentalist traditionalism with regard to the historical past. In the sixteenth century, a Moroccan scholar named Ridwan ibn 'Abdallah al-Januwi (d. 1583) suffered discrimination from the religious elites of Fez because his father was a converted Christian and his mother was a converted Jew. Commenting on the contradictory values of his time, he said, "Soon you will see, when the dust clears, whether a horse or an ass is beneath you!"[17] Today's alternative is more lethal; it may be a bomb, not an ass, on which many Muslims are riding.

CRITICAL HISTORY AND THEOLOGY

In order to overcome the epistemological crisis of contemporary Islam, Muslim intellectuals must look critically at the history of Islamic thought and formulate a theology and moral philosophy that has its roots in the classical intellectual tradition of Islam rather than in a utopian golden age or in a modern ideological construct such as the "Islamization of knowledge." Whether such utopias refer back to the time of the Prophet and his companions, or to nostalgia for past imperial glory under a Pan-Islamic Caliphate, both alternatives focus more on politics and social control than on spirituality. Neither fundamentalism nor perfectionism provides an adequate response to the theological and moral challenges of pluralism and globalization. Muslims must learn to be more intellectually open about their own doctrinal differences and about the memories that they make of their past before they can be theologically hospitable with believers in other religions. Especially now, in the midst of the culture war between Islam and the West inaugurated by the terrorist attacks of September 11, 2001, Muslims need to reopen the question of what Mohammed Arkoun has termed the "unthought" and the "unthinkable" in Islamic discourse.[18]

However, the Muslim theologian or historian who adopts such a critical-theoretical approach risks rejection by many, if not a majority, of her co-religionists. Throughout Islamic history, the actual diversity of theological, juridical, and philosophical views was repeatedly contradicted by persistent, if unrealistic, attempts to create a unifying orthodoxy. This move toward orthodoxy began with the jurist Muhammad ibn Idris al-Shafi'i (d. 820), who systematized Islamic legal reasoning by limiting both the scriptural sources of knowledge and the forms of logic that were used to approach them. It was continued in the attempt by certain Abbasid Caliphs (ca. 832–847) to abolish traditionalism and impose by force a rigid form of Mu'tazili rationalism. It came closest to succeeding in the centuries following the Seljuq vizier Nizam al-Mulk's (d. 1092) attempt to institute a common hermeneutic and theology in state-sponsored religious colleges.[19] Although some scholars have maintained that the concept of orthodoxy is inappropriate in Islam, Nizam al-Mulk's use of the Persian term *niku i'tiqad* ("pure belief") to describe the type of Sunni Islam he advocated leaves little doubt as to what he intended.[20]

Since the second half of the twentieth century, another attempt to create an Islamic orthodoxy has been under way, this time directed by Wahhabi purists and Salafi integrists such as the Muslim Brotherhood, who in the 1960s formed an alliance of convenience under the rubric of the Muslim World League of Saudi Arabia.[21] The institutional sites of this movement are Islamic centers throughout the world, particularly in regions that either are new to Islam, or have just returned to Islam, such as Europe, the United States, and Central Asia. The libraries, bookstores, and classrooms of these institutions are remarkably uniform in the materials they disseminate and in the version of Islam that they advocate. In the United States, the work of Salafi reformists has been abetted by organizations such as the Islamic Society of North America and the Muslim Students' Association, which promote similar theological, epistemological and political agendas. Using a combination of peer pressure, modern marketing techniques, and the creation of authoritarian bodies such as the Fiqh Council of North America, such organizations have largely succeeded in marginalizing Muslim academics and representatives of the historical tradition of Islam who do not agree with them. Their targets include not only liberal or "progressive" Muslim academics but also those who self-consciously represent the premodern intellectual traditions of Islam, including Sufis and those who seek to revive and reform, rather than to replace, the Islam of the historical legal schools.[22] Using petrodollars, the institutional support of the Muslim World League, and now the mass media, modern Salafis, Wahhabis, and like-minded reformists have succeeded in making Islam more doctrinally homogeneous, and hence more orthodox, than ever before.[23]

A non-Muslim scholar, who does not have a personal stake in the form that Islam will take in the twenty-first century, might respond that this attempt to create an integrist Islamic orthodoxy is a normal part of the development of Islam as a religious tradition.[24] As Alasdair MacIntyre observes, "A tradition of inquiry characteristically bears within itself an always open to revision history of itself in which the past is characterized and recharacterized in terms of developing evaluations of the relationship of the various parts of that past to the achievements of the present."[25] In this sense, the Salafi and Wahhabi rejection of premodern Islamic institutions and the attempt to recuperate a lost sense of unity by rationalizing away past "accretions" are a normal part of the dialectic between the past and the present. As MacIntyre further observes, "Knowledge is possessed only in and through participation in a history of dialectical encounters."[26] Islamic integrist reformism is, on this view, only the most recent of such dialectical encounters. However, when such dialectic is based on an epistemological rupture between an idealized time of origins and the de-legitimization of intellectual traditions that dominated Islamic discourse for centuries, this can only be construed as a tacit admission by Salafi reformers that Islam, as a system of thought, has been a failure. It is neither fair to Islam nor historically justifiable to assert that the majority of Islamic intellectual history has been worthless, or that the soul of Islam can be recuperated by political and social means alone.

From a logical point of view, the rejection of the historical traditions of Islam by Salafist and Sunni integrist intellectuals constitutes a massive example of the fallacy of the excluded middle. To all intents and purposes, there are no epistemological "middle ages" for integrist Islam. According to the Salafi version of authenticity, there is only the era of the Prophet Muhammad and his companions and the current attempt to reconstitute that utopian period through the reestablishment of the Shari'ah. With the exception of the Hanbali traditions of law and theology, the intervening 1200 years of Islamic intellectual history are seen as a theological and moral dark age of unwarranted innovation. While there is much discussion of past Islamic glory by contemporary ideologues, it is seldom mentioned that the glory of Islamic civilization was built on foundations that have largely been rejected by present-day reformers. Such a position is both logically and historically untenable. One cannot ignore the fact that many of the traditions rejected by contemporary Salafis developed from the same roots that nurtured Salafism itself. How else can one explain how the same early ascetics cited by Wahhabis to promote Salafi values can also be cited by Sufis as forerunners of their own tradition? Such paradoxes are proof that Islam is not as simple as it is made to seem. It is not sufficient to take refuge from the problematic of the past in a fundamentalist revival of the "myth of the eternal return."[27]

As a matter of fact, Muslims have resorted to this myth throughout their history, starting as far back as the earliest intra-Islamic doctrinal conflicts in the seventh century CE. However, the "eternal return" to the Way of Muhammad was traditionally accomplished as much through the inculcation of inner moral and spiritual values as it was through outward action. Today's reformists forget that the Prophet Muhammad was a Messenger of God, not a social engineer. Social engineers start on the outside, by first creating political and social systems, and then move inside, toward the individual; by contrast, God starts on the inside, by first changing the individual person, and then leaving it to people to reform society by applying their new consciousness to the social world.[28]

Today's attempt by Salafi reformist movements to engineer Islamic society socially in the context of the modern nation-state has very little in common with the pre-modern history of Islamic reform. The current debate over the goals of Islamic reform is no longer a conversation or even an argument, but instead has become a shouting match among ideologues jockeying for exclusive power. Real arguments depend for their existence on shared assumptions, which are hard to find at the extremes of Islamic discourse. The concept of warranted assertibility, by means of which competing ideas are judged as rational arguments, means little if everyone has the warrant to assert whatever political power allows them to assert, whether it makes sense or not.

According to Alasdair MacIntyre, such chaotic emotivism, which is characteristic of contemporary Salafi reformist thought, is a quintessentially modern phenomenon. Thus, it can only be antithetical to Islamic tradition, conceived historically. This leads to the ironic conclusion that modern Salafi and neo-Hanbali integrism is just as emotivist, just as modern, and hence just as radically different from historical Islamic tradition as its main opponent, Islamic liberalism.[29] In the ongoing debate about who speaks for Islam, the integrist voice is no more authentic than that of the modernist, the Sufi, or the "progressive" legal traditionalist. Perhaps what is most ironic about this debate is that these competing versions of Islam are epistemologically so different from each other as to constitute separate systems of warrantability. When Muslims were first instructed by the Qur'an to say to unbelievers, "To you your religion and to me mine" (Qur'an 109:6), no one imagined that Muslims might one day be compelled to utter this phrase to each other. Because of this epistemological divergence, hostility toward the other within the Islamic community is as significant for the future of Islam as hostility directed toward the non-Muslim other outside of the community.

Authentic intellectual traditionalism in the Islamic world today exists primarily among the Shi'ite clergy and Sufis. Cultural traditionalism, in which local customs are cast as religious virtues, is found widely in the rural areas of the Islamic world, where it is mixed with Salafi or Wahhabi ideology in regions such as Saudi Arabia, Afghanistan, and South Asia. As for the rest of the world of Sunni Islam, the historical traditions of Islamic thought are a forgotten memory, and the great thinkers of the Islamic past are merely names that one learns in secondary school. Since modern Sunni thought has severed itself from its roots, the most practical way to confront the theological and moral challenges of modernity is to meet them head-on, and not to hide behind the veil of a supposedly "pure" time of origins that is itself a modern ideological construction. The deeper questions of "Islam and the other" must be answered by a new Islamic theology of difference, one that engages in the kind of dialectic by which all historical traditions develop and evolve, a dialectic that legitimately draws from the past yet transcends the past by taking full account of the possibilities of the present. Only in such a way can Islam share with other religious traditions in a common vision of human flourishing.

FINDING INTERPRETIVE SPACE

The dialectical process by which a tradition develops through time requires a hermeneutical space in which critical theology and the critical history of theology can operate. The Wahhabi and Salafi regimes of power that dominate contemporary Sunni discourse limit such space by rejecting foreign epistemologies and by branding all models of reform that do not fit their political agendas as unwarranted innovation. This is the same whether these "unwarranted" methods seek a neo-traditionalist revival of the juridical, philosophical, or Sufi approaches of the past, or whether they employ the tools of critical theory to come up with new solutions. The Salafi response to the problem of making Islam relevant in an increasingly pluralistic, globalized, and empirical world is to proclaim that "true Islam is simple" and to reduce religion to a calculus of ritual obligations, external symbols of group identity (such as modern "Islamic" dress), and social mores that are designed to promote political activism and creedal exclusivism. The consequence in Sunni Islam has been a pervasive anti-intellectualism that when combined with the tendencies described above, has turned Islamic integrism, if not the majority of Sunni Islam, into more of a sectarian cult than a world religion.

Before modern times, few Muslim scholars of repute would dare to assert, "Islam is simple." Islam, as it was lived and interpreted, was as simple or complex as it needed to be, and the level at which it was approached conceptually depended on what circumstances required. The institution of jurisprudence (*fiqh*), traditionally the most important intellectual discipline in Islam, was premised on the need to apply the Shari'ah in a multiplicity of different contexts and developed a sophisticated logic, derived largely from Aristotle, for interpreting the Law in different situations. The complexity of Islam in practice was acknowledged further through the establishment of Islamic jurisprudence in several methodological schools, which differed in their approach to textual sources, yet recognized each other's right to exist. The juridical hermeneutical method, known as *ta'wil*, was the subject of treatises within each school and could operate on different conceptual levels.[30]

An example of the hermeneutical space that could be created through *ta'wil* can be found in Abu Hamid al-Ghazali's (d. 1111) *Faysal al-tafriqa bayna al-Islam wa al-zandaqa* (The Decisive Criterion for Distinguishing Islam from Heresy). This work was written to counteract the tendency of partisan Muslim scholars to condemn their opponents as unbelievers or heretics. Although contemporary neo-Hanbali and Salafi activists have often criticized Ghazali for departing from the Sunnah, his writings were so influential in setting the standards of Sunni orthodoxy that he is popularly known as "The Authority on Islam" (*Hujjat al-Islam*). According to Ghazali, all phenomena, including the statements of God in the Qur'an and the traditions of the Prophet Muhammad in the Sunnah, can be understood, and thus interpreted, on five different levels: (1) ontologically-existentially (*dhati*), (2) experientially (*hissi*), (3) conceptually (*khayali*), (4) intellectually (*'aqli*), and (5) metaphorically (*shabahi* or *majazi*).[31] These five levels constitute for Muslims the boundaries of interpretive space: "Everyone who interprets a statement of the Lawgiver in accordance with one of the preceding levels has deemed such statements to be true. . . . It is [thus] improper to brand as an unbeliever anyone who engages in such hermeneutics, as long as he observes the rules of hermeneutics (*qanun al-ta'wil*)."[32]

Ghazali's rules of hermeneutics assume that the Muslim theologian will at times be compelled to acknowledge "the logical impossibility of the apparent meaning (*zahir*) of a [sacred] text."[33] Once this becomes the case, hermeneutical space is opened for a variety of alternative explanations. All that is required to render a particular interpretation religiously valid is to consider the five hermeneutical approaches listed above in turn, thus establishing a logical warrant for the interpretive method that one chooses to employ. The theologian should also establish a proper warrant (*burhan*) for each assertion by adhering as closely as possible to the original text of the Qur'an or Hadith tradition and not allow doctrinal or political prejudices to affect one's judgment.[34] Although Ghazali allows for differences of opinion, he does not assume that all interpretations are of equal value. Some conclusions may be misguided or even completely wrong; however, wrong interpretations must be disproved dialectically. Wrong interpretations do not constitute heresy and thus they should not be suppressed. An interpretation is deemed heretical only if it denies the truth of a sacred text on all five levels of interpretation. According to Ghazali, the hermeneutics of sacred texts constitute informed speculation (*zann*) and not truth (*haqq*). Thus, no one may claim an exclusive right of interpretation and no single interpretation of a text is definitive. Ghazali's hermeneutical method thus fulfills an important need in contemporary Islamic discourse by allowing dissident theologians the "right to be wrong." In this way, it preserves alternative voices that help move the dialectical process of interpretation forward.

SUFI HERMENEUTICS AND RELIGIOUS HOSPITALITY

The warrant to interpret sacred texts on more than one level of meaning must be maintained if Muslim theologians are to engage constructively with theologians of other religions in the quest for religious understanding. An important advantage of Ghazali's critical hermeneutics is that it potentially enables the modern theologian to examine the vast sweep of Islamic intellectual history, to reassess its successes and failures, and to draw on interpretive voices that had been silenced in the past. Today, these silenced voices include most of the intellectual tradition of medieval Islam: philosophers, systematic theologians (such as Ghazali himself), jurisprudential scholars working within the classical Sunni schools of Shari'ah, and Sufis. Although it would be a mistake to consider all Sufis "liberal" or "open-minded," Sufi theologians were more inclined than their exoteric counterparts to view Islam from a wider, more universalistic perspective and thus to deal more meaningfully with religious difference. Some of the most important Sufi writings on religious difference came from the theological school of the Spanish mystic Muhyi' al-Din Ibn al-'Arabi (d. 1240).[35] One example of this approach can be found in the book *al-Insan al-Kamil* (The Perfect Man) by the Iraqi Sufi 'Abd al-Karim al-Jili (d. 1428). Jili, who was one of the most important of Ibn 'Arabi's doctrinal successors, concludes an extensive discussion on the origins of religious differences with the following remarkable statement:

> Ten sects are the sources for all the religious differences (which are too numerous to count), and all differences revolve around these ten. They are: Polytheists, Naturalists, Philosophers, Dualists, Magians, Materialists, "Barhamites," Jews, Christians, and Muslims. For every one of these sects God has created people whose destiny is the Garden and people whose destiny is the Fire. Have you not seen how the polytheists of past ages who lived in regions not reached by the prophet of that time are divided into those who do good, whom God rewards, and those who do evil, whom God recompenses with fire? Each of these sects worships God as God desires to be worshipped, for He created them for Himself, not for themselves. Thus, they exist just as they were fashioned. [God] may He be glorified and exalted, manifests His names and attributes to these sects by means of His essence and all of the sects worship Him [in their own way].[36]

At first glance, this passage seems to promote a medieval version of the "transcendent unity of religions" thesis. However, after more careful consideration, one finds that it is a legitimate, if somewhat unconventional, interpretation of the following verses of the Qur'an:

> For each one of you we have made a Law (*shir'ah*) and a way of life (*minhaj*). If God had wished, He would have made you into a single community. Instead, He has done this so that He may try you with what He has given you. So strive against each other in good works, for to God is the return for all of you and He will inform you about that wherein you differ (Qur'an 5:48).

> If your Lord had willed it, everyone on earth would have believed. Would you then force people to become believers? (Qur'an 10:99)

Although Jili's interpretation of these verses is unconventional, it is valid according to Ghazali's rules of hermeneutics discussed above. First, Jili does not engage in the hermeneutical slight of hand sometimes ascribed to Sufis by their opponents, but takes the word of God at its literal meaning. By accepting the literal meaning (*zahir*) of these Qur'anic verses, he is able to interpret them (in Ghazali's words) "conceptually" and "intellectually," without having to resort to metaphor. Next, Jili takes a third Qur'anic verse, "God does whatever He wills" (2:253), and applies this theological truism to the fact of religious diversity. From here, the seemingly radical conclusions that he draws—that religious difference is God's will, and that all human beings practice their religion as God intends them to do—follow logically from his literal interpretation of the Qur'anic text.

At the end of his discussion of religious diversity, Jili provides a similar explanation for another famous verse: "There is no compulsion in religion; the way of guidance is clearly distinguished from error. But he who rejects false objects of worship and believes in God has grasped a firm handhold (*al-'urwah al-wuthqa*) that will never break. God is All-Seeing, All-Knowing" (Qur'an 2:256). In other words, for Jili, all religions are not of equal value; Islam alone is quintessentially the religion of God. However, the other religions should be respected and their followers should not be forced into Islam, because all religions, including those that are in error, exist by God's will. One may infer from this conclusion that the modern preoccupation with *da'wa*—actively "calling" people to the religion of Islam—is not for Jili a fundamental duty for Muslims, at least when compared with the other requirements of the faith.

Today's Muslims should carefully consider Jili's conclusions and the Qur'anic verses that support them. In the modern age, the chief religious problem for Islamic theology is not the proliferation of local religions as it was in the past, but the competition of rival world religions, each of which has a history longer than that of Islam and has developed sophisticated means of defense and interpretation. If God had truly intended to save the world through the message of Christ alone, then why would He have allowed the theological challenge of Islam? If Islam resolved all of the contradictions of Christian theology, then why is Christianity still the largest religion? Part of the answer to these questions, Jili would assert, lies in the recognition that each religious tradition contains a portion of universal truth, to which people respond in their own way. Theological hostility can never be transformed into theological hospitality until this fact is fully recognized. In an unpublished paper, Martin Lings, commenting on Mark 12:30 ("Thou shalt love the Lord thy God with all thy heart, and with all thy soul, and with all thy mind, and with all they strength."), notes that today's Muslim and Christian religious authorities are much too ready to risk "with all thy mind" for the sake of "with all thy soul and with all thy strength."[37]

THE CREATIVE COMMAND OF GOD[38]

The question of religious difference in the Qur'an involves two separate types of divine command, which entail two different kinds of human obligation. Each command involves a different way of approaching the inter-religious other. The first command conceives of the other in a universal sense, as a fellow descendant of Adam, the first human being. In this perspective, human beings share natural duties and responsibilities that result from the covenant contracted between God and humanity before the creation of Adam. The second type of divine command applies more specifically and narrowly to the Muslim believer. This constitutes the level of individual and collective obligations, and includes the Qur'anic verses of difference and discrimination, which separate Muslims from believers in other religious traditions. It is on this level that the most problematical Qur'anic verses for interfaith purposes are found, which discuss the relations between the historical Muslim Ummah and other religious communities, the theological relationship between Islam and other historical religions, and the rules of social interaction, including the rules of war.

Muhyi' al-Din Ibn al-'Arabi calls the first divine command the Creative Command (*al-amr al-takwini*).[39] This command is "creative" because it regards all creation as a product of divine mercy. The Qur'anic verses that best convey this command are: "My mercy encompasses everything" (Qur'an 7:156); and "His only command when he desires a thing is to say to it 'Be!' and it is" (Qur'an 36:82). This is because the act of creation, the creation of existing things out of nonexistence, is both the most powerful and the most merciful act that God performs. The Creative Command is thus prior to all other types of divine command because it expresses most completely the theological and ontological oneness that is the Qur'an's basic message. Under the auspices of this command, the most important duty of the human being is to recognize that insofar as she is human and created, she has one God, one origin, one ancestor (Adam), one race, and shares with all other human beings the same nature, dignity, and religion. This religion is Islam, in the universal Qur'anic sense of recognizing and submitting to the consequences of one's ontological dependence on God. This understanding also expresses what moral philosopher John Rawls might have called the Islamic "Original Position," because it is built on the fundamental relationship between self and other that is the basis of all natural duties, whether between the individual and God or between oneself and other human beings.[40] This "Original Position" is epitomized in the Qur'an by a verse that expresses humanity's assent to their ontological dependence on their Creator: "When thy Lord drew forth their descendants from the children of Adam, He made them testify concerning themselves [saying]: 'Am I not your Lord?' They replied, 'Yes, we do so testify'" (Qur'an 7:172).

Theologically, the normal human situation is to see God from the perspective of the world. To see God from a worldly perspective is to see God as the Lord and Creator of everything. This is the attitude expressed in the Islamic Original Position when the human being responds to God's query, "Am I not your Lord?" with "Yes, I do so testify." This event is interpreted by Muslim theologians as having taken place before the earthly creation of the human being, when all of Adam's future descendants were summoned to acknowledge God's Lordship and His role in their creation. The fact that this covenant was contracted before humans were on earth implies that human beings have a pre-eternal side to their nature, and thus have the ability to rise imaginatively above their earthly condition and view the world of creation as if from a distance or a height.[41] The higher one goes, the more the world appears as a whole, and differences that appear significant on the ground begin to disappear with the change in perspective. From such a vantage point, all of the world, including all people and all of their different beliefs, are part of the same reflection of God, whose "face" will abide forever (55:27), because "He is the First and the Last, the Outward and the Inward" (57:3). This view of the world, in which self and other are seen as part of the same whole, is an important aspect of the Creative Command, and gives rise to the natural duties that result from the Original Position: "Oh humankind! Keep your duty to your Lord, who created you from a single soul, and created its mate from it and from whom issued forth many men and women. So revere (*attaqu*) the God by whom you demand rights from one another and revere the rights of kinship" (Qur'an 4:1).[42] The duty to revere God by fulfilling the promise of this pre-eternal covenant implies reverence for the rights of kinship (*al-arham*, literally, "the wombs"). In the context of the Creative Command, this duty would apply to genealogical kinship, but it would also include the greater kinship of the human species, since all of humankind, as the children of Eve, were born "from the same womb."

To return to the terminology used by John Rawls, the "initial contractual situation" of humanity's covenant with God is the starting-point from which all concepts of right devolve, including the rights that people demand from each other. The fact that such rights are both mutual and reciprocal is also part of the Original Position and is a consequence of the shared ontology of humanity. This ontology includes a transcendent aspect, which constitutes the spiritual potential of each human being. The Qur'an says that God breathed His spirit into Adam (Qur'an 38:72), and "[God] created the heavens and the earth with truth and right (*bi-l-haqq*), and fashioned [Adam] in the best of forms" (Qur'an 64:3). Thus, human beings, who are composed of both divine spirit and matter, have a natural duty to respect the rights of both self and other, because both self and other share the same combination of material being and spirit. This duty pertains irrespectively of whether the other is one's biological kin or belongs to another race or religion. To objectify the other means to forget that all human beings are made up of the same combination of spirit and clay. This is the mistake that led Satan, in the form of Iblis (Diabolos or the Devil), to disrespect Adam by saying, "I am better than [Adam]. You created me from fire, whereas you created him from clay" (Qur'an 7:12).

According to Rawls, a conception of right "is a set of principles, general in form and universal in application, that is to be publicly recognized as a final court of appeal for organizing the conflicting claims of moral persons."[43] In Islam, this conception of right is a corollary of the Original Position. As the Qur'an reminds us, not only was Adam created with rights, but the entire cosmological universe ('the heavens and the earth') was similarly created with *haqq*, an Arabic term that can mean "right," "truth," or "justice." This term expresses the most general and universal application of the Qur'anic conception of right. The duty of mutual respect is similarly general and universal, and the right of human dignity cannot be claimed exclusively by Muslims. Thus, the tendency of some exoteric Muslims to deny moral personhood to the non-Muslim or dissenting other is a breach of God's Creative Command.

Another basic right that is derived from the Original Position is the right to life: "Do not take a human life, which God has made sacred, other than as a right; this He has enjoined upon you so that you might think rationally" (Qur'an 6:151). Another is the right of free choice, without which the standards by which human beings are judged by God would be meaningless: "Had God willed, they would not have attributed partners to Him; We have not made you their keeper, nor are you responsible for them" (Qur'an 6:107); "The truth is from your Lord. So whosoever wishes shall believe, and whosoever wishes shall disbelieve" (Qur'an 18:29). It would make a mockery of the God-given rights of dignity, life, and free choice for Muslims to restrict the political and social rights of confessional minorities or to assign collective guilt to a group of people because of their religion, ethnicity, or system of government. All three of these rights—the right to life, the right to freedom, and the right to dignity—recall a second duty that arises from the Qur'anic Original Position. This is the duty of mercy (*rahmah*), which is prior to all duties in Islam except the acknowledgement of humanity's ontological dependence on God.[44] God says, "My mercy encompasses everything" (Qur'an 7:156), and every *Surah* of the Qur'an except one begins with the formula: "By the name of God, the Beneficent (*al-Rahman*), the Merciful (*al-Rahim*)."[45]

It is often forgotten by contemporary Muslims, especially those who wish to introduce the Islamic Shari'ah into modern legal systems, that the duty of mercy applies to each and every obligation that God enjoins upon human beings. What this means in practice is that when the performance of an obligation calls for severity, it is the duty of Muslims to temper that severity with mercy in any way possible.

THE COMMAND OF OBLIGATION

The divine command that is most clearly understood by most Muslims is not the Creative Command, but the Command of Obligation (*al-amr al-taklifi*).[46] This command forms the basis of the Shari'ah and is divided by the juridical tradition of Islam into injunctions covering acts of worship (*'ibadat*) and acts of interpersonal behavior (*mu'amalat*), including business transactions, criminal justice, and the laws of nations. The Arabic term, *taklif,* is a legal and moral concept that refers to the responsibility of individuals to carry out their obligations. Thus, the Command of Obligation imposes specific obligations on Muslims, either individually or collectively. It is a matter of debate whether such obligations should be obeyed simply because they come from God or because they are intrinsically good. Muslim liberals, following the teachings of Muhammad 'Abduh, who was Mufti of Egypt from 1899 until his death in 1905, assert that all divine statements, including divine commands, are subject to empirical verifiability, and serve a necessary function that can be proven rationally. Extreme literalists, such as the partisans of the Islamic Liberation Party (*Hizb al-Tahrir al-Islami*), consider it sacrilegious to put God's commands to such a test and assert that Muslims should obey them unquestioningly, simply because they come from God. What is perhaps most significant is that neither side presently discusses this question in the context of moral philosophy. While the classical juridical tradition of Islam dealt with questions of moral choice on a pragmatic case-by-case basis, it was primarily philosophers and Sufis who attempted to assess the Islamic concept of obligation within the context of more universal conceptions of right and justice.[47] The marginalization of philosophy and Sufism in contemporary Islam, and the resulting lack of debate on the wider philosophical issues surrounding the concept of obligation, have become, I believe, contributing factors to the rise of extremism in the Islamic world.

The natural duty that governs the moral obligations of Muslims under the Command of Obligation is justice. An alternative reading of the Qur'anic verse, "[God] created the heavens and the earth with truth and right (*bi-l-haqq*)," is "God created the heavens and the earth with justice." Justice is a secondary meaning of the Arabic term, *haqq* and is enjoined on human beings as a natural duty in a number of Qur'anic verses: "Verily, God commands justice and kindness" (Qur'an 16:90); "Make peace between them with justice, and act equitably" (Qur'an 49:9). The Arabic term for justice in these verses, *'adl,* corresponds closely to the Aristotelian notion of justice, which carries the connotation of "fairness" or "equity."[48] For the modern political philosopher John Rawls, all obligations arise from the principle of fairness, because the concept of fairness "holds that a person is under an obligation to do his part as specified by the rules of the institution whenever he has voluntarily accepted the benefits of the scheme."[49] In Islam, what Rawls calls "voluntary acceptance of the scheme" is entailed in the Islamic Original Position as a consequence of the pre-eternal covenant discussed above. Justice is thus a natural duty in Islam because human beings are "born into" justice from before their creation; the concept is, in effect "hard-wired" into the physical and social worlds that all humans occupy.[50] All three concepts that are included in the notion of justice in Islam also appear as Divine Names. God is thus characterized as The Truth (*al-Haqq*), Justice (*al-'Adl*), and The Fair or Equitable (*al-Muqsit*). This is particularly significant because for the Sufi theological school of Ibn 'Arabi, the essential qualities of existence are imparted as manifestations (*tajalliyyat*) of the Divine Names.

A problem with applying justice to specific obligations in Islam is that justice is most often understood as a moral duty, whereas a Command of Obligation is understood as a legal duty. Because the exact relationship between duties and obligations has not been philosophically defined in contemporary Islamic discourse, there is a tendency to fall into a confusion of priorities in the attempt to apply one or the other to specific cases. Ibn 'Arabi was one of the few Muslim thinkers to address the problem of duty versus obligation systematically and to prioritize their requirements in light of the two types of divine command. The natural duty of mercy is exercised through what Ibn 'Arabi called "Mercy as a Specific Obligation" (*rahmat al-wujub*).[51] Unlike the more ontological "Mercy as a Gratuitous Gift" (*rahmat al-imtinan*), which extends over creation by virtue of the act of creation itself, Mercy as a Specific Obligation refers to the mercy that is required in all individual human actions, according to God's statement: "Your Lord has prescribed mercy for Himself" (Qur'an 6:12).[52] Ibn 'Arabi relates the concept of mercy to the divine names *al-Rahman* and *al-Rahim*, with Mercy as a Gratuitous Gift corresponding to *al-Rahman* and Mercy as a Specific Obligation to *al-Rahim*. However, since all human obligations ultimately flow from the act of creation, any act of mercy bestowed by one human being on another constitutes a gift for both the receiver and the giver. For the receiver, the gift of mercy compensates for the severity of justice. However, for the giver, even the duty to act mercifully is a gift from God:

> God exercises mercy as a gratuitous act under the name *al-Rahman,* while he obligates Himself (to requite with mercy) under the name *al-Rahim.* Obligation is part of the Gratuitous Gift, and so *al-Rahim* is contained within *al-Rahman.* "God has written upon Himself mercy" in such a way that mercy of this kind may be extended to His servants in reward for the good acts done by them individually—those good works which are mentioned in the Qur'an. This kind of mercy is an obligation upon God with which He has bound Himself

toward those servants, and the latter rightfully merit this kind of mercy by their good works.[53]

To summarize the ethic of Mercy in Islam as outlined above: The natural duty of mercy is part of the Islamic Original Position by virtue of the Creative Command, which corresponds to the divine name *al-Rahman*. Similarly, the exercise of mercy by human actors is made obligatory through the Command of Obligation by virtue of the divine name *al-Rahim*. Just as human mercy (*rahmah*) is implicit in the idea of mercy as a universal principle (*al-Rahim*), so the obligation to act mercifully on all possible occasions is a necessary consequence of the idea of mercy as a natural duty. However, most people are not aware of the logical priority of natural duties that arise from the Creative Command. Mired as they are in a world of difference and subjectivity, they interpret the Command of Obligation in an exclusive sense, and overlook the logical priority of the Creative Command and the natural duties that derive from it:

> The divine effusion is vast, because [God] is vast in bestowal. There is no shortcoming on His part. But you have nothing of Him except what your essence accepts. Hence, your own essence keeps the Vast away from you and places you in the midst of constraint. The measure in which His governance occurs within you is your "Lord." It is He that you serve and He alone that you recognize. This is the mark within which He will transmute Himself to you on the day of resurrection, by unveiling Himself. In this world, this mark is unseen for most people. Every human being knows it from himself, but he does not know that it is what he knows.[54]

The Muslim who views the world from a narrow exoteric perspective can only perceive God through his or her personal experiences in the world. How God is to be conceived and what His commands entail are questions whose answers are constrained by the limits of one's sense of self. The interpretations that the believer gives to the commands of God in the Qur'an may be justifiable in a limited sense, but are likely to lead to injustice if they are applied universally and uncritically. This is because normal human understanding reflects one's personal worldview more than it reflects an understanding of God. In a commentary on the famous tradition, "He who knows himself, knows his Lord," Ibn 'Arabi explains: "You are the one who becomes manifest to yourself, and this gives you nothing of [God]. . . . You do not know other than yourself."[55]

Even for the exoteric jurist who considers a scriptural obligation to be prior to a moral duty, each obligation must be assessed as to whether the divine command that produced it is general or specific; and if it is specific, what is the historical context of its revelation?[56] An example of this problem of priorities can be found in *Surat al-Tawba* (Repentance), in which some of

the most apparently hostile verses concerning Muslim and non-Muslim relations appear. How is a Muslim to respond when the Qur'an commands:
"Fight against such of those who have been given the Scripture as believe not
in Allah or the Last Day, and forbid not that which Allah has forbidden by
His messenger, and follow not the religion of truth, until they pay the tribute
(*jizyah*) readily, being brought low" (Qur'an 9:29)? In interpreting this verse,
it is helpful to know that it was revealed at a time when polytheists and Jews
in Arabia had broken their treaties with the Muslims and banded together
against the Prophet in a military assault on Medina. However, the Muslim
Brotherhood activist Sayyid Qutb, who was fully aware of the historical
context of this verse, interpreted it as a general command to compel non-
Muslim minorities to pay the *jizyah* tax. Even more, he defined the *jizyah*,
not as an exemption from military service as Muslim apologists have often
done, but as a protection tax and token of public humiliation that only tempo-
rarily exempted Jews and Christians from persecution by the Islamic state.[57]

Christian theologians studying the question of usury refer to a "double
standard" in the biblical Book of Deuteronomy, which objectifies the non-
Jewish other by imposing discriminatory rules and practices on him.[58] In the
same vein, *Surat al-Tawba* can be seen as displaying a similar double standard, in which the *jizyah* tax levied on Jews and Christians replicates the
tarbit that Jews took from Gentiles. Jewish and Christian fundamentalists
might contend that this "double standard" is only a problem from the standpoint of secular notions of equality and citizenship, and that the idea of
"sameness before the law" is a humanistic ideal that does not correspond to
scriptural notions of justice. For such individuals, the Law of God always
trumps the laws of men. Theologians who advocate better interreligious relations cannot dismiss this objection out of hand, but must take it seriously. It
is not enough to simply ignore a problematical text from sacred scripture,
wishing that it would go away. For the most part, this has been the strategy of
Muslim apologists, who for years kept repeating the mantra, "Islam means
peace," until they themselves believed it, only to be rudely awakened from
their reveries in the aftermath of September 11, 2001. Such contradictions
will not be resolved until a new theology is formulated that can deal authenti-
cally with difference and the problem of religious hostility in new and creative ways.

BUILDING A BRIDGE TO HOSPITALITY
AND HUMAN FLOURISHING

The first step toward a theology of hospitality in Islam is for Muslims to
remember that ultimately, as Jili said in the passage discussed above, everything happens because God wills it to happen. This includes human diversity,

which the Qur'an mentions as having been created for the purpose of reflection and learning:

> Among [God's] signs are the creation of the heavens and the earth, and the differences of your languages and colors. Herein indeed, are portents for those with knowledge (Qur'an 33:22).

> Oh humankind! We have created you male and female, and have made you nations and tribes so that you may come to know one another. Verily, the noblest of you, in the sight of God, is the most God-conscious of you. Verily, God is the Knowing and the Aware (Qur'an 49:13).

Included in the diversity of which the Qur'an speaks are differences of ideas, world views, and religions, all of which are allowed to exist because of God's Creative Command. However, the acceptance of plural perspectives on the Absolute does not mean that all religions are ultimately the same, or even that some religions might not be more effective ways to knowledge of God than others. By the same token, prioritizing the natural duty of mercy by acknowledging the dignity of Buddhists and Christians or accepting the divine origins of Judaism and Hinduism does not mean that Muslims cannot oppose the actions of the Israeli government in Palestine or that they should accept the destruction of the Babri mosque in India. Such actions may still be seen as evil, because they contradict universal principles of social justice that are embodied in the Qur'an as well as in other scriptures. The point is that evil actions should be opposed in and of themselves: they should not be seen as inescapable consequences of alternative religious perspectives. No religion that God has allowed to exist is bad per se, and no one has the right to exclude a believer in another religion from the brotherhood of the Islamic Original Position. Individual Christians and Hindus can do bad things, but so can Muslims as well. Saying that "the Jews" are enemies of Islam or that American foreign policy is driven by "Crusader" goals is a moral and theological error of profound proportions. This error is caused on the moral level by ignorance of the relationship between the Creative Command and the Command of Obligation, and on the theological level by ignoring the full meaning of the human being as vicegerent (*khalifah*) of God on earth.

Acceptance of religious difference and disagreement does not mean that Muslims have to abandon their belief in the theological superiority of Islam, nor does it mean going against God's will. In fact, the situation is quite the opposite. The Creative Command, without which no religious differences can exist, acknowledges the theological permissibility of religious pluralism in the following Qur'anic passage: "For each one of you we have made a Law and a way of life. If God had willed, He would have made you into a single community" (Qur'an 5:48). In the context of this verse, "Law" (*shir'ah*) is a synonym for religion, because it refers to what philosophers call "primary commitments"—the duties and obligations that provide a framework for the moral life. In premodern Islam, the subject of "the Law before Islam" constituted what we today would call the history of religions. [59] The verse goes on to say: "Strive against each other in good works, for to God is the return for all of you and He will inform you about that wherein you differ." A literal interpretation of this statement would suggest that the only interreligious competition that truly counts in the sight of God is competition in good works, such that Muslims would compete with Jews, Christians, and others in the alleviation of human suffering. This is very different from the belief, expressed by (for example) contemporary Palestinian extremists that strapping on a bomb belt and blowing up a bus of Israeli school children will earn the martyr a reward in heaven because the children are potential Israeli soldiers.

All acts, whether they are performed by Muslims or others, must be judged by weighing the requirements of the Command of Obligation against the duties of the Creative Command. Every sane individual is morally responsible (*mukallaf*) and carries out her obligations in the context of the religion or moral standard (*shir'ah*) that she accepts by virtue either of choice or of birth. The Qur'anic verse, "He it is who has sent His Messenger with guidance and the religion of truth so that it may prevail over all religion, even if those who assign partners to God disapprove" (Qur'an 9:33), is usually interpreted by Muslims as a general obligation to proselytize and as an assurance of the ultimate victory of Islam. However, without interpreting this expression of the Command of Obligation in the wider context of the moral priority of the Creative Command, how is one to resolve its apparent disagreement with the previously quoted Qur'an 5:48, which seems to defer the resolution of religious difference until the Day of Resurrection? Which verse is theologically more fundamental? How is one to understand the fact that Islam has not prevailed over all other religions after fourteen centuries? If all one perceives is the Command of Obligation, is it logically permissible to assert, as Wahhabis and Salafis do, that Islam has not prevailed because Muslims are not "Islamic" enough? This preoccupation with obligation and the lack of a moral philosophy that takes account of the context of natural duty has prevented Muslims from viewing the divine will in a wider perspective. This error of shortsightedness, coupled with an obsession with victory, has plunged the world into its present religious crisis and threatens in the end to deprive Islam of both its spirituality and its morality.

Ibn 'Arabi reminds us, despite the objections of those who have sought to silence his voice, that all human beings "assign partners to God" in one way or another, and on this view, believers in all religions are equally far from the "Religion of the Truth" that will prevail at the end of time. The will of God is not one-dimensional, nor are history or human nature. If limiting the interpretation of God's word to a single dimension was theologically untenable for medieval Islamic scholars, it is even more untenable today, when human knowledge has better tools for analyzing and reflecting on the meaning of revelation. Five centuries ago, the Sufi and jurist Ahmad Zarruq of Fez (d. 1493) wrote: "He who practices Sufism without the Law is a heretic; he who practices the Law without Sufism is a reprobate; but he who combines the Law and Sufism has attained the truth."[60] What Zarruq meant by this was that the practice of scriptural hermeneutics demands a multi-dimensional perspective, in which individual obligations are viewed in the context of the creativity of God's will, and in which the outer word of the Law is interpreted in light of its inner spirit.

This understanding of multi-dimensionality is an important aspect of the human being's cosmically assigned role as vicegerent (*khalifah*) of God on earth. The role of God's vicegerent has been stressed often enough by Islamic integrists, but they see it primarily in terms of dominion over the earth rather than in terms of knowledge. In the passages of *Surat al-Baqarah* where vicegerency is discussed (Qur'an 2:30–39), what makes the human being rise above the "bloodshed and mischief" that the angels fear he will create is God's gift of "all of the names" (*al-asma'a kullaha*) and "words" (*kalimat*). In Qur'anic terms, the "names" symbolize the essences of things, whereas the "words" symbolize the actualization of the essences. As such, the names correspond to God's Creative Command, which brings things into being, and the words correspond to God's Command of Obligation, through which the divine will is made manifest. Whether one accepts Ibn 'Arabi's framework for interpreting the divine will or not, it is clear from the Qur'an that what made Adam special was that he could uniquely bridge the gap between the angelic and terrestrial worlds, and that the keys to his bridge-building are to be found in the transcendent intelligence and understanding (the "names" and "words") that God imparted to him.

As vicegerent of God and as a unique combination of spirit and matter, the human being is by his very nature a *pontifex*, a "builder of bridges" between conceptual worlds. Beneath the differences that obtain among religious doctrines, sacred laws, and world views, all people share the same transcendental nature; all have access to the "words" that allow them to communicate with each other across religious divides. Because the human being is a *pontifex* it is not logical to assume that religious misunderstanding is normal or that religious differences cannot be bridged. If believers in different religions cannot come to an understanding, it means that one or both of them are lacking in spiritual insight, or that one or both are in fundamental error. Among the rights bestowed upon us by God, the right not to understand each other is nowhere to be found. Not surprisingly, the Qur'an warns Muslims about this state of affairs: "Be not of those who ascribe partners to God (*mushrikun*), who split up their religion and become schismatics, each sect exulting in its doctrines" (33:31–32).

An important task of the contemporary Muslim theologian is to show how Muslims themselves can ascribe partners to God; Muslims do this by calling not on God Himself but on their personal Lord, through the narrow vision of their own ego. This mistake, which is the root of all the theological hostility and evil that the human being can create in the name of religion, is ultimately due to the *pontifex/khalifah* losing sight of the meaning and end of his personal existence. Through this error, he mistakes the contingent for the absolute, the false for the real, the secondary for the primary, the outer for the inner, and the particular for the universal. As the above verse of the Qur'an indicates, this is what it means to commit the theological sin of *shirk*, a Qur'anic term usually defined as "assigning partners to God," but which literally means, "sharing." It consists, in other words, of letting contingent ideas, concepts, and prejudices share in God's will and sovereignty, and as such, it is the greatest impediment to theological hospitality and the hope of human flourishing. As the Qur'an affirms: "God does not forgive your *shirk*, but he forgives all else, as He wills" (Qur'an 4:48).

NOTES

1. Alon Goshen-Gottstein, in an earlier draft of "Judaism: The Battle for Survival, the Struggle for Compassion."
2. See Steven M. Wasserstrom, *Religion after Religion: Gershom Scholem, Mircea Eliade, and Henry Corbin at Eranos* (Princeton: Princeton University Press, 1999).
3. Hans-Georg Gadamer, "The Elevation of the Historicity of Understanding to the Status of a Hermeneutic Principle," in *Truth and Method*, Joel Weinsheimer and Donald G. Marshall trans. (New York, 1994), pp. 265–307.
4. See John Wansborough, *The Sectarian Milieu* (Oxford: 1978). This work suggests that most of the text of the Qur'an is not a product of the seventh century CE as Muslims believe, but that it was written in the early Caliphal period, under the influence of religious polemics among Muslims, Christians, and Jews.
5. For a Marxist approach to Islamic history that removes consideration of religious motives, see Mahmood Ibrahim, *Merchant Capital and Islam* (Austin, Texas: 1990). For a Weberian study of the same period, see Hamid Dabashi, *Authority in Islam: from the Rise of Muhammad to the Establishment of the Umayyads* (New Brunswick, New Jersey: 1989).
6. See Patricia Crone and Michael Cook, *Hagarism: The Making of the Islamic World* (Cambridge: 1977). This work produced a firestorm of controversy when it first appeared, because it denied the authenticity of the historical tradition of Islam and seemed to suggest that Islam was a product of traditions that first developed in Samaritan Judaism.
7. See, for example, Muhammad Mahmud Taha, *The Second Message of Islam*, Abdullahi Ahmad Na'îm trans. and ed. (Syracuse, New York: 1987). Taha takes the concept of the created Qur'an to its outer limits by suggesting that all Qur'anic verses revealed at Medina be rejected, because their relevance is limited both historically and culturally. This would have the effect of removing the textual basis for most of Islamic law.
8. This is a major thesis of Alasdair MacIntyre, *Three Rival Versions of Moral Enquiry: Encyclopedia, Genealogy, and Tradition*. (Indiana: Notre Dame, 1990).
9. For a more nuanced view of MacIntyre's critique of the genealogical perspective, see the discussion in ibid, pp. 32–57.
10. Amir Taheri, "Al-Qaeda's Agenda for Iraq," *New York Post Online Edition*, September 4, 2003.

Islam 95

11. In *Ma'alim fi al-Tariq* (1962), usually translated as "Milestones" or "Signposts," the Muslim Brotherhood activist Sayyid Qutb (d. 1966) condemns all non-Muslim societies as beyond the pale of Islam, "not because they believe in other deities besides God or because they worship anyone other than God, but because their way of life is not based on submission to God alone. Although they believe in the unity of God, still they have relegated the legislative attribute of God to others and submit to this authority, and from this authority they derive their systems, their traditions and customs, their laws, their values and standards, and almost every practice of life." Sayyid Qutb, *Milestones* (Damascus, no date), pp. 82–83. The South Asian Islamic activist Abu al-Ala' Mawdudi (d. 1979), understood the concept of *tawhid* to include even the denial of free will: "Man in this kingdom is by birth, a subject. That is, it has not been given to him to choose to be or not to be a subject . . . nor is it possible for him, being born a subject and a natural part of this kingdom, to swerve from the path of obedience followed by other creations. Similarly he does not have the right to choose a way of life for himself or assume whatever duties he likes." Seyyed Vali Reza Nasr, *Mawdudi and the Making of Islamic Revivalism* (Oxford, 1996), p. 58.

12. The Iraqi-born legal specialist Taha Jabir al-'Alwani defines the "Islamic paradigm of knowledge" as "concerned with identifying and erecting a *tawhid*-based system of knowledge, a *tawhidi* episteme." See Idem, "The Islamization of Knowledge: Yesterday and Today" (Herndon, Virginia and London: International Institute of Islamic Thought, 1995), p. 14. 'Alwani, who received his degree in the Sources of Islamic Jurisprudence (*usul al-fiqh*) at al-Azhar University in 1973, was for ten years professor of Islamic law at Muhammad ibn Sa'ud University in Riyadh, Saudi Arabia, the premier educational institution of Wahhabism. He was a founder in 1981 of the International Institute of Islamic Thought and is a founding member of the Council of the Muslim World League in Mecca. Since 1988, he has been president of the Fiqh Council of North America, which he also helped create. The Islamization of Knowledge movement is popularly identified with the late Dr. Ismail Farouqi of Temple University. However, the most intellectually sophisticated presentation of this theory can be found in Syed Muhammad Naquib al-Attas, *Prolegomena to the Metaphysics of Islam: An Exposition of the Fundamental Elements of the Worldview of Islam* (Kuala Lumpur, Malaysia: International Institute of Islamic Thought and Civilization, 1995).

13. Vincent J. Cornell, "Religion and Philosophy," in *World Eras, Volume 2: The Rise and Spread of Islam*, 622–1500, Susan L. Douglass, Ed. (Michigan: Farmington Hills, 2002) p. 368.

14. Dimitri Gutas, *Greek Thought, Arabic Culture: The Graeco-Arabic Translation Movement in Baghdad and Early 'Abbasid Society (2nd–4th/8th–10th Centuries)* (London and New York: 1998) pp. 156–157.

15. Gilles Kepel, *Muslim Extremism in Egypt: The Prophet and Pharaoh* (Berkeley: 1993) p. 47.

16. In more than twenty-five years of teaching university-level Islamic Studies in the United States, I have often been told by Muslim students that their parents strongly discouraged them from taking courses in philosophy and literary criticism, because of the potential effects of these disciplines on their creedal (*'aqidah*) adherence to Islam. They are sometimes also warned away from Islamic Studies courses, partly out of fear of being identified as Islamic activists, but also out of fear of what one local imam in Durham, North Carolina, termed "academic Islam."

17. Muhammad ibn Yusuf as-Sijilmasi, *Tuhfat al-ikhwan wa mawahib al-imtinan fi manaqib Sidi Ridwan ibn 'Abdallah al-Januwi* (Rabat: Bibliothèque Générale, ms. 114K), p. 86.

18. For Arkoun's critique of what he called the "memoire-tradition" of Islam, see "Comment Étudier la Pensè Islamique?" in Mohammed Arkoun, *Pour une Critique de la Raison Islamiquee* (Paris, 1984), pp. 7–40. Khaled Abou El Fadl has recently criticized Arkoun's "rethinking" of the structure of Islamic reason for "using the Islamic tradition as a text upon which to continue a debate about Western epistemology." Idem, *Speaking in God's Name: Islamic Law, Authority and Women* (Oxford, 2001), p. 133 n. 8.

19. See George Makdisi, *The Rise of Colleges: Institutions of Learning in Islam and the West* (Edinburgh, 1981), esp. pp. 80–148.

20. See Omid Safi, "Power and the Politics of Knowledge: Negotiating Political Ideology and Religious Orthodoxy in Saljuq Iran" (Duke University, Ph.D. dissertation, 2000) pp. 7–11.

21. The first constituent council of the Muslim World League, which met in December 1962, was headed by Muhammad ibn Ibrahim ibn Al al-Shaykh, a direct lineal descendant of Muhammad ibn 'Abd al-Wahhab, the founder of the Wahhabi movement, and included Said Ramadan, the son-in-law of Hasan al-Banna', founder of the Muslim Brotherhood. See Hamid Algar, *Wahabbism: A Critical Essay* (Oneonta, New York: 2002), 49.

22. *The American Muslim*, a magazine published by the Muslim American Society in Falls Church, Virginia, carries a regular *fatwa* (juridical advice) column by Sheikh Muhammad al-Hanooti. The September 2003 issue contains a question (p. 38) by a woman who has been approached by "a good Muslim man" for marriage. Unfortunately, the man happens to be a Sufi, and the woman does "not want to end up with someone who does something wrong against Islam." Hanooti's reply clearly illustrates the marginalization of both Sufism and historical Islamic tradition mentioned above: "I do not know what sort of Sufi he is, but, in general, I advise you to marry a person who has good knowledge of Islam, and one who is not merely following culture and tradition. In general, I would caution you against marrying a Sufi, for a great many of them do not have a good knowledge of Islam and are tilted toward lives of inconvenience." By counseling the woman to not marry a Sufi, Hanooti is asserting, in effect, that Sufis are heretics.

23. The same tendency can be found in Shi'ite Islam as well, where the dominance of the religious establishment (*al-hawzah*) has been reinforced through the influence of Ayatollah Khomeini's ideology of "governance of the jurist" (*wilayat al-faqih*).

24. This was a common point of view in apologetic works on Islamism written before September 11, 2001, such as John L. Esposito, *The Islamic Threat, Myth or Reality?* (Oxford: 1992). See, for example, the chapter entitled, "Islamic Organizations: Soldiers of God," where the Islamist critique of traditional "stagnation" is accepted without questioning its assumptions (pp. 119–187).

25. MacIntyre, *Versions of Moral Inquiry*, p. 150.

26. Ibid, p. 202.

27. See Mircea Eliade, *The Myth of the Eternal Return, or, Cosmos and History* (Princeton, 1974). Although Eliade championed the perspective of "traditional" man, this book is still a useful comparative study of the "mythemes" that are employed by Islamic revivalists.

28. Contemporary Muslims would do well to heed the warnings against "utopian social engineering" in Karl Popper, *The Open Society and Its Enemies: Volume One: the Spell of Plato* (London: 2003 reprint of 1945 original). See especially chapter 9, "Aestheticism, Perfectionism, Utopianism."

29. See Alasdair MacIntyre, *After Virtue: A Study in Moral Theory* (Indiana: Notre Dame, 1984) pp. 6–22.

30. An important work in this genre is Abu Bakr Muhammad Ibn al-'Arabi al-Ma'afiri (d. 1149), *Qanun al-Ta'wil* (The Rules of Hermeneutics), edited by Muhammad al-Slimani (Beirut: 1990).

31. Sherman A. Jackson, *On the Boundaries of Theological Tolerance in Islam: Abu Hamid al-Ghazali's* Faysal al-Tafriqa bayna al-Islam wa al-Zandaqa (Oxford: 2002). I have altered Jackson's translation of terms slightly to better fit the present discussion. Ghazali's full discussion of the terms noted above is on pp. 94–100.

32. Ibid., p. 50.

33. Ibid., p. 104.

34. Ibid.

35. These polemics are detailed in Alexander D. Knysh's excellent study, *Ibn 'Arabi in the Later Islamic Tradition: The Making of a Polemical Image in Medieval Islam* (Albany, New York: 1999).

36. Abd al-Karim al-Jili, *al-Insan al-kamil fi ma'rifat al-awakhir wa al-awa'il* (Cairo: 1981), vol. 2, p. 122.

37. Martin Lings, "With All Thy Mind," an unpublished paper disseminated at the second "Building Bridges" seminar hosted by His Highness the Emir of the State of Qatar and Archbishop of Canterbury Rowan Williams, Doha, Qatar, 7–9 April, 2003.

38. Portions of this section and the following section appear in Vincent J. Cornell, "Practical Sufism: An Akbarian Basis for a Liberal Theology of Difference," *Journal of the Muhyiddin*

Ibn 'Arabi Society, volume 36, 2004, pp. 59–84. This chapter was reproduced with permission in *Sophia: The Journal of Traditional Studies*, Volume 15, Number 2, Winter 2010.

39. William C. Chittick calls this the "Engendering Command," because it results from the manifestation of the divine name *al-Rahman* (The Engendering). The source for this idea is Ibn Arabi's *al-Futuhat al-Makkiyyah* (The Meccan Revelations). See William C. Chittick, *Imaginal Worlds: Ibn al-'Arabi and the Problem of Religious Diversity* (Albany, New York: 1994) p. 142.

40. See John Rawls, *A Theory of Justice* (Cambridge, Massachusetts: 1999) pp. 10–19. The covenantal assent of humanity in the Qur'an is, of course, not a secular social contract, as in Rawls's version of the Original Position. However, equality of subservience before God, in the Qur'anic sense, does impart a basic equality of human beings in the sense that they all share the same qualities, whether these qualities are defined positively or negatively.

41. This could be a possible metaphorical interpretation of Qur'an 7:46, "And on the Heights are men who know all of them by their signs."

42. For the Jewish perspective on the creation from one soul see page 23; for the Christian view, see page 54; for the Buddhist perspective on the unity of humanity, see page 126.

43. Rawls, *Theory of Justice*, 117.

44. For the Jewish view on compassion, see page 40.

45. In *Fusus al-hikam* (The Ring-Settings of Wisdom) Ibn 'Arabi calls this type of mercy the "Mercy as a Gratuitous Gift" (*rahmat al-imtinan*). It is a mercy which God bestows on things simply because they exist. For Ibn 'Arabi, all existence is ultimately good, since it comes from God. Evil is nonexistence (*'adam*). See Toshihiko Izutsu, *Sufism and Taoism: A Comparative Study of Key Philosophical Concepts* (Berkeley: 1983) p. 121.

46. William Chittick calls this the "Prescriptive Command." See Idem, *Imaginal Worlds*, p. 142.

47. This is not to say that Muslim jurists did not discuss such questions. However, those who did so most successfully, such as Ghazali, Ibn Rushd (d. 1198), or even Muhammad 'Abduh, combined their juridical backgrounds with studies of either Sufism or philosophy.

48. Alasdair MacIntyre, *Whose Justice, Which Rationality?* (Indiana: Notre Dame, 1988). See especially the chapter entitled, "Aristotle on Justice," pp. 103–123.

49. Rawls, *Theory of Justice*, p. 301.

50. Ibid., p. 302. The fact that the Arabic term, *'adl*, connotes justice, fairness, and equity alike removes Rawls's problem of drawing a lexical distinction between justice and fairness. In Islam, one cannot say that justice is qualitatively distinct from fairness, because etymologically they are the same thing.

51. Izutsu, *Sufism and Taoism*, pp. 121–122.

52. This passage could also be translated literally as: "Your Lord has written mercy upon His own Spirit."

53. Izutsu, *Sufism and Taoism*, p. 122. This discussion is found in *Fusus al-Hikam*.

54. Chittick, *Imaginal Worlds*, p. 152. This passage is from *Futuhat* (IV 62.23).

55. Ibid., p. 163. The passage comes from *Futuhat* (IV 421.34).

56. Mohammad Hashim Kamali, *Principles of Islamic Jurisprudence* (Cambridge: 1991) pp. 139–148.

57. See the discussion in Sayyid Qutb, *Fi Zilal al-Qur'an* (In the Shade of the Qur'an) (Beirut: 1980) pp. 1220–1250. A less severe perspective, which represents the views of Pakistan's Jamaati Islami, can be found in Abdur Rahman I. Doi, *Non-Muslims under Shari'ah (Islamic Law)* (Lahore: 1981).

58. Benjamin Nelson, *The Idea of Usury* (Chicago: 1969) pp. 3–28.

59. This subject is discussed in detail in A. Kevin Reinhardt, *Before Revelation: The Boundaries of Muslim Moral Thought* (Albany, New York: 1995).

60. Abu al-'Abbas Ahmad Zarruq, *Qawa'id al-Tasawwuf* (Principles of Sufism), Edited by Muhammad Zuhri al-Najjar and 'Ali Ma'bid Farghali (Beirut: 1992) p. 8.

Chapter Five

Hinduism

Unity, Diversity and the Other:
Advaita and Madhva Vedanta Perspectives

Ashok Vohra and Deepak Sarma

PART 1:
METAPHYSICAL UNITY, PHENOMENOLOGICAL DIVERSITY
AND THE APPROACH TO THE OTHER:
AN ADVAITA VEDANTA POSITION

ASHOK VOHRA

Hinduism contains no notion of the "other"—the one outside of the religion to which we belong, the "unfaithful," the *kafir*. It posits that all the diversity we see and experience resides only at the level of phenomena. At the metaphysical level is absolute unity; everyone is nothing but Brahman. Consequently, there is no notion of the other in Hinduism. This leaves no place for hostility toward anyone; it spreads the message of love toward one and all and extends hospitality to aliens, even those who are critical of Hinduism and leave its fold.

The principles and practices of Hinduism are derived from the Vedas and Upanishads, which are called *shrutis* (the revealed texts) and *smritis* (the remembered texts). As *Taittiriya Aranyaka* says, the Vedas "register the intuitions of the perfected souls" (i 2). Vedas are *apaurusheya* (not created); they are eternal and revealed. They are, as *Purushasukta* says: *dhata yatha-purvam akalpayat* (presented without addition or subtraction), as it is revealed to the rishis (the seers).

Man, his nature, growth, development, and realization (or emancipation) are the central concerns of the Vedic literature, which consists of the Vedas, Upanishads, and Puranas. Questions like: "What is the true nature of man?" "How can man realize this true nature?" "What is man's destiny, and how can he achieve it?" and "Is spirituality the prerogative of only a few, select, gifted individuals, or is it the privilege of everyone?" are raised time and again in the Vedic literature. It is primarily with these concerns in mind that the Vedas, Upanishads, and other texts study nature, creation and other metaphysical and transcendental phenomena.

The Vedic literature presents an integrated scheme of life in which the metaphysical and the real are thoroughly merged. It upholds the unity of the macrocosm and the microcosm. Hinduism differentiates between empirical and transcendental existence, primarily because the Hindu religion, culture, and way of life are peculiar in that they do not distinguish between philosophy, theology, and religion. Therefore, Hinduism represents for its followers not just a religion but a total way of life. In order to work out the attitude in Hinduism toward the one whom we regard as the other—that is, issues of hospitality or hostility—I have divided my presentation into three broad sections. After outlining the metaphysical presuppositions of Hinduism in the first section, in the second I apply the findings to show that *mlecchas*—the foreigners as well as the outcasts—cannot be treated as the "Other." Due to our *avidya* (ignorance) of the real nature of the concept of person, we treat him as the Other and express hostility toward him. Once *avidya* is removed, we see everyone as an extension of ourselves. [1] Through training of the mind, Hinduism removes *avidya* and teaches love and hospitality toward all the living and the nonliving. Having done this in the third section, I trace the history of the term Hinduism to show that, because of its peculiar all-inclusive nature, it logically cannot maintain a place for hostility toward anyone. Its tolerant and accommodating approach has the seeds of human flourishing and universal love and brotherhood.

Metaphysical Presuppositions of Hinduism

In this section, I show that Hinduism believes that, underneath the diversity of class, caste, creed, skin color, and language, lies an essential metaphysical unity. Each of us is divine in character; each has the same indwelling *atman* (self, soul).

Hinduism begins with the axiom that reality is one and the wise men interpret it in various ways (*ekam sat viprah bahudah vadanti*). The differences that emerge from the interpretations of the one ultimate reality by various philosophers, sects, and religions appears only at the surface level of terminology used by each of them in their own contexts and cultures, determined by their individual needs. Deep down, each religion maintains the quest for the ultimate truth. If we penetrate beneath the surface grammar of each of the expositions and interpretations of the ultimate truth or reality, we find that each of the sects or religions articulates one universal truth or reality. The apparent diversity is superficial; deeper down, one finds only unity.

Each interpretation of the ultimate reality represents a form of life. The Hindu believes that class, caste, and religious affiliation have no unique spiritual function other than making many positive contributions to the individual's sense of identity, social support, and integration. This is because Hinduism upholds that "God can be realised through all paths. All religions are true. The important thing is to reach the roof. You can reach it by stone stairs or by bamboo steps or by a rope. You can also climb up by a bamboo pole."[2] Moreover, Hindus believe that God Himself has provided different forms of worship. He who is the Lord of the Universe has arranged all these forms to suit different men in different stages of evolution and having different degrees of knowledge.[3]

Hinduism therefore abhors the idea of superiority of any one religion over any other, because the believers in God cannot maintain that God has bestowed on them all wisdom and truth and appointed this small body of men as the guardians of the whole of humanity. Accordingly, "Religion is realisation: but mere talk—mere trying to believe, mere groping in darkness, mere parroting the words of ancestors and thinking it as religion, mere making a political something out of the truths of religion—is not religion at all."[4] With minor variations, the realized souls of all religions—big or small, ethnic, national, or even international—say: "Thou art the Lord of all, Thou art the heart of all, Thou art the guide of all, Thou art the Teacher of all, Thou art the savior of all, and Thou carest infinitely more for the land and welfare of Thy children than we can ever do." The Hindu attitude toward the perfection or imperfection of every religion, which is the sole cause of the feeling of superiority in different religions, is best explained by Ramakrishna in the following way:

> You may say there are many errors and superstitions in another religion. I should reply: Suppose there are. Every religion has errors. Everyone thinks that his watch alone gives the correct time. It is enough to have a yearning for God. It is enough to love Him and feel attached to Him. Don't you know that God is the Inner Guide? He sees the longing in our hearts and the yearning of our soul. Suppose a man has several sons. The older boy addresses him distinctly as 'Baba', or 'Papa', but the babies can at best call him 'Ba' or 'Pa'. Now will the father be angry with those who address him in this indistinct way? The father knows that they too are calling him, only they cannot pronounce his name well. All children are the same to the father. Likewise, the devotees call the one God alone, though by different names. They call on one Person only. God is one but His names are many.[5]

Thanks to these inclusive attitudes and the tendency to treat all faiths as equal, Hinduism projects no zeal for proselytizing and no enthusiasm for conversion. Not being exclusive, it enables its followers not merely to respect all other religions, but also to admire them and to assimilate whatever may be good in them. Because of its all-inclusive nature, conversion is alien to Hinduism. In fact, the Hindu mind finds the idea of converting the members of other faiths to its own—which seems so natural to the members of proselytizing religions—to be an act of moral, intellectual and cultural aggression. Conversion to Hinduism is sacrilegious. The Hindu attitude toward conversion is best encapsulated by Gandhi: "I do not want you to become a Hindu. But I do want you to become a better Christian by absorbing all that may be good in Hinduism and that you may not find in the same measure or not at all in the Christian teaching."[6] The same is applicable to Islam, Judaism and other religions.

Hinduism considers all doctrines, all sects, all modes of prayers, all places of worship—temples, churches, and mosques—as peripheral to religion. It regards spirituality and its realization and an individual's development and spiritual growth as the core of all religions. "For the Hindu," according to Radhakrishnan, "the aim of religion is the integration of personality which reconciles the individual to his own nature, his fellowmen and the Supreme Spirit. To realise this goal there are no set paths. Each individual may adopt the method which most appeals to him, and in the atmosphere of Hinduism, even inferior modes of approach get refined."[7] All religions and all sects and sub-sects, through their individual and sometimes unique, sometimes complementary, and at times even contradictory practices, try to bring out the latent divinity in each of us. Sri Aurobindo sums up this attitude of the Hindus in the following words:

> To the Indian mind the least important part of religion is its dogma; the religious spirit matters, not the theological credo. On the contrary, to the Western mind a fixed intellectual belief is the most important part of a cult; it is the core of meaning, it is the thing that distinguishes it from the others. It is formulated beliefs that make it either a true or false religion, according as it agrees or does not agree with the credo of its critic. This notion, however foolish and shallow, is a necessary consequence of the Western idea which falsely supposes that intellectual truth is the highest verity and, even, that there is no other. The Indian religious thinker knows that all the highest eternal verities are truths of the spirit. The supreme truths are neither the rigid conclusions of logical reasoning nor the affirmations of creedal statement, but fruits of the soul's inner experience.[8]

It follows that a religion is a form of life that represents the soul of the people, its peculiar spirit, thought, and temperament. Rather than being merely a theory of the supernatural that we can adopt or reject as we please, it is actually an expression of the spiritual experience of the race, a record of its social evolution, an integral element of the society in which it exists. Once we consciously or unconsciously recognize these traits of religion, it dawns on us that "religion is not a simple spiritual state of the individual. It is the practice of the divine rule among men. The believer in God loves his fellow men as he loves himself, seeking their highest good as he seeks his own, by redemptive service and self-sacrifice. He will put justice above civilisation, truth, patriotism."[9] Once we realize this, the idea of a single religion for all mankind—one set of dogmas, one cult, one system of ceremonies that all individuals must accept on pain of persecution by the people and punishment by God—becomes the product of unreason and the parent of intolerance.

In Hinduism, there is no "other." There is no place for the fear of or hatred of the Other; there is no need to be inhospitable to the Other; there is no room for xenophobia. Everyone is nothing but an extension of oneself or one's creed. The "other" results from looking at reality in a different way, from a different perspective. Once the multiplicity of perspectives and standpoints is admitted, no competing views remain, because all of them merge into one and become complementary. The Other and his creed is embraced into one's own. The Other is regarded as the one belonging to a different *jati*. By making the other realize that aham brahmasmi, *tat tvam asi* (I am *brahman* so art thou), Hinduism becomes all-encompassing and totally inclusive.

Hindu View of a Person

The concept of person in the Hindu tradition differs radically from how it has developed in the Judaeo-Christian traditions. In the Hindu tradition man is essentially divine (*amritasya putrah*), the child of the immortal bliss. In fact, he is *Brahman*, the ultimate reality itself. *Taittiriya Upanishad* III.1 describes Brahman as "that from which all these beings are born, by which after being born they live, and into which they merge when they cease to be." A man is essentially *nitya, shuddha, buddha, mukta Paramatman* (the eternally pure, awakened and free Self).

Hindu tradition recognizes that man lives in an external and an internal environment. He forgets his true nature, because of the external environment in which he lives. His body is a part of the external world, and his spirituality constitutes his internal world and represents his true potential. As long as man is under the sway of his sensate nature, he allows himself to be conditioned by the body, the senses, and the fruits of their actions. He is affected by the pulls of lust, fear and greed, with the result that he is lost in the world of the ephemeral and the perishable. But he has the capacity to transcend this situation and to explore the world of spirituality, which leads him to freedom from the sensate nature, offers fearlessness, and provides him breadth of vision, sympathy and immortality. Hinduism views man both as an actor and a spectator, as both *drishya* and *drik* (the object and the subject). In order to know himself, he must transcend himself. By such transcendence and the ability to realize the truth, he is able to know that he is *atman, brahman* and therefore, he is essentially infinite and immortal.

Once man ceases to look at himself as a conglomerate of different senses alone, he realizes that he is not merely a physical entity. He shares his sensuality with other primates, and his unique distinguishing characteristic is spirituality. As a physical entity, like other physical entities, man is acted upon and governed by forces outside him. Sensate view thus looks upon man from the outside and is very narrow. It is finite and trivial, because life at the level of ego "is only a shadow life." It ignores spirituality, which, as noted above, is the most profound distinguishing feature of man. Spirituality lies in his capacity to delve deep into himself; to look at his own self from within and not only from without.

This sensate view of man is restricted to the fact that the sense organs can give us knowledge of the external world alone. Being subject to physical laws, its findings are subject to change. The senses do not and cannot provide knowledge of what is eternal and abiding. Shankara in his commentary on the *Brihadaranyaka Upanishad*, II.1.20, says:

> This self of man, which is of the same category as the supreme Self, but separated from It like a spark of fire (from the fire) has entered this wilderness of body, sense-organs, etc. and although really beyond all relativity and finitude, takes on the attributes of the body and the sense-organs, which are characterised by relativity and finitude, and thinks itself to be this aggregate of body and sense-organs, regards itself to be lean and stout, happy or miserable—for it does not know itself as the supreme Self.

This Supreme self, the *brahman*, the *Prajapati*, according to *Isha Upanishad* verse 8, is "the self existent, one, is everywhere. He is the pure one, without a subtle body, without blemish, without a gross body, holy and without a taint of sin. He is the all-knowing, the all-encompassing. He has duly assigned their respective duties to the eternal *Prajapatis* (cosmic powers)."

The differences among persons belonging to different religions, tribes, classes and castes are superficial; deeper down exists only unity, identity; each is nothing but *Brahman*, each is *atman*. In fact, like the *rishi-s* of the *RigVeda* (IV.40.5) and *Katha Upanishad*, the person who sees everyone like himself (*atmavata*) as the manifestation of one true reality sees the identity of all beings. For him there is no other. He realizes that the *atman* that is in the sun, the air, and the fire is also in man, in gods, in sacrifices, and in the sky. The same is true for the aquatic creatures, insects, reptiles, and mammals, as it is for the fruits of the sacrifice. It is the rivers flowing from the mountains. It is *ritam*, truth, and *mahat*, great. It is the infinite. Shankara summarizes the above in his commentary on the second verse of *Katha Upanishad* as follows: "Atman, verily is not the indweller of the 'city' of only one body; what then? He is the indweller of all the cities. The meaning of the verse is that the entire universe has only one Atman; there is no possibility of a plural in atman." It is not as if one starts seeing unity in all living and non-living beings or one identifies oneself with the Others only after such a realization; this identity is there even before that awareness comes to fruition. Regardless of one's knowledge of this unity, every person is really one with the universe. In his commentary on I.iv.10 of *Brihadaranyaka Upanishad*, Shankara says, "Even before knowing Brahman, everybody, being Brahman, is really always identical with all, but ignorance superimposes on him the idea that he is not Brahman and not all, as a mother-of-pearl is mistaken for silver, or as the sky is imagined to be concave, or blue, or the like."

By treating everyone as ultimately *atman* or *brahman*, the Indian seers have advocated equality of all men and women, old and young. That the Upanishads believe in the sameness of everyone can be seen from verse IV.3 of the *Shvetashvatara Upanishad*, "Thou art the woman, Thou art the man; Thou art the youth and the maiden too; Thou art the old man tottering on his stick. Thou art born in diverse forms." Since the same *atman* dwells in all, none is superior and none is inferior. This condemnation of the idea of separateness and the idea of the essential unity and kinship of men and other creatures of the universe recurs in the Vedic literature repeatedly. Verse 6 of the *Isha Upanishad* also emphasises that "the wise man who realizes all beings as not distinct from his own self, and his own self as the self of all beings, does not, by virtue of that perception, hate anyone." Accordingly he realizes that the differences in the universe perceived by the senses reside only at the surface level, but deep down, regardless of the positions held by the individuals—the social or other functions performed by them; the *varna* or *jati*, class or caste to which they belong; or the money earned by them— is absolute unity. At that level there is an essential identity among all men. Shankaracharya has very aptly explained this in Verse 244 of his *Vivekachudamani*: "One man with the *upadhi*—limiting adjunct of the dress and function of governance is called a king; another man with the different *upadhi*, and function of the lowest military rank is called a soldier. But when the particular *upadhi* of each is taken away there will remain neither king nor soldier, but only man." When we realize that all the differences are only apparent and not real, that they belong only to the "outer" and not the "inner," and that the "inner" is common to all, we realize the essential oneness of all mankind. Once this realization dawns on us, the sense of "otherness" disappears and with it hatred, delusion and sorrow.

For a person who knows and has realized that underneath the vast superficial diversity lies an essential unity of all beings, "there is no difference between service of man and worship of God, between manliness and faith, between true righteousness and spirituality. All his words, from one point of view, read as a commentary on this central conviction."[10] For such a person, the notions of "mine" and "thine" (the source of separateness), *raga* (attachment), *dvesha* (covetousness), and *vaira* (animosity) leading to hatred, violence, and war is non-existent. He has an attitude of equanimity and friendliness toward all; he is at peace with himself and with his environment. Thanks to this *manasaivedam aptavyam*, the right training of the mind, which emphasizes seeing oneself and others as Brahman, a Hindu does not care about the caste, creed or religion to which one belongs, provided that one achieves excellence and has something to contribute to his own and to the corporate life. This is evident from the high esteem in which Mother Teresa, Sister Nivedita (born Margaret Elizabeth Noble), The Mother (born Mira Richard), Annie Beasant, and Father C. F. Andrews, who were all Christians, and several Sufi Saints are held by the Hindus.

Mlecchas as the Possible "Other"

In this section, I show that the Hindus actually put into practice their doctrine of unity in diversity. This can be best seen from their treatment of the foreigners with whom they came in contact long ago. They called the people whose origins were traced to lands outside Bharta (modern-day India), who could not use the Sanskrit language and who belonged to an alien culture, by the term *mlecchas*. In what follows, I deal with the notion of otherness in the classical Hindu literature by examining the concept of *mleccha*. I show that, though the surface grammar of the term *mleccha* gives one an impression of the other and some kind of hostility toward him, upon deeper analysis we find that *mlechha* is a value-neutral cultural term.

Though in the course of history Hindus came in contact with many cultures, religions and civilizations, they never made any special effort to explore or understand them; indeed, they were almost indifferent to their principles and practices to the point that they barred their followers from crossing the boundaries of Bharata or Aryavarata. *Brihadarnyaka Upanishad* 1.iii.10 says, "one should not approach a person, nor go to that region beyond the border lest one imbibe that evil, death," because contact with these persons and the region they inhabit has a polluting effect on all those who come in contact with them and go to the places inhabited by them.

They called the places located outside their own territory Asura *pradesh*, *mleccha pradesh* (the area inhabited by the barbarians, the uncultured populace). *Manusmriti* II.23, differentiates Aryavarata from the *mleccha Pradesh*: "That land where the black antelope naturally roams, one must know to befit for the performance of the sacrifices; (the tract) different from that (is) the country of the *mlecchas* (barbarians)." Describing the traits of the *mlecchas*, it says in X. 45: "All those tribes in this world, which are excluded from [the community of] those born from the mouth, the arms, the thighs, and the feet [of Brahman], are called Dasyus whether they speak the language of the *mlecchas* or that of the Aryans." This means that all who do not believe, at least in some measure, in the philosophical doctrines of *avidya*—ignorance, *karma*—action, *punarjanma*—rebirth, and *moksha*—liberation, which form the kernel of Hinduism and other religions of Indian origin, is a *mleccha*. In addition to these philosophical principles, anyone who does not believe in the social norms prescribed by different *smritis* and popularly known as *varnashrama dharma* (duties relating to the class, caste and the stages of life) is also a *mleccha*. But from this it does not follow that these are the essentials of Hinduism, because no two *smritis* agree about the content of each of them. For example, there is no universal agreement, other than the use of the word, about what *dharma* itself is.

The Hindus were directed neither to have a dialogue with the *mlecchas*, nor to learn their language, nor to visit their dwelling places or their countries. This was done to maintain ritual purity and to preserve the Hindu culture. Free intermixing in a primarily oral tradition would certainly have affected the distinction maintained by the Hindus between the sacred and the profane. A free intermixing would certainly have ruined the age-old *smriti*, as well as the *shruti* tradition. It would have corrupted if not destroyed their *sanmskaras* (sacraments). *Sanmskaras* include education, cultivation, training, refinement, perfection and grammatical purity, cognitive tendency (which gives rise to recollected knowledge), purificatory rites, sacred rites or ceremonies, consecrations, sanctifications, and the like. Thus the directive to avoid the *mlecchas* was practical and not due to their being considered less than part of the divine. Swami Ramakrishna put succinctly the dislike for foreigners thus, "All is God, but tiger-God is to be shunned. All is water, but we avoid dirty water for drinking."[11]

Apparently the term *mleccha* had nothing to do with those who did not follow the principles and precepts of *Sanatana dharma* or *Vaidika dharma*. Were it so, the Charvakas, the Buddhists and the Jainas would have also been called *mlecchas*, because none of them believes in the authority of the Vedas. But nowhere in the cipher of the canonical literature of the Hindus have they been described as *mlecchas*. Rather we find that every effort is made to show how they can be accommodated within Hinduism. On the contrary, we find that the Buddhist and Jaina canonical literatures use the term *babbhra* and *milakkhu* respectively to refer to those who are outside their fold. This shows that all the religions of Indian origin treated foreigners differently from their own class and that the notion of cultural otherness was deeply rooted in them. Jainas classify *mlecchas* into those who are "born in other continents" (*antaradvipaja*) and those born in Bharta (*karmabhumija*). Jaina *Acaranga-sutra* II.3.1.8 describes *mlecchas* (*milakkhu*) as "the jungle tribes and other groups of outsiders." The "other group of outsiders" apparently refers to the Yavnas (Greeks), Sakas (Scythians), Kushanas (Central Asian nomadic tribe), Turks

(Iranians), Hunas (Epthalites) and Portuguese, French, British, Persian, as well as nationals of other countries who visited India either as travellers or traders or even as conquerors.

Often the term *mleccha* is used to connote one who cannot use the Sanskrit language properly or who suffers from the linguistic deficiency in the lingua franca of the native Hindus. He is one who speaks confusedly, indistinctly or barbarously. A person who cannot see contradictions in his own speech (*virodha adarshane*) is also a *mleccha*. In his *Dharma Sutra*, Baudhayana defines *mleccha* as a person who consumes beef, speaks contradictorily, and is devoid of all conducts. Patanjali, in his *Vyakarna Mahabhashya*, says that, in order to avoid falling down to the level of *mleccha*, one must learn the grammar of the Sanskrit language. He says, "*mleccha ma bhuma-ity adhyeyam vyakaranam.*"[12]

All foreigners who did not know Sanskrit were called *mleccha*s. Accordingly, it served as an ethno-cultural term used to distinguish the nobility and aristocracy of character and the temperament of the natives of Bharata from those who belonged to other regions and were not proficient in Sanskrit. It was never used in the sense of the "other," as we understand in the context of Semitic religions. In Islam, the other refers not to the cultural "other" but to the one who belongs to a different religion. He is a *kafir* and needs to be redeemed through conversion. One is either hostile to him or extends hospitality to him in order to win him over; one cannot be indifferent to him. In Hinduism, one is indifferent to the Other's beliefs, faith and ways of worship; the Other is not at all necessary for establishing one's own identity.

That is why, as J. L. Mehta puts it, "Hinduism has at no time defined itself in relation to the other, nor has acknowledged the other in its unassimilable otherness."[13] On the contrary, Hinduism has always attempted to assimilate the foreigners into its fold. The exact procedure of giving the *mleccha*s a place in the *chaturvarnaya* (fourfold classificatory) system, or purification (*shuddhikarana*) has differed from time to time and from text to text. Therefore, only a general outline of the process adopted for such assimilation can be described. There are no set rites and ceremonies associated with such assimilation. Manu (X. 43-44) regarded the *mleccha*s to be the offspring of inter-caste marriages or as originally belonging to the *kshatriya* class and losing their status either due to heretical tendencies or non-observance of sacred rites. *Mahabharata* (XII. 65.13.22) elaborates the duties of the *mlecchas*—Yavnas, Shakas, Tusharas, Pahlavas, Chinas, and other alien people. These are obedience to parents, preceptors, kings, and hermits; performance of Vedic rites; digging of wells; making of presents to the *dvijas* (twice born); abstention from violence of any kind; absence of wrath; truthfulness, purity, and peacefulness; maintenance of wives and children; and performance of sacrifices in honor of the *pitrs* (ancestors); and performance of *paka-yajnas*. This shows that the *mleccha*s were also expected to perform the same normal acts of piety as the Hindus.

During the Bhakti period, the barrier between the native Hindu and the *mleccha*s (the outsiders) was further broken down. *Bhagavata Purana* II.4.18 clearly states that taking resort to Vishnu and his devotees is enough for the purification of the Kiratas (Mongoloid or Sino-Tibetan), Hunas, Andhras, Pulindas, Pukvasas, Abhiras, Suhmas, Yavnas, Khasas, and others. According to Ramanuja, to be eligible for liberation, all that is required of everyone, may he be a *mleccha* or a *shudra*, is wholehearted surrender (*sharanagati*).

The Hindus hold the *mleccha*s in high esteem and not with contempt, even though they dislike their way of life. They are ready and willing to learn from the *mleccha*s whatever they know better than the Hindus. The attitude of Hindus toward the *mleccha*s is best summed up in the *Gargi Samhita*. Acknowledging that the Yavanas have a better knowledge than the Hindus in astronomy and are more skilled in astronomical calculations, the *Brihat Samhita* II.32 implores the Hindus thus: "The Greeks are *mleccha*s, but amongst them this science is duly established; therefore even though they are *mleccha*s they are honoured as *rishis*; much more than an astrologer who is a Brahmana." Shabara and Kumarila, the two chief exponents of the Mimamsa school of Indian Philosophy, also assert that the *mleccha*s have equal and, in some cases, superior skill and proficiency in some secular (*laukika*) matters—that is, areas in which there can be no real conflict with the sacred tradition of the Hindus—and worldly activities, like agriculture and the catching and rearing of birds. Therefore, there is nothing wrong in learning from them these techniques and entering into empirical transactions with them. This capacity of the Hindus to learn from everyone is based on the maxim: *Antyadpiparam dharmam* ("Supreme knowledge can be learnt even from the man of low birth").

From this, it is clear that a Hindu is keen to learn from anyone, regardless of his class, caste, or origin. There is no sense of hatred; at the most, a sense of indifference and no theoretical hostility toward the other. If for some reason one cannot be friends with the foreigner, or cannot rejoice (*mudita*) in his achievements, one must have compassion (*karuna*) toward him. If that is impossible, one must ignore (*upeksha*) him but never have feelings of animosity toward him.

Even in their epistemology and metaphysics, the Hindus distinguish between the *vyavaharika* (phenomenal, empirical level of existence, truth and knowledge) and the *paramarthika* (the transcendental or supra-phenomenal plane of existence, truth and knowledge). Only at the *vyavaharika* level do we see the world of *nama* and *rupa* (name and form)—the plurality of selves and things. We see these differences because of *avidya* (ignorance) and *maya* (illusion). The knowledge we derive here is the result of our senses; it is *aparavidya*, lower knowledge. At this level of existence, we find multiplicity: there are "others," there are *mlechhas*, there are *shudras*, there are out-casts, and the like. But at the *paramarthika*—that is, supra-phenomenal lev-el—there is no multiplicity, only unity, oneness. There is neither self nor the absence of self. Once the *para vidya* (higher knowledge) dawns on an indi-vidual, he becomes *mukta* (free from all dualities). For him there is no "oth-er." With the help of the distinction between the *vyavaharika* and *pramathika* levels of existence, Hinduism is able to explain the differential treatment it recommends to its followers against the *mlecchas*. The differential treatment to different people belonging to different creeds, castes, and classes—as per the prevalent social laws and customs—is applicable only at the phenomeno-logical level, but once one transcends that, there is no difference between one and the Other. Like the salt or sugar dissolved in water, all of us at that level are one.

Thanks to this distinction between the *vyavaharika* and *paramarthika*, Hinduism has been able to maintain its non-proselytizing character; it neither seeks nor avoids any doctrine, practice, or custom but assimilates everything that comes its way. For example, the *Bhavishya* (Future) *Purana* narrates the story of Christ and the development of Christianity and the downfall of some of the practices of Hinduism. It also narrates briefly the story of Prophet Mohammad. Both these stories are told in ways that portray both Christ and Muhammad like the other incarnations of the Hindu pantheon, the incarna-tions of Narayana, the Supreme Being itself. It asserts that Nyuh worshipped the Supreme in the form of Lord Vishnu, who in turn blessed him with prosperity and extensive progeny. It then narrates the lineage of Nyuh in the same manner in which the genealogy of the Hindu kings is given. This shows how keen the Hindus are to assimilate the "other" religions into their own.

The Term "Hinduism" — An Historical Survey

This tendency of Hinduism to welcome one and all to its fold unconditionally and to assimilate them is best illustrated by the analogy of the bull. Accord-ing to Vivekananda, Hinduism is like the bull on whose horns a mosquito sat for a long time. The bull apparently was not affected by his presence. But eventually the mosquito's conscience started troubling him. He said to the bull, "Mr. Bull, I have been sitting here for a long time, perhaps I annoy you. I am sorry, I will go away." But the bull replied, "Oh no, not at all! Bring your whole family and live on my horn; what can you do to me?" In this section, I show that the all-inclusive attitude of Hinduism is a product of its own history.

Let me begin with an explanation of the use of the term "Hinduism." The word "Hinduism" is derived from the term "Hindu." Both are of relatively recent origin. Traditionally the two have no meaning, as they are not found in the ancient literature or in the scriptures of the people to whom they refer and to the religion they connote. These names were used by foreigners—earlier by the Persians, to refer to the people living in the geographical region lying on the eastern side of the river Sindhu, and later by Muslims, to refer to the people who had not converted to Islam. The use of the terms "Hindu" and "Hinduism" were thus developed from geographic designations into religio-cultural ones (as occurred with so many other geographic designations over the centuries) by outsiders who were not the practitioners of the religion or the way of life which was meant to be described by it.

Historians like Jackson[14] have traced the earliest mention of the term "Hindu" to the first chapter of *Zend-Avesta*. In the chapter, entitled *Avestan Ven-didad*, the fifteenth of the domains created by Ahur Mazda was called *Hapta Hindu* (Seven Rivers) a region of abnormal heat. Similarly, *Rig Veda* VIII, 24, 27 describes this geographic region as *Sapta Sindhavas* (Seven Rivers). The use of the term "Hindu" by foreigners has been dated by some historians like H. W. Rawlison[15] to c. 518 BC. According to historical records, the term "Hindu" continued to be used to refer to the inhabitants of the geographical region until the early twentieth century in phrases like "Hindu Christian" (as opposed to "Christian") and "Hindu Muslim" or "Hindu-Mohammedans" (in contrast to "Arab Muslim" or "Turkish Muslim") were in vogue.

The inhabitants of the eastern side of the river Indus had no name for their own religion. One reason was that, to the practitioner of Hinduism, one's temporal and spiritual life should form one integral and harmonious whole. To separate them is to destroy their organic unity. "All life to him was religion and religion never received a name from him, because it never had for him an existence apart from all that had received a name."[16]

According to J. N. Mohanty, this religion "may best be called a natural religion," because it was not founded by a prophet or based on a book produced at an identifiable point of time. Moreover, "the corpus of the texts of this religion is much unlike the Bible and the Qu'ran. Rather, the texts record everything that the community knew (*vid* = to know) and serve as the founding texts from which the entire culture began. Not having an author, the texts—compiled into the various Vedas in course of time—came to be characterized as *apaurusheya* (not having a human author)."[17]

The other and stronger reason for not having a name for this religion was that it was the most universal and unique religion. It was the most universal, as it had no beginning in time and no founder. It was the first religion followed by humankind. It is *sanatana* (perennial and eternal). It has been there since eternity. It is unique in the sense that it is not dominated by theology and gives ample freedom to the followers in matters relating to faith, belief, and way of religious life. As a result, it is all-inclusive and represents a comprehensive way of life. In the words of Shri Candrashekharendra Sarasvati, the sixty-eighth Shankaracharya of the Kanchi Kamakoti peetha, the reason for this religion not having a name is:

> Other religions did not exist before the time of their founders.
> Ours is a religion which existed long before the founded religions. [18]

Obviously, it was the only religion in the world ministering to the spiritual needs of mankind as a whole. There was no second religion from which it was required to be distinguished. Hence there was no need for a name for it. It was, and even now continues to be nameless. [19]

The above argument relies heavily on the presupposition that a unique thing—a thing which does not have any other in the same category—does not need to be named, because the purpose of naming is to distinguish one thing from another. Individuation is needed only when more than one thing belongs to a particular category. Whether one agrees with the above argument or not, the fact remains that there was no name of the religion practiced by the habitants on the eastern side of the Indus, the "Hindus."

"Bharata" is the term used in the classical Indian literature to represent the geographical region in which the Hindus lived. *Vishnu Purana* II.3.1 describes the geographical boundaries of *Bharata* thus:

> *Uttaram yat samudrasaya himadreschaiva gacchatam*
> *Varsham tad bharatam nama bharati yatra santatih.*

(That is, the area, which is to the north of the sea and extends up to the Himalayas, is called Bharata and its inhabitants are known as Bharatis.) From this it can be concluded that not only the foreigners identified the inhabitants of this region by the geographical region occupied by them but even the local inhabitants described themselves in terms of the geographical contours of the physical area they occupied, not the religion they practised.

However, in the course of time, when various religions (*panthas*) came into being and came to be known by the names of their founders or inspirers, the ancient Indians felt the need to distinguish their mode of individual, spiritual, ethical, and social life from the newly founded religions. They called their religion *Sanatana Dharma* (eternal religion). Since their individual and social way of life was determined by the teachings of the four Vedas (*Rigveda*, the book of adulations; *Yajurveda*, the book of rituals; *Samaveda*, the book of songs; and *Atharvaveda*, the book of wisdom), the Hindus sometimes called their form of life Vaidika Dharma (the Dharma which is based on the doctrines contained in the Vedas and which derives its authority from them). "Dharma" means "to sustain," "to maintain," and "to support." It encompasses the duties, obligations, and justice in the given society and lays down the rules of conduct and guide for action. In short, it represents a way of life or what Wittgenstein calls "a form of life." In fact, the use of the term "religion" in the Indian context is itself problematic, because there is no corresponding term in the traditional Sanskrit doxographies. But some works contain chapters entitled *Ishvaravada*, whose approximate translation would be "doctrine of God." The term used for religion is *pantha* (the path), while the Dharma is one of the *panthas*. That is to say, there are many religions to lead us to the divine. If the goal is spiritual perfection, the paths to achieve it may be many. Each may be equally efficacious. This distinction shows that the pluralism and respect for all faiths and creeds is built into Hinduism.

The term "Hindu" was first used to connote the follower of a religion in c. 712 AD by Mohammad ibn Quasim in the administrative treaty known as "the Brahmanabad settlement." As well, Al-Biruni (973–1048), in the Preface of his *India*, uses the term to connote the religious principles and practices of "our religious antagonists." He goes on to say that these theories and observances may sound "utterly heathenish, and *the followers of the truth*, i.e., the Muslims, find them objectionable."[20]

It was not until the thirteenth century that the Hindus started using the terms "Hindu" and "Hinduism" or "Hindu Dharma" to describe their own religious principles and practices. Saint Namdeva first used the term in his writings, later included in the *Guru Granth Saheb* of the Sikhs. It says: *Hindu pooje dehura, musalmaan masid; Name soi poojya na dehura na masid* (that is, a Hindu worships in the temple, a Muslim in the mosque; but the real worship is of only those who worship the name alone, without the confines of the temple or the mosque). The same is the case with the Hindus' use of the term "Muslim." It is reported by Romila Thapar that "the name 'Muslim' does not occur in the records of the early contacts (with the followers of Islam). The term used was either ethnic (*turuska*, referring to the Turks), or geographical (Yavanas, Greeks), or cultural (*mlecchas*)."[21]

Functionally, Hindu use of the term "Hinduism" refers to the people who follow a religion other than the religions of foreign origin like Islam and Christianity. This continues to be so. The Hindu Marriage Act of 1952 defines a Hindu as a category including not only all Buddhists, Jainas and Sikhs but anyone who is not a Muslim, Christian, a Parsee, or a Jew. The use of the term "Hinduism" in place of *Sanatana Dharma* has the singular merit of avoiding the implication that it is Brahmanism, which in turn implies that it owes its origin to the Brahmanas. The use of the term "Hinduism" makes it convenient for the user and hearer to understand that it refers to the Indian's mode of life, inclusive of religion in the strict sense of the term.

Hindu practice contains no absolute list of descriptive and prescriptive regulations; none of its prescriptions and proscriptions, imperatives and taboos is codified permanently. There are some well-documented *sadharana dharmas* (normal duties) for all *varnas* (classes and castes) and *ashramas* (stages of life), but in an emergency or exceptional circumstances all the *sadharana dharmas* can be replaced by *apta dharmas*. For example, there are rigid standards for the sacred and the profane with respect to eating, worshipping, performing daily ablutions, marriages, rules of governance, and so on, but in an exceptional situation each can be abandoned in favor of an entirely opposite course of action.

Moreover, there is no single prescribed deity or prescribed text to which one must adhere in order to be called a Hindu. One may worship one god or many gods, one may be a Vaishnavite (follower of Vishnu) or a Shaivite (follower of Shiva), or one may be Shakta (follower of Shakti, the female goddess), or one may not believe in any god or goddess at all, yet he can call himself a Hindu. Without losing his Hindu identity, one may go to a temple to worship once or twice a day, once a week, once a month, once a year or never. Likewise, one is free to believe in the authority of the Vedas and to accept them as the text by which to conduct one's life or to totally reject them—as did the Charvakas, Buddhists, and Jainas—without ceasing to be a Hindu. One may be a strict vegetarian, a non-vegetarian, or even an Aghori—the follower of a sect who eat not only human flesh but also human excreta—still he remains a Hindu. A traditional or a set idea of Godhead or conventional form of worship has no place in Hinduism. Underlying the acceptance of a plurality of Godheads and methods of worship lies a principle. Though the Truth or God or the Supreme may be one, we can and in fact we do see and apprehend it differently from various perspectives. This attitude removes antagonism and also promotes forbearance and sympathy for all religions.

Hinduism does not cramp the growth of its followers by limiting them to the confines of a text or a practice but allows them the freedom to accept all that is good, regardless of where it is found. In the words of Vivekananda, it allows this freedom to the individual because it realizes that, in human progress, development, and realization, "no theories ever made men higher. No amount of books can help us to become purer.[22] The only power is in realisation and that lies in ourselves and comes from thinking. Let men think" (CW II, p.336). Mahatma Gandhi summarized these qualities of Hinduism in the following way.

Hinduism is not an exclusive religion. In it there is room for the worship of all prophets in the world. It is not a missionary religion in the ordinary sense of the term. It has no doubt absorbed many tribes in its fold, but this absorption has been of an evolutionary, imperceptible character. Hinduism tells every one to worship God according to his own faith or Dharma and so it lives at peace with all the religions (*Young India*, 6.10.1921)

Hinduism considers all religions to be equal and different paths (*panthas*) for reaching the same goal; it does not attribute any superiority or exclusivity to its own theories and practices. This is clear from its assertion in the *Bhagvata Purana* III.27.2: "As different rivers originating in different mountains, running along crooked or straight path, mingle their waters in the ocean, so do the different sects, with their different points of view, their different ways of worship at last all come unto Thee." The Hindu mindset with respect to different religions is represented by the following stanza from a Vaishanva prayer in the *Vishnu Sahstranam* 16: "Just as all rain water dropping from the sky ultimately reaches the ocean, so the obeisance made to each god in whatever form reaches Keshava (God—the Supreme) ultimately." It may be noted that Keshava is just one of the names of gods in the Hindu pantheon. Keshava is neither superior nor inferior to other Gods; it is merely used in a figurative sense, as a metaphor. The idea is that all offerings are made to the One, the Supreme, the formless Brahman.

Hospitality and Flourishing

From the above discussion, it follows that a Hindu is "not someone with a particular set of beliefs or practices, but rather someone who is not in any way a foreigner."[23] This implies that, with the exception of those who by "origin or self identification" look to some tradition like Christianity and Islam, whose origin lies outside the geographical boundaries of South Asia, everyone is by default a Hindu. Hinduism treats everyone as equal, welcomes all the noble ideas, examines them on merit and adopts them. One of the prayers in the *Yajurveda* says: *"aa no bhadrani kratavo yantu vishvatah"* (Let noble thoughts come to us from all over the world.) It treats and prays for each and every individual. The invocation to the *Kena Upanishad* states:

Om saha navavtu; saha nau bhunaktu; sahaviryam karavavahait. Tejasvina-vadhitamastu; ma vidvishavahai.

May Brahman protect us both; may He nourish us both; may we both achieve energy; may we never hate each other.

Hinduism tolerates no hostility toward anyone. It extends its hospitality to everyone; it accommodates everyone. The fact that one can follow its principles and precepts without in any way altering one's own shows us the way to human flourishing.

PART 2: HINDUISM AND THE OTHER: A MADHAVA POSITION

DEEPAK SARMA

Dichotomy and Irony: "Hinduism" and the Other

"Hinduism is the oldest religion." This claim is made by many Hindus when comparing their "tradition" with other well-known religious traditions, such as Buddhism, Judaism, Christianity, and Islam. This claim is problematic, as it is also possible to argue that "Hinduism" is the youngest religious tradition among the so-called "great" religions of today. How can this be the case when the Vedas, argued to be the most important texts in Hinduism, are believed by secular historians to be more than 3500 years old? How is this possible when people have been practicing what we now call "Hinduism" in the subcontinent since at least 1500 BCE?

The answer to these and related questions revolves around the phrase "what we now call." That is, the term "Hindu" is a relatively new one and only came into vogue in the last two centuries when British colonizers sought a generalizing umbrella term to describe those traditions in India that were neither Christian nor Muslim.[24] The term "Hindu," invented in the eighth century CE, was first used by Muslim thinkers merely as a geographic term but then evolved into a religious term to refer to those people and traditions in the subcontinent that were not Muslim. The term "Hindu" is one that was thus employed by outsiders, first as a geographic characterization, and then to refer to the religions of others. Ironically, the term has been adopted and adapted by the non-Muslim people of India itself in order to differentiate themselves from the very people who first used it to differentiate. What was once a product of alterity is now a creator of the same!

But does the relatively recent use of the term "Hindu" demarcate the beginning of notions of "otherness" in Hindu[25] thought?

Antyajas and Mlecchas: Those Excluded from the Class System

Given the importance of varna (class) and jati (caste) in the history and development of Hinduism, it should come as no surprise that Hindus have been, and continue to be, highly aware of the boundaries that surround their communities. The internal awareness of class and caste has meant that alterity was always part of the Hindu mindset. One might mistakenly think that this meant that Hindus were ignorant of, or ignored, communities that did not have a place in the class system. This is not the case as Hindus have established taxonomies that also include those outside of the Hindu social system. In the thirteenth century, for example, Madhvacarya, the founder of the school of Vedanta that bears his name, used the term *antyaja* as a way of referring to the "other." Jayatirtha, his most well-known commentator, explained that the term meant "excluded from the class system."[26] *Mlecchas*, on the other hand—a term first used in 800 BCE—were understood to be foreigners or barbarians, and these were strictly distinguished from antyajas.[27] Though excluded from the class system, antyajas were nevertheless considered part of the community of sentient beings dwelling within approved or immediate areas, while *mlecchas* applied to those living in non-Sanskrit-dominated cultures. Such terminology was used to differentiate and maintain exclusivity, purity, and insularity. The existence of such taxonomies proves that Hindus have always thought in terms of alterity. Do Hindus accept this today?

Stereotypes and Inclusivism

One of the most common responses to questions concerning Hindu alterity is that such differences are superficial, the product of illusion (maya) or ignorance (avidya), and that ultimately, all humans, in fact all things, are identical and/or equal to Brahman (the all-pervasive divine force). Such responses are either modified or simplistic versions of the metaphysic propounded by Shankaracarya, the founder of the Advaita School of Vedanta in the eighth century, which will be referred to here as the "neo-Advaita Vedanta position." Though the metaphysical position may be a desirable one, it identifies, some might say confuses, metaphysics with conventional reality. Shankaracarya's position has undergone various incarnations and has largely been appropriated and put forth by leading Hindu intellectuals and politicians as the essential doctrine of Hinduism. From such a perspective, perceived differences are explained away as cognitive errors. According to this position, notions of otherness appear foreign to Hinduism.

People who do not agree with this position or hold a different belief are placed in a hierarchy that situates the Advaita perspective at the pinnacle.[28] Competing views are incorporated into the Advaita position, which, according to its proponents, has the purest version of the Truth. For example, any kind of theism, whether it is Hindu or Abrahamic, is deemed only partly true and at a lower level on the epistemic hierarchy than the Advaita position.

Those who do not subscribe to the neo-Advaita position point to several weaknesses in this position. The all-inclusivist position is, to a large degree, itself as exclusive as any other position. While it seeks to include other, less advanced, forms of religious understanding in its world view, the danger of a total view of reality becoming exclusivist always lurks. It too could lend itself to a hostile alterity, based on negative images of the other, as a consequence of its affirmation of its religious superiority and the inferiority of the religiously different. Furthermore, though the metaphysics is ultimately against alterity, conventionally it exists. The social and historical reality of alterity cannot be dismissed by purely metaphysical arguments. Metaphysics aside, only a segment of the historical Hindu population has adhered to this position. To construe this position as the prototypical or exemplary Hindu position would therefore be incorrect.

While neo-Advaita Vedanta does offer an important perspective on otherness, the complexity of Hindu life and the wealth of positions articulated in the course of its history require exploring alternatives. This leads us to an examination of the theological landscape, prior to the domination of neo-Advaita Vedanta.

Tradition? Tradition!

Pre-modern India was filled with diversity and difference. Innumerable religious communities thrived in this context, overlapping with each other, and yet distinct from each other. While some traditions were well formulated or were producers of systematic doctrines, others were amorphous conglomerations of beliefs and practices. They were distinguishable by the importance they gave to class, caste, particular gods or goddesses, and even to particular context. Unlike many other world religions, the many Hinduisms were not unified under one leader or one set of texts. Rather, diversity was the unifying element.

Alterity is also evidenced among the so-called "viewpoints" (darshanas) which developed into religio-philosophical schools. These schools produced doxographies, collections of philosophical opinions, such as Haribhadra's Saddaranasamuccaya (eighth century CE), that were obvious indicators of an awareness of the Other—in this case, intellectual opponents.[29] Though such "viewpoints" were literati communities, the fact remains that alterity was part and parcel of the outlook of pre-modern Indians.

The closest proximity to "religious tradition" was the *sampradayas*, which were largely Brahmin communities founded by one leader who was believed to have propounded a systematic and coherent theological system. Such *sampradayas*, such as Madhva Vedanta, established monasteries wherein virtuoso religious leaders and practitioners were trained and knowledge could be handed down from one generation to the next. Though there were overlaps (shared texts, metaphysics, and so on), these *sampradayas* saw one another as rivals, as "Others."

How did these sampradayas interact with one another? How did they confront the Other? Before addressing internal solutions to the problems of religious diversity and alterity, it is essential to address the current complexity of "Hindutva"—an ideology that is based on and fosters hostile alterity.

Hindutva and the Religious Other

The British impact on the traditions of the subcontinent cannot be underestimated. The presence of Christian missionaries and scholars presented challenges for the religious diversity of India. Christian missionaries were able to present a relatively monolithic tradition to the leaders of the various sampradayas—something they themselves could not do. The pre-modern traditions of Hinduism, as suggested above, did not present many universally held identifying characteristics. The end result was that Hindu intellectuals, such as Rammohan Roy and others trained by the British, sought to reify "Hinduism" in order to battle against their Christian counterparts. Such moves to standardize and homogenize what was once diverse were taken to another extreme when the attempts at doctrinal systematicity were combined with politics. This led to the development of '"Hindutva" or Hindu-ness (-tva is an abstracting suffix), which saw and sees itself as a rival to Christianity and Islam. The Hindutva movement and accompanying "Syndicated Hinduism"[30] has resulted in many Hindus defining themselves in opposition to other traditions—only possible after Hinduism was co-opted and reified. In recent times, when the Bharatiya Janata Party, the dominant and governing party until its defeat in the 2004 parliamentary elections, sought to enforce and propagate reified Hindutva, they did so via somewhat violent means. These activities, atypical in the history of India, were directed toward Christians and Muslims who had suddenly become a threatening "other." This current incarnation of Hinduism is a far cry from the inclusivism of neo-Advaita Vedanta since it is founded upon presumed alterity rather than unity.

Are there better, less hostile or more fruitful ways for the Hindutva supporters and others to deal with the "other"? What sorts of indigenous responses are there to religious diversity and alterity?

Debate, Dialogue, and Conversation

The various traditions and "viewpoints" of India have often sought to resolve or confront alterity and diversity through debate (samvada). These are formalized conversations that required participants to be more than familiar with the positions of their opponents. The debates were (and are) a way to humanize opponents and to welcome alterity. To illustrate debate, a brief examination of such practices as found in the Madhva School of Vedanta is here offered.

The Madhva sampradaya, a theistic school, proposes a position that is dialectically opposed to its most well-known predecessor—namely the Advaita school of Vedanta referred to above. Not only do Madhvas disagree with the basic tenets of Advaita Vedanta, namely that reality is ultimately non-dual and that differences are not real, but they are also perpetually in search of debate with Advaitins.

Madhvas are famous for polemics against their rivals. In fact debate and argument with other schools is an integral part of being and becoming a proper citizen of the Madhva world. Madhvacarya was not the first to propose the importance of debate. Such an instruction is found in Vyasa's Brahma Sutras, a text central to the commentarial traditions of Vedanta, in the section known as Samayavirodha (The Contradictions [In Other] Doctrines). The Brahma Sutras, composed in the fifth century CE, is a summary of the teachings of the Vedas, specifically the Upanishads, and, indirectly, an explanation of how to obtain liberation. It contains arguments against numerous schools of the day, including Buddhism and Jainism. According to Madhvacarya: "[Vyasa, who is] the Lord of knowledge, composed refutations of [rival] doctrines for [his] own devotees in order to sharpen their intellect."[31] Sharpening the intellect helps devotees to not only learn the intricacies of their own tradition, but also to defend it against others. To return to the themes of this study unit, religious identity in Madhva Vedanta is thus inextricably bound to debate with outsiders. Recognizing and embracing alterity is essential for Madhvas. And, as argued elsewhere, communication forces those involved in the dialogue to recognize the human element all too often ignored.[32]

In the Madhvacarya text known as the *Kathalaksana*, types of debate are defined, along with the context within which they are to take place. Such manuals were not uncommon among the schools of Indian philosophy, and Madhva Vedanta is no exception. This treatise on polemics is useful as a dialectical handbook for adherents who wish to debate and wish to learn about the type of arguments one can use. The debate was to be conducted with respect for the opponent and with knowledge of the opponent's position:

> In the dialogue [when there is opposition] there should be praise and respect given to the other [person] who won.
> 21–22. If the vadins, disputants, [show] the signs of having no knowledge, there will be an immediate failure. . . .

The debate was a civil and considerate form of dialogue. Though it is true that not all traditions are so doctrinally motivated, it is equally true that members of most traditions each can speak in depth about their belief systems or practices. Whether they can argue or not, they certainly can aspire to convey the basic beliefs of their respective traditions.

Fostering Inter-religious Dialogue and Conversation

The tradition of debate can serve as an important alternative to the philosophical dismissal of alterity and to the political accentuation of alterity and the violence it leads to. Respectful debate is a means of acknowledging and seriously engaging the alterity of the other. When two people speak to one another directly, facelessness disappears and trust and hope can be fostered. Beliefs and concerns can be shared more freely, and compromise may even emerge. Participants in dialogue can learn that their conversation partners are not cold and heartless killing machines or inhuman or even juvenile, but that the participants have families, children, loves, and are also committed to preserving these and not destroying them. Though it is possible to kill someone with whom you have shared ideas, it is much more difficult when one recognizes that the person is human too.

Inter-religious dialogue is thus especially suited to serve as a means to preventing violence, toxic othering, and hostile alterity. Many religious traditions, such as the Madhva tradition, have themselves made such activities an integral part of their institutions. Dialogue is often believed to be an important part of becoming a citizen of a particular religious world. Followers of Madhvacarya's school of Vedanta, for example, are encouraged to debate with members of other traditions in order to gain a better understanding of and certainty in their own religious identity. As long as the conversation is alive, then so too are the participants. As long as there is a conversation between people who respect one another, an explosion of violence can be prevented. As long as there is conversation, there may be no bloodshed.

NOTES

1. Compare to the Buddhist view on ignorance, page 125.
2. The Gospel of Sri Ramakrishna, p. 39.
3. Ibid., p. 5.
4. Vivekananda, "My Master," *The Complete Works*, Volume IV, pp. 182–183.
5. Ibid., p. 39.
6. *Collected Works of Mahatma Gandhi* , volume XXXVII, p. 224.
7. T. M. P. Mahadevan, *Outlines of Hinduism* (Bombay: Chetna Publications, 1971) p. vii.
8. Birth Centenary Library, Sri Aurobindo Ashram Trust, Vol. XIV, 1972, p. 123–24.
9. Radhakrishnan, *The Religion We Need* (Banaras Hindu University, 1963) p. 25.
10. Sister Nivedita, Introduction, *Collected Works of Vivekananda* , pp. xiii–xiv.
11. *The Gospel of Sri Ramakrishna*, trans. Swami Nikhilananda, New York: Ramakrishna Vivekananda Centre, 1952, p. 39.
12. Volume I, edited F. Kielhorn, 3rd edition, BORI, Poona, 1962, p. 2.
13. J. L. Mehta on Heidegger, *Hermeneutics and Indian Tradition*, edited William J. Jackson, EJ Brill, Leiden, 1992, p. 224.
14. Jackson, A. V. Williams, "The Persian Dominions in Northern India Down to the Times of Alexander's Invasion," *Ancient India*, ed. E. J. Rapson (Cambridge: Cambridge University Press, 1922) pp. 324–325.
15. Rawlinson, *India: A Short Cultural History* (London: The Cresset Press) pp. 53–54.

16. Bankim Chandra Chatterjee, *Aspects of Our Religion* (Bombay: Bhartiya Vidya, 1966) pp. 1–2.

17. Mohanty, *Classical Indian Philosophy* (London: Oxford University Press, 2002) p. 125.

18. R. Balasubramanian, "Two Contemporary Exemplars of the Hindu Tradition: Ramana Maharishi and Shri Chandrashekharendra Saraswati" *Hindu Spirituality: Vedas through Vedanta*, Ed. Krishna Sivaraman, Crossroad, New York, 1989, p. 381.

19. *Aspects of our Religion*, pp. 1–2.

20. National Book Trust, 2008.

21. *A History of India*, vol. I. New Delhi: Penguin, 1966, p. 27.

22. For more on Vivekananda, see in the chapter on Buddhism, page 142.

23. Mary Searle-Chatterjee, "Caste, religion and other identities," *Contextualising Caste*, ed. Mary Searle-Chatterjee and Ursula Sharma (Blackwell Publishers, 1994) p. 161.

24. For more see von Stietencron, Heinrich, "Hinduism: On the Proper Use of a Deceptive Term," in G. Sontheimer and H. Kulke (eds.) *Hinduism Reconsidered*, Manohar: Delhi, 2001, 32–53.

25. Having deconstructed the term "Hindu," it will now be used as a convenient designation rather than a reified system. Quotation marks around the term are therefore no longer required.

26. Jayatirtha, Tattvaprakasika 1.1.1.

27. See Halbfass's "Traditional Indian Xenology" in his *India and Europe: An Essay in Understanding* (NY: State University of New York Press, 1988), for an introduction to the xenological thought and categories of classical India.

28. So in actuality, neo-Advaita Vedanta is an exclusive position that is hidden behind a thin veneer of metaphysics.

29. See Halbfass's "The Sanskrit Doxographies and the Structure of Hindu Traditionalism" in *India and Europe* for more on this topic.

30. For more on syndicated Hinduism see Romila Thapar's "Syndicated Hinduism" in G. Sontheimer and H. Kulke (eds.) *Hinduism Reconsidered*, Manohar: Delhi, 2001, 32–53.

31. Anuvyakhyana 2.2.9.

32. See Deepak Sarma's "Viewpoint: Fostering Interreligious Dialogue and Conversation," *Hindu-Christian Studies Bulletin* 16 (2003), pp. 58–59.

Chapter Six

Buddhism

Views on Overcoming Obstacles to Universal Friendship:
Pali Theravada and Mahayana Perspectives

Richard P. Hayes and Dharma Master Hsin Tao

One of the principal themes of the Conference on Actualizing Human Potential has been that of hospitality. While hospitality has always been an important theme in Asian cultures, a more common theme in Buddhist texts has been the closely related notion of universal friendship: that is, friendship toward all sentient beings, without exception. The opposite of friendship, of course, is enmity or hostility. The Theravādin scholastic Buddhaghosa refers to hostility as the far enemy of friendship; that is, hostility is as far from friendship as one can get, and as the opposite of friendship, it is destructive of it. Equally destructive of universal friendship is what Buddhaghosa called its near enemy, namely, a kind of friendship that is similar enough to universal friendship to fool one into believing one has attained the ultimate in friendship when in fact one has stopped short of it. The near enemy of universal friendship, says Buddhaghosa, is preferential or particular friendship, the sort of friendship one might have toward members of one's own family or immediate neighbors or members of the same tribe or nation. This lesser kind of friendship manifests itself as a tendency to look after the needs of one's own people before (or in some cases to the detriment of) looking after the needs of strangers or people from a different people or a foreign nation.

HOSPITALITY AND UNIVERSAL FRIENDSHIP

When the Buddha's devoted personal attendant Ānanda made the observation that friendship is half the religious life, the Buddha reportedly said "Friendship is not half the religious life, Ānanda, it is the the whole of the religious life" (Samyutta Nikāya 45.2). Given the importance of universal friendship as a key aspect of Buddhist practice, therefore, this chapter will focus on that theme rather than the theme of hospitality. Hospitality will never be far in the background, however, since it can easily be seen as one of the natural manifestations of friendship, especially friendship toward the stranger or the perceived "Other." This chapter will begin with a discussion of the principal hindrances to friendship, namely the aforementioned near and far enemies of friendship. Next there will be a discussion of how, according to the teachings of Buddhism, these hindrances can be removed, the removal of these hindrances being seen as the actualization of the human potential to achieve universal friendship. Along the way, it will be necessary to explain some of the basic teachings of Buddhism for the benefit of those to whom Buddhist teachings are relatively unfamiliar.

HOSTILITY AND XENOPHOBIA

The Nature of the Problem

> Fear has arisen of him who has taken up weapons.
> Look at the people making war!
> I shall talk about my grief
> For I am deeply aggrieved.
> Seeing people contending
> like fish in shallow water—
> Seeing them in war with one another—
> I am very afraid. [1]

In these opening couplets of a poem entitled "Attadaṇḍa" (accumulated weapons), attributed to Gotama the Buddha, the stage is set for an investigation into the question of why there is so much conflict among people that, as he puts his situation in a subsequent verse, he found no place of safety and stability anywhere in the world. In this poem the Buddha goes on to say that as he looked into the hearts of human beings he saw there a barely visible dart, a subtle and yet deep wound that makes human beings run around frantically and crazily, a wound that tragically undermines all human efforts to find peace. The dart that has wounded us so is identified as the dart of arrogance and self-importance. It is our pathetic need to see ourselves as special that makes us set ourselves apart from others, to denigrate others and eventually to go to war with others.

In numerous other poems in the Suttanipāta, the same collection from which the poem cited above is taken, the Buddha talks at greater length about the human malaise. All conflict, whether in the form of quarrels among individuals or wars among peoples, ultimately stems from the universal tendency to measure oneself up against others. When we do this, we either feel inferior to others and then resent them, or we feel superior to others and then scorn them, or we feel equal to them and then compete with them until one gets an advantage over the other. The principal ways that the Buddha says we have of measuring ourselves against others are to compare our experiences, to compare the extent of our knowledge and the depth of our thinking and reasoning, and to compare our purity in conduct. So whoever has seen more of the world lords it over those who have seen less. The intellect also becomes an arena in which people constantly compete against one another, each trying to show the superiority of his understanding and wisdom, each trying to show that the other's way of thinking is flawed and inadequate, each trying to show that his knowledge is better in both quality and quantity. As if that is not enough, we even compete with one another as to who can be the most pure, the most righteous and the most pious. But the wise person looks at all this competition and says "Let them contend with one another all they wish. They shall get no quarrel from me."

In this chapter I shall examine several human tendencies that the Buddha saw as being at the root of all human conflict and suffering. I shall argue that xenophobia, the fear of the other, is seen in Indian Buddhism as an affliction that comes from a failure to see reality clearly.[2] And finally I shall look at the issue of whether these ancient Indian insights are applicable in the modern world.

A Critique of Making Unwarranted Divisions

Among the stock characters in the Pali canon are a pair of young men named Bhāradvāja and Vāseṭṭha, who appear in several narratives as foils to the Buddha. Both men are portrayed as being very proud of the high place in society that their being Brahman affords them, and they are often seen in narratives discussing the special duties and the privileges that are theirs as a result of the fact that they are Brahmans. Although they agree that they are special human beings, they do not always agree with each other as to what it is that makes them special.

In one of the narratives of the Pali canon, a text called *Vāseṭṭha Sutta* in the Suttanipāta, we find Bhāradvāja holding the view that what makes someone a Brahman is purely genetic and has only to do with pedigree. If a person's parents are Brahmans, and if all ancestors of both parents have been pure Brahmans for the past seven generations, then he or she is a Brahman. Vāseṭṭha, on the other hand, takes the position that pedigree is not sufficient; to be a Brahman, one must act like a Brahman, which means doing certain ceremonies and keeping pure by doing all the necessary purification rituals at the designated times. When neither is able to convince the other of the correctness of his position, they agree to go ask the Buddha which of them is correct. The Buddha's response, given in poetic couplets, is as follows:[3]

> I shall explain to you in proper order and in accordance with the fact the different kinds of living things, since there are diverse species. (600)

> If you look at trees or grass, although they may not be conscious of it, there are lots of different kinds and species. There are divergent species. (601)

> Then there are insects, large ones like moths and small ones like ants: with these creatures too you can see that they are of different kinds and species. (602)

> And in four-footed animals, whatever the size, you can see that they are of different kinds and species. (603)

> Now look at the creatures that crawl on their bellies, the reptiles and the snakes—you can see that they are of different kinds and species. (604)

> Look at the fish and water life—look at birds and the breeds that fly—you can see that they are of different kinds and species. (605–6)

> There is not among men different kinds and species in the manner that they are found among other species. (607)

> Unlike in other species there is not among men differences in kind or species with regard to their eyes, ears, mouths, noses, lips, eye-brows and even their hair—all are the same type. (608)

> From the neck to the groin, from the shoulder to the hip, from the back to the chest—it is all of one kind with men. (609)

> Hands, feet, fingers, nails, calves and thighs are all standard, and so are the features of voice and of colour. Unlike other creatures, men do not have characteristics which distinguished them at birth. (610)

> They do not have the variety of inherited features that other creatures have. In fact, in the case of humans, differences are differences only by convention. (611)[4]

The Buddha's contention—that the racial and ethnic and cultural divisions among human beings are purely conventional and are not natural (in the literal sense of belonging to one by nativity) in the way that differences among species are—became a point that Buddhists argued with increasing sophistication for as long as Buddhism remained in India. Although it can be admitted that there are observable differences among human beings, these differences were typically seen by Buddhists as trivial in the context of the overwhelming similarities in both the physical and psychological attributes that men and women have in common. While all human beings belong to the same species, the Buddha does acknowledge that there do exist differences in name only (*samaññaya*). These differences in name, he then goes on to say, are based in differences in occupation. A man who herds cows is called a cowherd, a man who cultivates fields is called a farmer, and a man who performs religious ceremonies for a living is called a Brahman.

At first glance, it would appear that the Buddha agreed with Vāseṭṭha as opposed to Bhāradvāja, for he has dismissed the latter's claim that what makes one a Brahman is just that one's ancestors are Brahmans. But disagreement with Bhāradvāja does not entail complete agreement with Vāseṭṭha. The Buddha would agree with Vāseṭṭha so far as acknowledging that it is behavior and conduct, rather than nature and heredity, that makes one a Brahman. He would not, however, go so far as to agree that it is the performance of ritual baths and adhering to dietary restrictions and so forth that make one a Brahman. Rather than these external observances, says the Buddha, it is one's inner character that truly makes one a Brahman. The true Brahmans of this world are not those who observe all the purity rituals that differentiate them from other men and women. Rather the true Brahmans are those who cultivate such qualities as wisdom, compassion, tranquility and emotional and intellectual flexibility internally, and who externally promote social harmony and human unity instead of conflict and division of the human species into castes, classes, clans, tribes and races. These points are made repeatedly in Buddhist literature, but probably the best known loci are the last two chapters of the *Dhammapada*, entitled *Bhikkhuvaggo* and *Brāhmaṇavaggo*.

In the *Bhikkhuvaggo* it is argued that what makes someone a genuine monk is not a shaved head and orange robes or the taking and periodic recitation of various vows, but the cultivation of inner virtues that manifest outwardly in acts of kindness and thoughtfulness of the needs of others. In the *Brāhmaṇavaggo* it is argued that what makes one a true Brahman is precisely the same as what makes one a genuine monk. In an earlier chapter of Dhammapada we find this two-line summary of the teachings of the wise:

Sabbapāpassa akaraṇam, kusalassa upasampadā
sacittapariyodapanam, etaṃ buddhāna sāsanaṃ [5]

Not doing any harmful thing, promoting health, purifying one's thoughts—this
is the discipline of those who have awakened.

A moment's observation will make it clear that not everyone in the world is
dedicated to avoiding harm to others, promoting health and purifying the
mind by eliminating greed, hatred and delusion. Those who are doing so, or
who are at least aspiring and attempting to do so, may be seen as practitioners
of goodness (*dhammacārī*). But what of those whose attention and efforts are
directed to enterprises that cause harm and keep the mind disturbed with self-
indulgence, animosity and muddled thinking? To those who are following his
path of discipline, the Buddha recommends that they avoid too much contact
with such people. In other words, while associating with like-minded people
is the best way to cultivate all the recommended virtues, associating with
other-minded people is the best way to undermine one's efforts to cultivate
virtue. And so it would appear that after all the talk of the unity of the human
species we have the basis for a distinction between self and other— between
us (the good folk) and them (the bad people)—of just the sort that could
undermine the project of seeing the unity of the human species.[6] We must
therefore turn our attention now to how the Buddhist self is advised to regard
the non-Buddhist Other.

Outsiders: The Foolish Masses

In the post-canonical Pali texts of the Theravada school of Buddhism one
encounters several references to the term *puthujjana*. This word is subject to
interpretation, because the first element of the compound, *puthu*, is homony-
mous. That is, there are two separate Pali words with a single pronunciation,
one corresponding to one Sanskrit word and the other to another Sanskrit
word. Some traditional scholars in the Theravada tradition have taken *puthu*
as the counterpart of Sanskrit *pṛthu*, which means extensive, numerous, plen-
tiful and so forth. On this account the compound *puthujjana* means the multi-
tudes, the masses, the majority of people. Other traditional scholars have
taken puthu as the counterpart of Sanskrit pṛthak, which means different,
separated, outside. On this interpretation the *puthujjana* are the outsiders:
that is, those who have not chosen to become Buddhist.[7] It is worth noting
that the logic of the texts we have examined so far leads to the conclusion
that one can be a true monk, and therefore a true Brahman, only by choice,
never by birth; this amounts to saying that one cannot be a birthright Buddhist but can only be a convert, and therefore being a non-Buddhist can also
be only through not choosing to become a Buddhist—or choosing not to be a
Buddhist. So the question that was asked earlier can now be rephrased slightly: How is a person who has chosen to pursue virtue advised to regard

someone who has either not chosen to pursue virtue or has perhaps even chosen to pursue vice?

A hint to the answer to this rephrased question is found in the adjective most commonly found with the expression *puthujjana*, namely the adjective *bāla*. This expression means childish or adolescent, immature, not fully developed. The use of this adjective suggests that the Other is not to be regarded as "other" in the sense of belonging to an alien species or perhaps another race or social group, but rather as "other" in the sense that an adult is "other" than a child of the same species. The Other, then, is just a being much like oneself in an earlier stage of development, therefore someone to be nourished and protected and helped along until maturity and refinement sets in.

That the *bāla putthujjana* is to be seen more as an infantile or adolescent version of oneself than as an alien is supported by the fact that it is not only non-Buddhists who are referred to as *puthujjana*. The term is also sometimes used with reference to Buddhists who have not yet achieved the first fruits of Buddhist practice, the first manifestations of wisdom. Having said this, let me now turn to a brief discussion of what those first fruits are said to be.

Entering the Stream

The ultimate goal of all Buddhist practice is nirvāṇa, which is defined as the cessation of all psychological afflictions (*kilesanirodha*), the afflictions being such drives as appetite for comforts and possessions, animosity and aversion and the clinging to beliefs. This goal is seen as remote for most people; most people, including most serious practitioners, are usually said to be unlikely to achieve *nirvāṇa* in this lifetime. There are, however, several stages along the way to attaining the ultimate goal. The first of these important stages along the route is called "entering the stream." This expression occurs only three times in the Pali canon, but the participial form *sotāpanno* (which means "having entered the stream" or "stream-entrant") occurs just over two hundred times. This word is used in two different senses. First, the term "stream-entrant" can be applied to anyone who recognizes the Buddha as the best of all teachers and strives for *nirvāṇa* and recognizes that there are people who have achieved higher stages of character refinement. In this first sense stream-entry may be akin to religious conversion, since it is linked to what Buddhists call going for refuge, which is the formal act by which one becomes a Buddhist. Second, the term "stream-entry" may refer to three specific changes in one's character. It is this second sense of the term that has most relevance to our topic.

The three specific changes in one's thinking that constitute stream-entry in canonical and later scholastic literature consist in abandoning three habits of thought that are known as fetters (*saṃyojanāni*):

sak-kāya-diṭṭhi: the view that collections are real or that wholes are greater than the sums of their parts, and especially the view that one has a self that is more than the collection of all the physical properties of one's body and all the various traits of one's mentality;

vicikicchā: doubt, indecisiveness, irresolution, spiritual paralysis;

sīlabbataparāmāso: addiction to good conduct and to religious vows

The third of these fetters requires some explanation. Two standard explanations are given by the traditional commentaries. First, most commentators make the reasonable suggestion that what is meant here is that it would be a form of bondage to be as obsessed with literal observance of all the Vedic rituals as Brahmans are portrayed as being. In Buddhist texts a good deal of fun is poked at Brahmans' preoccupation with maintaining ritual purity by following all the rules. Brahmans are depicted as people who have become so intent on following the letter of the rules that they have lost track of what the rules were designed to do, namely to aid people in the cultivation of such virtues as thoughtfulness of others and moral integrity. But a second explanation is also given. According to it, addiction to good conduct and religious vows refers not so much to particular types of rituals as to the general human tendency to seek for personal rewards for doing the right thing. Breaking this addiction, then, consists in cultivating virtue for its own sake rather than calculating the benefits for oneself of being virtuous.

Taking stock of what we have seen up to this point, the process of maturing is seen as a long and gradual continuum with more or less well-defined stages along the way. The transition from spiritual adolescence to adulthood, called the transition from being a foolish ordinary person to being a stream-entrant, is characterized as leaving behind the relatively self-centered preoccupation with following rules and reaping their rewards and moving into a more altruistic mood of cultivating kindness either for its own sake or because kindness makes life more pleasant for others. Typically in Buddhist texts the ritualistic Brahman is seen as being on the more childish or adolescent end of the spiritual spectrum. He is seen not as a spiritual Other but more as a less sophisticated and refined version of the spiritual aspirant who has reached stream-entry.

In later Buddhism, such as in the satirical Mahāyāna text called the *Teaching of Vimalakīrti*, we find instances of Buddhists being aware of the danger of being excessively rule-bound that lurks within the Buddhist tradition itself. In the text, the hero, a lay person named Vimalakīrti, whose name ironically means "in praise of purity," is portrayed as a man who apparently flouts all the conventions expected by pious Buddhists. He lives in the lap of luxury with a number of beautiful wives and servants. He spends his time in casinos, taverns and brothels, and when he studies he studies the works of non-Buddhist teachers. The story goes that when Vimalakīrti falls ill, the

Buddha sends his most senior and best-respected monks to inquire after his health. The monks refuse to go, for fear of being contaminated by his impurity. The Buddha, however, insists that they go. En route to his house, the monks have a number of misadventures, all of which are illustrations of the theme that people who allow themselves to be obsessed with purity inevitably invite unto themselves the very kinds of impurity they most fear. In one comical episode, for example, some heavenly beings cause flowers to fall out of the sky and land on the monks. The monks, aware of the rule that they must not wear garlands or ornamentation, try to brush the flowers off their robes. The more they try to rid themselves of the rule-breaking flowers, however, the more persistently the flowers stick. The flowers from heaven fall from the clothing of all other people, but to the ornament-dreading monks they stick like glue. The monks, then, in the very effort to liberate themselves, become slaves to rules that not only entrap them but make it impossible for them to respond to the afflictions of others. By insisting on being monks who obey all the monastic rules, they fail to respond to another's pains. Fortunately, the story ends happily. The apparently ailing and scandalous layman heals the monks of their scrupulosity and helps them grow up into a more mature spirituality. Once again we see the common Indian Buddhist theme of spiritual practice being a method of growing to maturity, and the recognition that another man's practice may well be suited to his stage of development and will be a means of his continued growth—provided that he does not become stuck forever in a stage of relative immaturity.

What we find in Indian Buddhism is not much different from what we find in religions of India in general. No matter which system of religious thought or practice one looks at, the most commonly encountered pattern is that a school will see itself as the model of maturity and will see other religious systems as being at earlier stages of development through which it is natural to pass on the way to greater maturity. There may be a somewhat paternalistic attitude towards people following paths other than one's own, but hardly ever is the practitioner of another religion seen as a threat or even as an annoyance that must be tolerated. Such is the prevailing ethos in Indian religions.

Given that we are not living in ancient India but in the modern world, what I should like to do now is to turn to a discussion of how we in the modern world might benefit from some reflection on these aspects of classical Buddhism that have been discussed above.

A PRESENTATION OF TWO PROGNOSES

Like Gotama the Buddha, we live in a time in which one can look everywhere for safety but never find any such place. Earlier in the period that is
now called modernity, Immanuel Kant also lived in dark and dangerous
times. For Kant, however, it was possible to muster an almost cosmic optimism, for he was convinced that the ultimate purpose of the human race was
to achieve a perfect and perpetual peace and that this would come about,
oddly enough, precisely through conflict. In an essay entitled "Idea for a
Universal History from a Cosmopolitan Point of View," Kant advanced nine
theses, the first and fourth of which were as follows:

> All natural capacities of a creature are destined to evolve to their natural end.[8]
>
> The means employed by Nature to bring about the development of all the
> capacities of men is their antagonism in society, so far as this is, in the end, the
> cause of lawful order among men.[9]

Kant's hypothesis was that the special natural capacity of the human being is
reason, and that it was this faculty of reason that was destined to evolve to its
natural end. The natural end of reason is the development of full and lasting
peace on earth. Although the faculty of reason can figure out in the abstract
that peace would be a good idea, the desirability of peace is not fully apparent to people until they have had their fill of conflict. And therefore war, he
argues, is the means that Nature has provided to human beings to assist their
reason in finding a way to peace. It is often said of Kant that his contempo-
raries observed that he was a man of extraordinary cheerfulness and optimism, and this line of argument would seem to bear that observation out. Be
that as it may, I would like to use the Kantian position as a standard of
optimism against which to assess the classical Buddhist position described
above. I have chosen to use this Kantian standard because, as I shall argue
more fully below, it seems to be that some version of his optimistic vision is
still shared by many people today.

Let me begin that assessment by returning to the Attadaṇḍa Sutta, the
poem cited at the beginning of this chapter. After the two lines quoted above,
Gotama the Buddha goes on to say this:

> samantam asāro loko, disā sabbā samerita
> icchaṃ bhavanam attano, nāddasāsiṃ anositaṃ.[10]
>
> The world is entirely unstable. Every quarter is trembling. Wishing safety for
> myself, I saw no such thing.

After this graphic depiction of the state of the world, Gotama sees only one
solution: renunciation, leaving the world and its cares behind and seeking the

bedrock stability of solitude in which one has left every form of craving and striving and struggling behind. This solution is evidently for the individual. True, society as a whole would be better off if every individual took this solution, but the solution is decidedly individualistic. Moreover, as the Buddha is said to have thought to himself shortly after his own personal liberation, the solution is one that only a very few individuals are likely to see as a living option. The vast majority (the foolish masses?) will go on striving, individually and collectively, for possessions, comforts, influence, recognition and social status. Human beings will therefore find peace only one at a time, and when they do find it, most of the people around them will not even notice that someone once in their midst has found it. The Buddha's conviction is, in this point, precisely the opposite of Kant's, whose second thesis is:

> In man (as the only rational creature on earth) those natural capacities which are directed to the use of his reason are to be fully developed only in the race, not in the individual.[11]

Human beings, then, are, according to Kant, destined to quarrel and make war together until their reason, spurred on by the painful results of this experiment with conflict, collectively matures, at which time people will collectively usher in an era of uninterrupted peace. Until that happens, admits Kant, the world will seem pretty dismal to reflective people. To them it will seem that

> everything in the large [is] woven together from folly, childish vanity, even from childish malice and destructiveness. In the end, one does not know what to think of the human race, so conceited in its gifts.[12]

Despite the fact that the world will seem bound up in folly, the philosopher of Kant's persuasion will have confidence that in the end Nature, which provided humanity with reason, will triumph. The key to Kant's optimism was that he could not admit of the possibility that Nature operates blindly and without a plan, nor could he admit of the possibility that Nature's plan is anything but to provide what is good for all creatures. Perhaps the greatest difference between Kant and the Buddha on this score was that the Buddha could easily conceive of the natural world unfolding without any plan or purpose whatsoever. This is indeed one of the ways of taking his observation that the world is *asaro*, a term that means not only lacking stability but also lacking a foundation, lacking a plan, and lacking a purpose. The world for the Buddha was entirely pointless, so how could it be the point of Nature, which is after all nothing but the world taken as a whole, to make everyone who happens to live there happy?

So far we have seen that Kant and the Buddha had different predictions for the future course of human history and different assessments of the relationship between the individual and the collective, but we have not yet seen why. Kant's reason for stating his second thesis, that the human being's natural capacities are fully developed only by the species as a whole rather than by the individual, is stated as follows:

> Reason in a creature is a faculty of widening the rules and purposes of the use of all its powers far beyond natural instinct; it acknowledges no limits to its projects. Reason itself does not work instinctively, but requires trial, practice, and instruction in order gradually to progress from one level of insight to another. Therefore a single man would have to live excessively long in order to learn to make full use of all his natural capacities. Since Nature has set only a short period for his life, she needs a perhaps unreckonable series of generations, each of which passes its own enlightenment to its successor in order finally to bring the seeds of enlightenment to that degree of development in our race which is completely suitable to Nature's purpose. [13]

Kant's idea seems to have been that each generation adds to the collective wisdom of the human race until eventually the amount of wisdom achieves a critical mass and dispels once and for all the kinds of folly that lead to war. At that time each individual will benefit from the collective wisdom of the human race.

That each generation leaves a legacy of wisdom for future generations is something with which the Buddha would surely agree. He would add, however, that each generation also leaves a legacy of folly and of what Kant called childish maliciousness and destructiveness. Moreover, since the number of spiritually mature people is always going to be significantly smaller than the number of childish people, the folly and other aspects of childishness are bound to grow more rapidly than wisdom. It is no more realistic to assume that the human race will become collectively more wise and mature than it is to assume that the human race will become collectively elderly and that as this happens each individual in society will simultaneously participate fully in this elderliness. Therefore, whereas Kant's vision was one of incremental progress, the Buddha's vision of human history was one of incremental degeneration. In such texts as the Aggaññasutta of the Dīghanikāya, the Buddha is portrayed as predicting that the human race will become generally more prone to destruction and warfare. The principal reason for this, he says, is that selfishness, which is the principal feature of the childish masses, will lead to more selfishness more rapidly than generosity will beget more generosity. As people become more selfish, they will become more determined to defend themselves and their possessions and their territory against intruders, and they will perceive more and more people as intruders. As the perception of intrusion increases, people will acquire more and more weapons. As more people have more destructive weapons, fear will increase, which will in turn lead to people acquiring even more weapons. Governments will become so preoccupied with protecting their citizens against attacks from enemies that they will neglect to provide citizens the resources they need to make a livelihood. In this atmosphere of the panicky acquisition—and use—of destructive weapons, people will naturally become even more preoccupied with their own personal safety and thus less concerned with Others. The downward spiral is described in sobering detail in the *Aggaññasutta* and in several other texts in the Pali canon.[14]

Up to this point it would appear that the Kantian and the Buddhist views of human history are beyond reconciliation. There is, however, more to the Buddhist vision. The downward spiral into increasing violence and selfishness cannot go on forever. The Buddha's prediction is that it will continue until the average human lifespan is just barely more than the time it takes to reach sexual maturity; at this point most people will just barely live long enough to reproduce themselves once. The general human condition will be so violent and unpredictable that some people will begin to seek alternatives to selfishness and its resultant conflict. They will form small groups and retire as far away as possible from the rest of the world, and together they will develop the skills necessary to live together. On this point the Buddha's vision is similar to Kant's in that in both cases it is a weariness with conflict that is said to lead to a collective discovery (or rediscovery) of the human virtues that make peace possible. Where the two visions remain dissimilar is that Kant is convinced that Nature has provided the means for human beings eventually to achieve perpetual peace, whereas the Buddha predicts that human history will forever oscillate in large periods between degeneration and regeneration, between Dharmic peace and anti-Dharmic conflict.

The collective name for these virtues in Buddhist texts is *Dharma*. In a famous discussion with his aunt, who was also his stepmother and the first woman to become a Buddhist nun, the Buddha offers a brief set of guidelines on how to tell whether or not a human characteristic is a virtue. It is a virtue, says this text, if it promotes dispassion rather than passion, self-reliance rather than dependence on alliances, wishing for little rather than wishing for much, harmony rather than divisiveness, a love of seclusion rather than a love of company, energy rather than indolence, and frugality rather than wastefulness.[15] In this list of criteria we see the suggestion that individuality and self-reliance tend to promote social harmony, whereas forming alliances and fostering solidarity with any group smaller than all of humanity tends to promote disunity and conflict among people. The spiritually mature fare through life alone but with an eye out for the needs of others; spiritual adolescents form gangs that contend with one another.

Two Prognoses, Two Kinds of Hope

Kant's views on history have been brought into this discussion because it seems to me that a good many people in our times, and particularly a good many of those who are making war or preparing to do so, are acting as if they are convinced that there will be an eventual end to war and that this will somehow come about by making war on those who are perceived as enemies of the very idea of making peace. And this conviction seems to be particularly prevalent among those who see operating behind human history something very much like Kant's Nature—that is, an intelligence that has a good purpose and that has provided human beings with the means necessary to rescue themselves collectively from the human condition, but only after making themselves very miserable.

If Buddhism has anything to offer the world in its present condition, it is a critique of that conviction. The classical Buddhist view extends an invitation to reconsider the evidence of history. It is not that Kant was blind to this evidence. Indeed, he was profoundly aware that anyone who looked at the world would see much more folly in practice than wisdom. What, then, was the source of his optimism? It was an *a priori* principle. If it is not the case that Nature is nudging man to greater wisdom by exposing him to unbearable conflict, said Kant, then

> his natural capacities would have to be counted as for the most part vain and aimless. This would destroy all practical principles, and Nature, whose wisdom must serve as the fundamental principle in judging all her other offspring, would thereby make man alone a contemptible plaything. [16]

The Buddha, in looking at the evidence of history, simply refrained from making this assumption that man's capacities are not for the most part vain and aimless and that man is somehow special in the world of nature.

The Buddha's message may seem bleak, particularly to those who hold on to the view that an intelligent and benign Nature has provided all the uniquely human requisites whereby human beings will eventually find peace and harmony. On the other hand, his perspective may offer a different kind of hope than that provided by Kant's *a priori* assumptions about what Nature must be like. The hope provided by the Buddha's vision is that it is possible for at least some people to attain to a state of maturity wherein they will be able to learn that dividing the naturally uniform species into unnatural divisions such as clans, tribes, races and nations leads only to xenophobia, that xenophobia leads only to conflict, and that conflict leads only to further conflict. These mature people will appreciate the words found in the opening chapter of what is probably the best-known and most frequently quoted Buddhist text, the Dhammapada (1:3–6):

He insulted me, he hurt me, he conquered me, he robbed me. The wrath of those who never think like that will end.

For wrath is not conquered by wrath; wrath is conquered by leaving it behind. This is a universal principle.

Others do not know that we can live here in harmony. Those who do know it leave fighting behind.

OVERCOMING THE HINDRANCES

In the preceding section we saw the claim made that partiality or less-than-universal love is regarded as the greatest hindrance to the sort of friendship that is naturally expressed as hospitality toward those who are other than oneself. We saw that an extreme form of the absence of friendship is hostility. We saw that Buddhist texts claim that there are those who know how to leave fighting behind. To do so is to learn to live in harmony with all other sentient beings, and this can be seen as what Buddhist teachings would regard as the actualization of the human potential, or at least as the most palpable manifestation of having actualized the human potential for attaining enlightenment.

Before considering the potential that Buddhism may have in the task of actualizing the human potential, it is necessary to clarify just what it means to be a Buddhist. In dealing with this issue, I shall follow a text called Abhidharmakośa, a title that is rarely translated into English but could be rendered The Receptacle of Highest Principles. Written by Vasubandhu in the fourth century CE, this Indian Buddhist treatise was studied and considered authoritative by most of the schools of Buddhism in India. The text was written in Sanskrit and was eventually translated into Chinese and Tibetan. In Chinese translation it was widely studied by most schools of Chinese Buddhism that evolved not only in China but also in Korea, Japan and Vietnam. The Tibetan translation was, and still is, studied by most traditions of Buddhism in Tibet and Mongolia.

Going for Refuge

According to Vasubandhu, who follows a long-standing tradition within Buddhism, being a Buddhist consists in going for refuge to the Buddha, the Dharma and the Sangha. Each of these terms is explained in some detail by Vasubandhu; I shall offer an abbreviated explanation based on what he wrote. Before doing that, however, let me lay down a little background information to put this whole issue into context.

During the time when the Buddha was alive, going for refuge to him simply meant becoming his disciple, and usually the understanding was that being the disciple of one teacher precluded being someone else's disciple at the same time. After the Buddha's death, however, there was a need to redefine what it means to be a disciple of and to go for refuge to the Buddha. The principal way of redefining the act of going for refuge to the Buddha was to acknowledge that the Buddha was worth taking on as a teacher because he had a particular mentality. That is, he possessed a set of qualities that enabled him to serve as a teacher. When one formally becomes a Buddhist, it is customary to declare that ideally one incessantly honors and respects all buddhas of the past, all buddhas who may arise in the future and all buddhas who exist in the present time. This declaration that one will always honor all buddhas naturally invites one to ask: just exactly what is a buddha?

Just before his death, Gotama Buddha, the founder of the religion we now call Buddhism, reportedly told his disciples that everything he had ever taught could be summarized in several lists of practices and the virtues that those practices are designed to cultivate. This list of lists has altogether thirty-seven items. Collectively, these thirty-seven items are known as the wings to awakening (*bodhi-pakkha*) or the factors in awakening (*bojjhaṅga*). In his discussion of what it means to go for refuge to the Buddha, Vasubandhu makes it clear that it is not the physical person or the historical figure of the Buddha that one honors; rather, it is this set of thirty-seven characteristics. It was possession of these characteristics that made the Buddha a buddha, and it is possession of these thirty-seven features that makes anyone else a buddha as well. Vasubandhu also observes that there are many repetitions of individual items in the list of lists given by the Buddha. If one were to eliminate all the redundancies, then the list would in fact amount to ten items. To be a Buddhist, then, consists first of all in respecting anyone who has these ten qualities and, more importantly, striving to cultivate these virtues within oneself. Moreover, the hope of human flourishing for anyone, whether officially a Buddhist in the sectarian sense or not, is said as being commensurate with the degree to which one has cultivated these ten virtues known as the ten factors of awakening.

The Ten Factors of Awakening

Let me turn now to a brief discussion of what these ten virtues are and how Vasubandhu characterizes them. The ten factors are wisdom, heroism, concentration, mindfulness, joy, flexibility, equanimity, faith, resolve and good moral habit. Vasubandhu explains them as follows:

1. Wisdom is defined as the investigation of virtue. This investigation consists in observing what kinds of attitudes and actions are helpful and beneficial to oneself and others, and which attitudes and actions are detrimental. So wisdom consists first of all in developing a discriminating awareness and then choosing the beneficial and eliminat-

ing the detrimental. On a practical level, this wisdom is cultivated by developing a clear awareness of one's bodily and mental states and their effects on oneself and others.

2. Heroism consists in having the energy to do beneficial actions and in having the courage to strive for virtue in a world in which virtue is not always highly valued. Heroism also consists in striving to establish harmony among people who are in conflict. The Buddha once observed, "If one remonstrates, educates and leads away from rudeness, Then one will be agreeable to good people and disagreeable to bad people" (Dhammapada 77). Heroism, then, includes having a willingness to educate others and to lead them away from coarse and unrefined attitudes and behavior, knowing that doing so entails the risk of becoming unpopular with those who are rude.

3. Concentration is the ability to keep a healthy mind focused on a single topic. A mind is said to be healthy when it is characterized by such attributes as modesty, humility, a sense of shame, and aversion to harmful actions. The healthy mind is always said to be free of anger and hatred and filled with love and a desire to serve and be of benefit to others.

4. Mindfulness is a term that one hears Buddhists talking about constantly. It consists first of all in remembering from one's previous experiences what kinds of attitudes and actions have proved to be beneficial and which have proved to be detrimental. Secondly, mindfulness consists in remembering to apply that knowledge gained from the past to situations that are currently at hand.

5. Joy is defined as having a zest and enthusiasm for virtuous thoughts and actions. It means appreciating the virtue in others and letting one's heart be filled with joy whenever one sees acts of kindness and generosity being done by anyone anywhere.

6. Flexibility is considered one of the most important qualities of the healthy mind. In the scholastic literature of Vasubandhu and others it is described as both intellectual and emotional dexterity. It is seen as the opposite of the sort of intellectual and emotional fixity and rigidity that might stand in the way of being fully open and responsive to the needs of others.

7. Equanimity is said to involve two things. First, as an attitude toward one's own experiences, it is described as indifference to one's own pleasure and pain. It is indifference in the sense of not having such a preference for pleasure that one is unwilling to undergo hardship in the service of others. Second, as an attitude toward others, equanimity is a spirit of impartiality. In practical terms it is said to manifest itself as not taking sides in disputes but being available to provide for the physical and psychological needs of both sides in a conflict.

8. Faith is described as the confidence that naturally arises when one has seen the benefits of generosity, kindness, equanimity and the various other virtues that we have been discussing. It is said to be the sort of confidence and conviction that can arise only from personal experience. This conviction that arises as a result of one's own experiences naturally gives rise to having trust in those who have provided guidance and leadership.

9. Resolve consists in the determination to cultivate healthy, competent mental states and to eliminate unhealthy, incompetent mental states.

10. Good moral habit is the conduct that naturally flows from the cultivation of the mentality characterized by the virtues described so far. It manifests itself as right speech, right conduct and right livelihood.

    a. Right speech is described as speaking in a way that conveys the truth of a situation and that establishes harmony among people. It is the opposite of speaking in such a way that deceives, abuses, creates factions, promotes anger, encourages carelessness and destroys concentration. A famous guideline for using speech well was given by the Buddha as follows:

        If you know that words are unfactual, untrue, unbeneficial, unendearing and disagreeable to others, do not say them. If you know that words are factual, true, and beneficial but disagreeable, then wait for the right time to say them. Even if you know that words are factual, true, beneficial and agreeable to others, wait for the right time to say them. [17]

    b. Right conduct, like right speech, is action that promotes harmony and avoids harm and abuse.

    c. Right livelihood means following a way of making one's livelihood that involves integrity and as little harm as possible to others.

        Let me turn now to a discussion of how these ten characteristics that a Buddhist is invited to admire in others and to cultivate within oneself fit in with the theme of this conference.

Realizing One's Potential as a Human Being

The first observation I would like to make is that the cultivation of these ten virtues is said to be a goal that can be achieved by anyone who strives to cultivate them. They are not seen as virtues that only the Buddha has or that only Buddhists regard as important. Rather they are seen as the principal focal point of a serious Buddhist; that is, a Buddhist ideally makes the gradual cultivation of these virtues the main work of a lifetime. Cultivating these virtues is never seen as easy, for there are numerous obstacles along the way.

It may be helpful to see all of them as being similar to a mathematical asymptote, a limit that one approaches but perhaps never realizes perfectly.

As a path of practice, the Buddhist tradition embodies a wide range of exercises and practices that are designed to help an individual cultivate these virtues. As a path of theory, the Buddhist tradition also embodies reflections on why it is that it may not be easy for an individual to experience rapid success in perfecting them. At the heart of all Buddhist theory is the observation that all things are interconnected, sometimes in obvious ways and sometimes in very subtle ways. Everything that takes place in the world has some effect on everything else in the world. As Buddhists like to put it, everything is conditioned by everything else, and this conditioning is sometimes extremely difficult to overcome. The environment in which one lives is so powerful as a source of conditioning that the most important first step for a person to take, according to the Buddha, is to seek out the company of good people. While being part of a community of good people is the most effective way to realize one's own potential for leading a helpful and beneficial life, it is not always possible to find such a community. If one cannot find one, says the Buddha, then the next best option is to seek a life of solitude. The worst thing that one can do is to allow oneself to be surrounded by those are are careless, self-centered, insensitive, abusive, destructive and violent, for unless one is very strong indeed, these qualities are contagious and will eventually undermine one's efforts. Because it is so important to be within an environment that promotes the health of all individuals who are in it, it is also important to try to create and maintain a community that will be a nurturing environment. So the second observation I would like to make is that realizing one's potential as an individual is seen as a task that cannot be separated from the task of helping all of humanity realize the human potential. It is necessarily a communitarian and cooperative venture.

The realization of the human potential is one that requires the combined efforts of all people. Moreover, cooperation is something that requires mental and emotional flexibility and a willingness to learn not only from one's own experiences but also from the experiences of others. From these two considerations, I claim that it follows that the healthiest human community is one that encourages individuals to benefit from the entire collective wisdom and experience of humankind as a whole. (I would go further and say that the healthiest community is one that also learns to benefit from the collective experiences of all species of living thing, but I will not develop that idea here.) So this leads to my third observation, which is that when Buddhist principles are taken to their logical conclusion, they must embody a spirit of religious pluralism and can never be seen from the narrow perspective of the Buddhist tradition alone.

So let me turn now to a few further reflections on religious pluralism.

Religious Pluralism

Pluralism can be described as not just the recognition but the celebration of a plurality. Religious pluralism, then, is not simply the recognition that there are many religions in the world, but the conviction that this plurality of religions is a sign of health and vitality in the human race. Among the many eloquent advocates of religious pluralism in relatively modern times was Swami VivekĀnanda.[18] The spirit of his type of religious pluralism is illustrated by the following quotation, taken from a talk that he gave at the Universalist Church in Pasadena, California, on January 28, 1900. In this talk VivekĀnanda observes that there are various grades of mind. Some people are rationalists who do not care for ceremonies and whose intellects are satisfied only by hard facts. Other people have more artistic temperaments, and they thrive on beauty of lines, colors, fragrance, flowers, lights and candles in worship rituals. Some see God in these forms of beauty, while others see God with the intellect in the wonders of nature. Some people are devotional by nature, and their greatest joy comes in worship and praise of God. At the other end of the spectrum, says VivekĀnanda, "there is the philosopher, standing outside all these things, mocking at them. He thinks, 'What nonsense! Such ideas about God!'"[19] At the end of his talk, Swami VivekĀnanda said this:

> Our watchword, then, will be acceptance and not exclusion. Not only toleration; for so-called toleration is often blasphemy and I do not believe in it. I believe in acceptance. Why should I tolerate? Toleration means that I think that you are wrong and I am just allowing you to live. Is it not blasphemy to think that you and I are allowing others to live? I accept all the religions that were in the past and worship with them all; I worship God with every one of them, in whatever form they worship Him. I shall go to the mosque of the Mohammedan; I shall enter the Christian church and kneel before the Crucifix; I shall enter the Buddhist temple, where I shall take refuge in Buddha and his Law. I shall go into the forest and sit down in meditation with the Hindu, who is trying to see the Light which enlightens the hearts of everyone.
>
> Not only shall I do this, but I shall keep my heart open for all the religions that may come in the future. Is God's book finished? Or is revelation still going on? It is a marvellous book—these spiritual revelations of the world. The Bible, the Vedas, the Koran, and all the other sacred books are but so many pages, and an infinite number of pages remain yet to be unfolded. I shall leave my heart open for all of them.[20]

On another occasion, Swami VivekĀnanda wrote: "Books are useless to us until our inner book opens; then all other books are good so far as they confirm our book."[21] Although some of his language seems dated, and his way of referring to Muslims as Mohammedans is no longer used by careful speakers, the overall message is one that is still worthy of reflection. At the

heart of VivekĀnanda's kind of pluralism was a recognition of the importance of poetic imagery and figures of speech that suggest but do not over-
specify, and also of myths as multi-layered stories that convey invitations to
reflect on questions of ultimate human value. In another essay, VivekĀnanda
wrote this:

> Then, if you can, lower your intellect to let any allegory pass through your
> mind without questioning about the connection. Develop love of imagery and
> beautiful poetry and then enjoy all mythologies as poetry. Come not to mythol-
> ogy with ideas of history and reasoning. Let it flow as a current through your
> mind; let it be whirled as a candle before your eyes, without asking who holds
> the candle, and you will get the circle; the residuum of truth will remain in
> your mind.
>
> The writers of all mythologies wrote in symbols what they saw and heard;
> they painted flowing pictures. Do not try to pick out the themes and so destroy
> the pictures; take them as they are and let them act on you. Judge them only by
> the effect and get the good out of them.
>
> Your own will is all that answers prayer; only it appears differently, under
> the guise of different religious conceptions, to each mind. We may call it
> Buddha, Jesus, Krishna, Jehovah, Allah—but it is only the Self, the "I."[22]

Although I have cited VivekĀnanda as a person who admirably captures
what I believe is entailed by Vasubandhu's understanding of the qualities
personified by the Buddha as one to whom a Buddhist goes for refuge, one
can find modern Buddhist writers expressing themselves in very much the
same vein. Among the best known of these Buddhists are the Dalai Lama of
Tibet, the Vietnamese monk Thich Nhat Hanh, and the British Buddhist
author Stephen Batchelor.[23]

REALIZING THE PROMISE OF BUDDHISM

In the final part of this presentation, I should like to return to the question of
what kinds of things Buddhism may have to offer people at this particular
time in history. The two principal features that I should like to focus on are
the Buddhist emphasis on what we might call practical psychology and the
emphasis on the importance of universal friendship. Let me begin with practical psychology.

Emphasis on Practical Psychology

A statement that I have heard many times during my life is along the lines of
"I am not at all religious, but I consider myself quite spiritual." It is very
much a sign of our times to be suspicious of formal institutions, authority
figures and other external features of organized religions, while at the same

time being drawn to exercises aimed at cultivating good character. The Catholic tradition has customarily used the term "spiritual practice" for exercises such as prayers and meditations that are aimed at cultivating personal virtue, and the word "spiritual" has now come to be used widely, even outside Christian circles. So when people say that they are spiritual but not religious, they seem to be saying that their emphasis is primarily on putting their energy into cultivating a refined mentality, a mentality so refined that it will eventually become freed of all the limitations that collectively make life less than satisfactory. Given this widespread modern Western aversion to organized religious institutions but attraction to spiritual exercises, it is not surprising that many Western people are turning to Buddhism, not as an organized religion, but as a collection of accessible and effective spiritual exercises.

In nearly all Buddhist writings, one finds the point being made that one's mentality can be changed for the better and that there are time-proven ways of bringing these changes about. In many Buddhist books one finds detailed exploration of the mentality of an ideal person who is dedicated to the unconditional love of and service to other beings. In the *abhidharma* genre of Buddhist texts, one finds maps of the terrain of the human mind, maps that will help the explorer discover that terrain effectively by pointing out what one is likely to find there.

Emphasis on Spiritual Friendship and Community

A friendship can be called spiritual when it is based primarily on the determined effort of each friend to cultivate a mentality characterized by wisdom and compassion and other healthy mental characteristics. [24] A true friendship features reciprocity—that is, each friend helping the other to learn and grow and find fulfillment. The British Buddhist writer Sangharakshita observes that a true friendship "can never involve any kind of power relationship." [25] In speaking in this way, Sangharakshita shows his indebtedness to the psychologists Carl Jung and Erich Fromm, who wrote that all relationships are based either on love or on power, and that one is operating toward others either in one of those modes or the other but never in both at the same time, since the two modes are incompatible. The power mode consists in using others as a means toward one's own ends, whereas the love mode consists in taking Others as ends unto themselves and therefore dealing with them without any ulterior motive. Treating Others as ends unto themselves and not as means toward one's own ends can have some paradoxical results, not the least of which is that, by all accounts, dealing with others in love mode rather than power mode turns out to be one of the most effective ways of doing what is really good for oneself. In the end, therefore, there turns out to be no distinction between truly serving Others and truly serving oneself.

Sangharakshita echoes Carl Jung also in his recurring preoccupation with distinguishing the mass-mind, the mentality of the person who develops an emotional dependency upon a group of people, from the mind of the individual. One of the goals of psychoanalysis, according to Jung, was to help the client become an emotionally independent individual with a capacity for interacting effectively with others without becoming psychologically dependent on them. Clearly, dealing with others as an independent individual entails dealing with others in the love mode, whereas needing others for one's own sense of self-worth usually results in dealing with others in the power mode. When a group is formed on the basis of the neurotic needs of its members, then the group itself tends to act in power mode toward all its own members, with the result that the survival of the group takes precedence over the health of its members.

Earlier mention was made of the Dalai Lama, Thich Nhat Hanh and Stephen Batchelor as contemporary Buddhists who hint at the most promising direction for humanity as a whole. That direction, I think, consists in seeking wisdom from whatever source it can be found. Stephen Batchelor has drawn inspiration from the writings and analytic techniques of Carl Jung; he has also explored the thinking of the existentialists. Sangharakshita draws on various Western poets, especially the romantics, and on a handful of mystics and on the reflections of Jung. The Dalai Lama has expressed great hopes for the potential insight that could come of the marriage of the natural sciences such as physics and biology with the traditional religions. As mentioned before, both the Dalai Lama and Thich Nhat Hanh have explored the important similarities between Buddhism and Christianity, and in this they have been followed by several prominent Buddhist academics such as Jose Cabezón. In a book dedicated to Christian-Buddhist dialog, Professor Cabezón made this observation:

> I consider my Christian brothers and sisters fortunate, and I rejoice in the fact that they have at the very core of their tradition—in the very life of their founder—such a clear and superb model of what it means to be a socially responsible person, a person of integrity, in the world. We Buddhists have a great deal to learn from this aspect of the life of Jesus. [26]

Cabezón's admiration for Jesus as a example of passionate social responsibility stems from more than the fact that Cabezón himself was a Cuban Catholic before he became a Buddhist monk as a young adult. He speaks, I think, for quite a large number of contemporary Buddhists, and not only those who come from Christian backgrounds.

Finally, I should like to refer to a hermeneutical principle that is commonly used by Buddhists. It is usually given as a guideline to Buddhists who are about to embark on the study of their own tradition, but it has applicability, I think, to anyone in our times who is going to undertake the study of any religious tradition in a spirit of openness and receptivity. The Buddhist doctrine is often called the four reliances. They are stated as follows:

1. One should rely on the spirit of a text more than on its literal expression.
2. One should reflect on the teaching itself, more than on the personality or character of the teacher who offers it.
3. One should rely on one's own intuitive understanding of a teaching more than on the exegesis of scholars.
4. One should rely on texts that can be taken in a straightforward way more than on texts written in a symbolic or circuitous language that needs to be unpacked or interpreted.

The first three of these principles are especially relevant to a religious pluralist, I think. The first principle, that one should rely on the spirit of a text rather than resorting to literalism, would be a welcome corrective to trends in recent times that have discouraged open inquiry into the meanings of religious texts. The third principle, that one should rely on one's own institutions more than on the understandings of scholars, has the potential to liberate individuals from traditions that may have imprisoned them. The second principle could be seen as a corrective to the disappointment people often feel in religious teachers whose flawed humanity has shown through to such an extent that their followers become ready to jettison the entire set of principles that the teachers teach. Following all these principles in opening oneself up to reflecting on the literature and practices of all peoples of the past, present and future would be, I claim, a sure way of realizing our highest human potentials both at the individual and at the societal level.

ADDENDUM: MORE ON THE MAHĀYĀNA PERSPECTIVE

DHARMA MASTER HSIN TAO

To address the topic of hostility and hospitality, we cannot limit ourselves to only look at the Theravada and Sautrāntika perspectives, but we must also look at major developments in the Mahāyāna and Vajrayāna traditions. For example, Lotus Buddhism, Pure Land Buddhism, Zen and the Tantric traditions of East Asia and Tibet, all of which exert major influence, also need to be considered for their attitude on hostility and hospitality. Also, rather than just dwelling on the textual sources and traditions, we need to consider the living context in which Buddhism has influenced culture and society in different epochs and regions of the world. From this perspective, there is much room for self-criticism from within the Buddhist perspective.

For example, in those regions where Buddhism has served to form the identity of an ethnic community, has it also functioned as a principle of exclusion of others who do not share such an identity? Sri Lanka comes as a case in point. We all know how Theravada Buddhism came to Sri Lanka and formed the basis of racial cohesion of Singhalese society. But this very fact has also given Singhalese nationalists a weapon to exclude Hindu Tamil communities from political participation. Some strands of Lotus Buddhism, specifically those deriving from the thirteenth-century prophet Nichiren, emphasize their version of Buddhist teaching as superior over others in a way that has led Nichiren's followers to denigrate other Buddhist schools. Scholars also have pointed out how Zen Buddhism was used by Japanese nationalists for war efforts. Also, in the long history of Buddhism influenced by patriarchal structures in Asian societies, women tended to be excluded or put into stereotypical roles. Full ordination is not yet available to women in the Theravada and Tibetan traditions, although steps in this direction are being taken in Sri Lanka and Thailand. Given the above, there is much room for Buddhists to be self-critical about their own tradition, and this remains a task for follow-up.

APPLYING THE CORE MESSAGE

The core message of Buddhism is one of loving-kindness and compassion. This message is contained in the early texts of Buddhism and further developed in the Mahāyāna and Vajrayāna traditions. For example, the Mettā Sutta, which is commonly recited from memory by monastics and lay followers in Theravāda countries alike, says the following:

> One should cultivate one's thoughts thus: May all beings be happy and secure. May their minds be contented. Whatever beings there may be—weak or strong, tall, stout, medium, short, small, or large, seen or unseen, dwelling far or near, born or yet to be born—may all beings, without exception, be happy. Let no one deceive or despise any person whatever in any place. In anger or ill will, let not one wish any harm to one other. As a mother would protect her only child even at the risk of her own life, let one cultivate a boundless heart towards all beings.

Buddhist compassion is not just an emotional attitude, but a dynamic principle based on an insight into reality, into what is. This insight is wisdom. It leads into our realization of the interconnectedness of all sentient beings. This interconnectedness is especially extolled and explained in the Avatamsaka Sutra, which is a basic text for the Zen Buddhist tradition. To see everyone as intrinsically connected with one's own being is thereby to embrace the suffering and pain of all as one's own.

The figure of the Bodhisattva Guanyin (Avalokiteśvara in Sanskrit) is a powerful symbol of this. The Bodhisattva figure, even though known in the earlier tradition, embodies the Mahāyāna ideal of the seeker of enlightenment who postpones his or her own entry into Nirvāṇa until he or she has saved all beings from suffering. Guan-yin is an awakened figure who embodies the Buddha's compassion. Her salvific actions are described in the Lotus Sutra, which is one of the most important and beloved texts in the Mahāyāna tradition. The Great Compassion Sutra of the thousand-armed and thousand-eyed Avalokiteśvara, a text that is also very important in the Tantric tradition, describes how Guanyin assumed the form with one thousand eyes and arms, which signify her compassionate embrace of all aspects of reality and of all sentient beings in different situations of suffering.

The Buddha's teachings ask more of us than to overcome hostility and practice hospitality. They ask us to give the whole of our selves for the happiness of all sentient beings, which is our very own happiness. This kind of happiness is the hope that the Buddha has to offer to the world. I want to end my response with a quote from the Bodhisattva vows of Santideva, an Indian poet who lived in the eighth century:

> I dedicate this self of mine to the happiness of all beings. Let them smite me, constantly mock me, or throw dirt at me . . .
>
> Let them do to me whatever pleases them, but let no one suffer any mishap on my account. Whether they direct thoughts at me that are angry or kindly, may those thoughts be a constant cause for their achieving all their aims.
>
> Those who accuse me falsely, others who do me wrong, and still others who deride me—may they attain enlightenment!
>
> May I be a protector of the unprotected, a guide for travelers on the way, a boat, a bridge, a means of crossing for those who seek the other shore.
>
> For all creatures, may I be a light for those who need a light, a bed for those who need a bed, and a slave for those who need a slave.
>
> Just as the Buddhas of the past grasped the mind-set of enlightenment and went on to follow the bodhisattva training, so too will I give rise of the mind sent on enlightenment for the well-being of the world, and so will I train in the stages of the bodhisattva discipline.

In a narrowly literal interpretation of the Suttanipāta, the dart that has wounded the hearts of human beings is explained as the "dart of arrogance and self-importance." The meaning of the dart however is more comprehensive. It stands for Dukkha, the suffering or dissatisfaction which the Buddha taught as the first Noble Truth. Dukkha is caused by the fact that all things are impermanent and that there is no self to be found in them. The text describes the dart or arrow as "the arrowhead of grieving, of desiring, of despair" and continues to say that "the One who has taken out the arrow, who has no clinging, who has attained peace of mind, passed beyond all grief—this one, free from grief, is still."[27]

Far from being "entirely pointless," this world with its suffering is upheld as the only place in the whole realm of Buddhist cosmology where the arrow can be taken out, where human beings can attain realization. Moreover, seen from the background of the rigid division of Indian society into the fourfold caste system, which excluded the despised group of the outcasts, the Buddha's rejection of the deterministic and hierarchical structure perpetuated by the priestly class of the Brahmins and his opening up of his teaching and Sangha to members of all groups and even to women provided not only a revolutionary message of hope for those who suffered most from discrimination and hostility, but also an alternative vision for society and the human existence.

NOTES

1. Suttanipāta 935–936. All translations in this chapter, unless otherwise indicated, are R. P. Hayes's.

2. For a Hindu view on the role of ignorance, see page 100.

3. The translation is that of H. Saddhatissa, *The Sutta-Nipata* (London: Curzon Press, 1985).

4. For the Jewish view on the unity of the human species, see page 23; for the Christian view, see page 54; for the Muslim view, see page 85.

5. All citations of Pali texts in this chapter are taken from the third version of the CD-ROM edition of the Pali canon produced by the Vipassana Research Institute.

6. Compare with Christian caution regarding "us vs them," page 55.

7. In Sanskrit Buddhist texts, whether of Mahāyāna or Śrāvakayāna affiliation, one finds only this latter interpretation. The *pṛthagjana* are the outsiders. In Tibetan also one finds that Buddhists are most commonly called "insiders" (*nang pa*) and that non-Buddhists are called "outsiders" (*phyi pa*).

8. Immanuel Kant, *On History*, translated by Lewis White Beck (Indianapolis: Bobbs-Merrill,1963), p. 12.

9. Kant, *History*, p. 15.

10. Suttanipāta 937.

11. Kant, *History*, p. 13.

12. Kant, *History*, p. 12.

13. Kant, *History*, p. 12.

14. A good translation of this text appears in Maurice Walsh, *Thus Have I Heard: The Long Discourses of the Buddha. Dīgha Nikaya* (London: Wisdom Publications, 1987). A detailed study can be found in Steven Collins, *Nirvāṇa and Other Buddhist Felicities* (Cambridge: Cambridge University Press, 1998). Some reflections on the text appear in Richard P. Hayes, "Classical Buddhist Model of a Healthy Mind" in *Psychology and Buddhism: From Individual to Gobal Community*, edited by Kathleen H. Dockett et al. (Kluwer/Plenum, 2003.)

15. This passage occurs in the Bhikkhun iupasampadanuj ananam section of the Bhikkhunikkhandhakam of the Cūlavagga of the Pali version of the Vinaya-pitaka.

16. Kant, *History*, p. 13.

17. Summary of Majjhimanikāya 21:11.

18. For more on VivekĀnanda, see page 114.

19. Swami VivekĀnanda. "The way to the realization of a universal religion." In *The Complete Works of Swami VivekĀnanda*, Volume 2, p. 373. Tenth edition. Calcutta: Avaita Ashrama, 1963.

20. Swami VivekĀnanda, *The Yogas and Other Works*, edited by Swami NikhilĀnanda (New York: Ramakrishna-VivekĀnanda Center, 1953), p. 386.

21. Swami VivekĀnanda. *The Complete Works of Swami VivekĀnanda* Volume 7, p. 89. Tenth edition. Calcutta: Avaita Ashrama, 1963.

22. VivekĀnanda, *Yogas*, p. 563.

23. All these authors have written numerous books. Let me refer to just one representative work by each of them: Tenzin Gyatso, the Fourteenth Dalai Lama, *The Good Heart: A Buddhist Perspective on the Teachings of Jesus* (Boston: Wisdom Publications, 1996); Thich Nhat Hanh, *Living Buddha, Living Christ* (New York: Riverhead Books, 1995); Stephen Batchelor, *Buddhism Without Beliefs: A Contemporary Guide to Awakening* (New York: Riverhead Books, 1997).

24. For a Jewish view on compassion, see page 40.

25. Sangharakshita, *What is the Sangha? The Nature of Spiritual Community* (Birmingham, UK: Windhorse), p. 200.

26. In Rita M. Gross and Terry C. Muck, *Buddhists Talk About Jesus; Christians Talk About the Buddha* (New York: Continuum, 2000), p. 20.

27. Suttanipāta 593.

Chapter Seven

Conclusion

Comparative Perspectives, Collective Tasks

Alon Goshen-Gottstein

The time has come for drawing together insights from the various chapters, in an effort to understand them in relation to one another, and to assess the overall contribution of our project to the theme of our religions' attitudes to other religions. Assessing our contribution will allow us to define the tasks ahead and to recognize where our project has layed the ground for future work. I shall undertake a comparative conclusion by focusing first on the three Abrahamic faiths, and then expanding the comparison to Hinduism and Buddhism.

JEWISH, CHRISTIAN, AND MUSLIM PERSPECTIVES — COMPARATIVE OBSERVATIONS

The chapters representing Judaism, Christianity and Islam suggest some important common features, leading us to examine the relations within the so-called Abrahamic family in their own right. All three writers are engaged in a similar attempt to deal with the history of hostility within their tradition, to contextualize the phenomenon historically, and to strike a balance between the historical dimensions that have given shape to their religions and the theological dimensions that constitute the religions.

For me, the battle for Jewish survival is the source of hostility shown by Jews to others. Sykes adopts a similar strategy with reference to the early Christian community. Cornell, by contrast, offers a historical critique of the particular forms of current Islam as these have led to hostility toward others. In all three cases, hostility is considered non-essential to the religion, a historical accretion that must be contextualized and accounted for in historical terms.

All three writers juxtapose the ultimate religious teaching of their traditions with these historical circumstances and thus view their traditions as historically and theologically complex, which presents them with a dual challenge. They recognize the negative components of tradition and the contingency of particular historical circumstances, and they must consequently account for the negative elements in their traditions, even as they develop more positive resources in relation to other traditions. They also have the task of constructing their traditions in a way that is hospitable to the Other, both the concrete cultural Other and the religious and ideological Other.

While each one of the constructive presentations appeals to elements that are particular to that tradition, one may point to some parallels in the positive resources offered by the three traditions. Two governing notions control the positive presentations of all three chapters: God and creation. Note how creation plays an important role in each of the three chapters. The notion of the image of God is central to my piece and to Sykes's, obviously representing a commonality of the two traditions. While Sykes struggles, through the lens of the Christian tradition, with the problem of the fall and its ultimate impact on the integrity of all of creation, and particularly on the notion of the image of God, it is ultimately the power of creation, even if reconstituted by the "new Adam," that offers humanity its common ground. The Muslim tradition does not refer to man as created in God's image, perhaps because the very consideration of a divine image was troubling. Nevertheless, as Cornell teaches us, the way we view creation shapes our religious lives. Much in the way I present the tension between creation and covenant, perhaps even resembling how Sykes describes tension between creation and the Christ event, Cornell speaks of the tension between God's creative command, pointing to a common basis for all of humanity, and the command of obligation, particular to Muslims. It seems that for all three traditions, one of the dangers is that of getting lost in the particularity of the religious community and losing sight of the universal perspective offered by the creation of the entire world.

The perspective brought about through the appeal to creation is also the means of recalling the greatness of God and His will. God's will is greater than any way in which a religious community may tend to limit it, as it projects God through its own particular lens. The point is perhaps most clearly made in the latter part of Cornell's chapter. My quest for a spiritual revival in Judaism aims to achieve precisely the same thing, the recollection of God as the central controlling feature of the religious system and hence as the ultimate reference point of Judaism. Also for Sykes, that which takes the religious community beyond its particularity and its own battle for continuing survival is God. The entire Christian faith is based on the actions of God, not the life of the community. And as Sykes teaches us, there is a strong basis in the tradition for recognizing the significance of this action for all of humanity. It is precisely because Christianity is rooted in faith in God that ultimately the universal implications must outweigh the sectarian tendencies. One might add that even the metaphor of "making space for the theological other" ultimately relies on the divine action of forming a common humanity, thereby mandating the listening to the testimonies of life and spirit offered by other parts of the body of the one humanity.

Several other striking similarities emerge from a comparative reading of the three chapters. In some significant way all chapters appeal to the language of command. Theirs are religions in which God spoke, and in some significant way it is the application of God's speech and its interpretation that provide the ultimate basis for extending hospitality. In the case of Judaism, it is the divine command concerning the *ger* that sets the stage for hospitality. Similarly, the early Christian community is shaped by constitutive commands to extend hospitality, such as those made by Jesus, the author of the Epistle to the Hebrews, or other early Christian writers. For Cornell, the notion of command is even more fundamental, extending from a particular commandment to a broad principle of law, God's creative command. The God who speaks and commands is thus considered by all three writers as the ultimate source of hospitality. If historical circumstances bring about a teaching of hostility, the ultimate religious ideal, grounded in God Himself and in His commanding presence, is that of hospitality.

But God seems to provide more than just a command. God's reality also provides the basis for emulation and the core attributes necessary for successfully overcoming hostility and implementing hospitality. One is struck by how all three chapters, each in its own way, makes an appeal to the concept of compassion. The latter part of mine is an extended attempt to describe Judaism in terms of compassion, grounding this attitude in the very understanding of God through the concept of *da'at*, the knowledge and understanding of God. It is also interesting to note how the relationship between the creative command and the command of obligation is presented by Ibn Arabi in terms of the two divine names expressing God's compassion and mercy. Further, as Cornell teaches us, the very significance of the distinction between the two commands is that it allows us to balance justice and to temper it with mercy, grounded in the creative command. Thus, while command defines obligations and informs the practical horizon, compassion shapes the spiritual vision, calling us to emulate God. While Sykes makes only passing reference to notions of grace in his presentation, would it not be fair to say that the entire faith of Christianity is based upon an act of profound compassion, undertaken by God?[1] And is not the obligation to treat others with love ultimately founded upon the fruits of such mercy and compassion? While there are obvious differences of nuance between the three traditions, it is very interesting to note how similar themes are played out in the three chapters, suggesting significant similarities between them.

Two further parallels should be pointed out. The first concerns the importance of community. All three chapters make a significant appeal to the community as the carrier of the spiritual message and as the ultimate agent of hospitality. The case is obvious with regard to Judaism, whose very self-definition is communitarian. Sykes appeals time and again to the role of the community in ancient Christianity. It is through the lens of the community that the formation of Christian hostility is accounted for. Community is also the means for extending hospitality, which, according to Sykes, cannot ultimately be administered outside the communal framework. In the case of Islam, one notes the repeated appeal to the Muslim Umma in Cornell's chapter. More significantly, the struggle for understanding Islam is one of defining the nature of the community. The problem, in Cornell's analysis, ultimately points to a false notion of how community is to be built, by attempting to impose monolithic standards on Islamic society. While the solution may be a return to the individual and to the riches that spirituality provides, one cannot ignore the fact that the context in which the Islamic problematic is articulated is one of community.

All three chapters share a belief in the importance of doctrine and religious teaching. They do so as part of a common process of recognizing imperfections within the historical manifestations of their traditions. These imperfections relate to the body of teaching, or perhaps rather to the ways in which teachings are misunderstood and misrepresented. The suggestion that teaching is faulty and in need of correction conveys both the centrality of doctrine and the belief in the potential to change through teaching and through the changing of teaching. While all three traditions do not necessarily share the same understanding of dogma or doctrine, an interesting commonality emerges regarding how teaching is addressed and redressed in the attempt to either present or reconstruct a better or an ideal form of the religion.

The comparison of these three chapters is not only illuminating in and of itself. It also sets in clearer focus the commonalities between the Abrahamic traditions, allowing us to recognize significant differences between them and the other two religions represented in this project: Hinduism and Buddhism.

THE ABRAHAMIC FAITHS AND HINDUISM COMPARED

There are some obvious differences between the foci of the chapters representing the Abrahamic faith and Vohra's presentation of Hinduism. As Vohra presents Hinduism, its two poles of orientation are the cosmos, or metaphysical Being, and the individual. The religious quest is a metaphysical one. Like that of Rabbi Nachman, it is a quest to gain knowledge, *Da'at*. Yet, its goal is that of the personal liberation of the believer from ignorance, *avidya*. Not only is the particular form of religion of little importance; community itself seems to play a secondary role. One wonders to what extent phenomenological religion can withstand such a divorcing of the social dimension of religion from a presentation of a religion. Sarma's response reminds us of phenomenological diversity, and of how Hinduism does in fact break down to distinct religious communities. The notion of community may, however, be different, if by community we mean, as does Sarma, different schools of thought and chains of tradition, *sampradayas*. Notwithstanding the recollection of the importance of the historical and sociological dimensions to an overall portrayal of Hinduism, it is significant that Hinduism, in Vohra's eyes, can be cast in terms that privilege epistemology and metaphysics over community and the specifics of way of life. One cannot but pose the following question: If Vohra's presentation is complete, does Hinduism really offer the possibility of less violent, less hostile religion? And if so, what is it about Hinduism that enables it to do so? Is it the relativity of all religious paths, considered from the perspective of absolute metaphysical unity? Is it the leap from the individual to the metaphysical absolute, making the importance of community secondary?

One notes with interest how, once again, an appeal to creation and its metaphysics serves the cause of hospitality and acceptance of the Other. Unlike the three Abrahamic traditions, which juxtaposed creation to some significant religious moment through which religious meaning is endowed, Hinduism was not presented here as exhibiting a similar tension. Presumably all forms of Hindu particularity would be nothing but expressions of a broader universal sweep, rather than points of meaning that stand in tension with its metaphysical roots. Thus an underlying recognition of the power of existence, an appeal to the metaphysical ground of all being, of all of creation, provides a common basis. The Hindu perspective is informed not by creation as an act of a sovereign God but by the appeal to creation as instructive of the very basis of existence. While remaining aware of this difference, it is still interesting to note that ultimately creation, variously understood, provides a common ground for all humanity.

INSIGHTS FROM AND CONTRASTS WITH BUDDHISM

While the Abrahamic and Hindu notions of God may not be identical, they provide sufficient common ground for theological exchange. By contrast, Buddhism's starting point is radically different. Neither God nor creation,[2] that figured so heavily in the efforts of other religious positions to grapple with the problems of hostility and hospitality, are operative notions within a Buddhist framework. Moreover, Hayes claims that one of the key concepts of the present project, the concept of hospitality, is not the most useful notion from which to explore Buddhist teachings, and he therefore prefers to concentrate on universal friendship. Buddhism thus comes across as being shaped by alternative categories, making the identification of common ground less obvious than in relation to the other religions examined in our project. Nevertheless, important points of intersection and possible sites of inspiration do arise from the juxtaposition of the four theistic traditions with Buddhism. Let us consider the importance of proper understanding. The comparison is particularly clear in relation to Vohra's presentation of Hinduism, to which Hayes's chapter provides an interesting complement. On the one hand, both share the same emphasis on the cultivation of the proper understanding in the individual. The Buddhist perspective too sees the root of all hostility in an inappropriate understanding that must be corrected through discipline of the mind. But, while Vohra's chapter focused on the metaphysical dimensions of Hinduism, that of Hayes highlighted the psychological processes that are characteristic of Buddhism. This difference is very suggestive of the unique emphasis of Buddhism and how it differs from the other traditions.

All traditions balance a recognition of the unity of creation, or of humanity, and the kind of particularity that could result in tension and violence. With reference to Buddhism, Hayes struggles with how distinction can arise within a view of reality that ought to uphold fundamental unity or equality. Where, after all the talk of the unity of the human species, do we have the basis for a distinction between self and other, between *us* (the good folks) and *them* (the bad ones) of just the sort that could undermine the project of seeing the unity of the human species? Despite the fundamental differences in metaphysics, the problem and the answer are strikingly similar to those offered by Sykes in accounting for Christian reality. The quest for perfection and the recommendations for a life that would lead to it inevitably lead to the formation of a distinction between an *us* and a *them*, thereby undermining a vision of the fundamental unity of humanity. Different kinds of behavior—virtuous and non-virtuous, moral and immoral—undermine a perceived unity of humanity, thereby posing a challenge to this unity and threatening it with hostility. Like Hinduism, Buddhism is not envisioned as possessing a fundamental theological hostility to others. Nevertheless, the challenges of the moral life and the need to keep the company of the good do in fact place before it challenges similar to those of other religions.

While there is no room within Buddhism to think of a chosen community, Hayes's perspective is communitarian, recalling the significance of the *sangha*, the Buddhist community, for achieving the goals of the religious life. Hayes reminds us of the power of community as a means of achieving the virtues and hence as an instrument of human flourishing. Hayes extends the recognition of the centrality of community to all people. Hence, the realization of human potential is one that requires the combined efforts of all people. Extending community to all humanity is a move that is made, within our collection of chapters, uniquely with reference to Buddhism. While Abrahamic perspectives call for a balance between community and creation or community and humanity at large, Hayes, who makes no appeal to the consequences of a common notion of creation, is able to suggest that the very boundaries of community be expanded to include other religions.

Buddhism, as presented by Hayes, is a sustained reflection on life and the human condition. It lacks the grand narratives, and along with them the great hopes and messianic ideals, that characterize the Abrahamic faiths, or even the mystical idealism that is typical of the Hindu faith. Instead, it emphasizes human psychology and the virtues as keys to a happy life. Its practical emphases make it a source of teaching on the human condition, which, as Hayes points out, is part of the current appeal of Buddhism, permitting it to touch people of other faiths. While its goals are ultimately individual and only individuals are destined to attain full perfection, its central emphasis on community as a vital component of the spiritual life allows it to dialogue with the other faiths that share a strong communitarian emphasis. In the framework of the present collection of chapters, Hinduism seems to be an exception, lacking or having a weak sense of community, as a constitutive dimension of the spiritual path (as opposed to recognizing its existence as part of social, hence also of religious, reality).

TOWARD A COMPOSITE MESSAGE

Having identified commonalities and discrepancies between the different traditions, we may now venture to explore whether it is possible to suggest a composite message that emerges from our project in its entirety. Clearly, the recognition that traditions must move from hostility to hospitality, that they must make room for the theological Other and that their vision for the hope of human flourishing ought to be expansive is the overall message of this project. However, while this message is argued or worked out in the various chapters, it is really a presupposition of this project, as much as it is its conclusion. Our authors seek not so much to demonstrate the thesis itself as to provide an argument for it from within the resources of their individual traditions.

Looking at our project in greater detail, I would like to draw together various insights that point to key notions that cut across our traditions. While they are configured differently in the various traditions and while not all authors emphasized all points to the same degree, an attempt to read our project synthetically leads me to highlight the following themes as components of a composite picture, that emerges from our project:

1. Community and identity. We have seen that almost all authors highlight the role of community as part of the workings of religion. Community is a means of fulfilling the goals of a given religion. It is,
   however, also the basis for exclusion of others. Communities are constructed around identities, and these clash with those of others, and are
   often constructed in conscious opposition to those. I note that in relation to each and every religion, without exception, violence and hostility is related, in some way, to identity construction. I have made this
   argument in relation to Judaism, ancient and contemporary. Sykes
   accounts for the deviation from the fundamental Christian vision of
   love in terms of the process of identity construction in nascent Christianity. Cornell's presentation of contemporary Islam as a program of
   social engineering is also relevant in this context. The attempt to impose a particular social vision on society involves one implicitly in
   issues of identity construction. The process is in many ways similar to
   the "Syndicated Hinduism," of which Sarma speaks. Othering and
   exclusion are fundamental strategies of some contemporary forms of
   Hindu identity construction. And finally, Dharma Master Hsin Tao
   reminds us that no matter how universal the Buddha's message may
   have been, once it became the fabric for a society's identity, it too
   became entangled in identity politics, bearing violent consequences.
   Thus, we are called to the recognition that religion, no matter how
   lofty and universal its founder's ideals may be, can become violent
   where it intersects with identity construction of a particular community. This is a valuable insight. It allows us to draw a distinction
   between religion and ideology. It invites us to revisit our traditions
   with an eye to their purification, a purification from the human tendency to exclusion and its attendant violence, in the quest of fulfilling our
   religions' higher vision.
2. A second thread that runs through many of our chapters concerns the
   significance of consciousness. If we seek to rise above the human/
   social dimension of our traditions, this involves a process of transformation of awareness, in conformity with or approximation of the divine perspective. This is the *Da'at* of which Rabbi Nachman of Breslav speaks. Cultivating proper understanding is the key response of
   both Hinduism and Buddhism to the threat of religious violence. In the
   case of Hinduism, it is proper metaphysical knowledge, in the case of
   Buddhism it is proper psychological insight into the human condition.
   In both cases, proper attunement of understanding and awareness
   holds the key to overcoming hostility. While not all chapters in this
   collection formulate their approach in terms of consciousness, I believe that the authors representing the Christian and the Muslim perspective would agree as well. Their respective constructions of their

traditions involve a return to its fundamental spiritual vision and a purification of forms of the tradition that have emerged through entanglement with human nature and society. This return involves a realignment with the higher vision of the tradition. Such realignment can only be attained through a reorientation of the believer's awareness to God's presence and purpose.

3. Complementing the more personal emphasis on consciousness is the theological or reflective process that all our traditions must undertake. Religious traditions are not simply givens, entities that can be accurately described and presented. Rather, they must be constructed through a process that seeks to identify what is core about them and what is a secondary accretion, stemming from misunderstanding, corrupting social influence, and so on. The fact is that all our traditions suffer in some way or another from the scourge of hostility and all must find ways of cultivating theological hospitality, hence of constructing the tradition. Such construction involves us in acts of selection and interpretation. We must select those features of tradition that we seek to highlight, and that we consider constitutive of its identity. We must interpret the sources that have supported alternative visions, as well as those sources whose vision we seek to amplify. It is important to recognize that none of our chapters simply "tell it as it is." They are all involved in a fine balancing act of reading the tradition, interpreting it, highlighting what they deem significant and above all relating all that to the concrete historical and sociological circumstances that have governed and that continue to govern their tradition's attitude to the Other. This balancing takes place within the chapters or in the dialogue between the chapter and the response to it. But the task is the same. Our common task is the task of traditions with a rich history of scriptural interpretation, philosophical reflection and complex relations with other religions that seek to restate their contemporary position in relation to the religious Other. This process requires revisiting and restating the message of our traditions, a task undertaken by all our authors.

4. Our project seeks to ground the cultivation of theological hospitality as a virtue that all our traditions can subscribe to. This is closely related to our authors' views on interreligious dialogue and its significance. Each of the contributors assumes the positive value of the interreligious exchange of ideas. While all authors recognize the importance of the dialogue, the Abrahamic chapters are clearly more hard pressed to justify it than the Eastern chapters, which almost take it for granted. In my chapter, I appeal to the crisis of Judaism as a background against which inter-religious exchange may play a constructive role. Jonathan Sacks, in the afterword, offers a powerful contemporary

midrashic reading that mandates dialogue, recognizing in it a contemporary religious necessity. Sykes develops the notion of making space for the other, as an extension of the notion of Christian hospitality. Significantly, none of us cite traditional precedent for such activity, though it obviously exists within our traditions. Cornell's presentation of Islam is a plea for the retrieval of earlier Islamic sources that recognized, accepted, and legitimated religious pluralism and the possibility of learning from other religious traditions. While for Vohra, dialogue is not a problem to be solved but a given of Hinduism's broad and inclusive nature, Sarma makes us aware of how central debate is to the culture of Indian philosophical schools and recommends it as a broader strategy for dialogue. Finally, for Hayes dialogue is a natural outcome of authentic Buddhist presuppositions, supported by the best practices of contemporary Buddhist leaders.

THE CHALLENGES AHEAD

Having identified significant currents that run through all our chapters, it is time to consider what work must be undertaken in the future, in order to advance reflection, research and education in line with the vision spelled out by our project. The way forward will be suggested in relation to the project's outcomes and conclusions.

1. Our project suggests hostility, animosity, hatred, violence and war are a common enemy. All religions here represented recognize that hostility has no room in the ideal construction of their religion. This calls us to continue reflecting upon why and under what circumstances our religions become violent and inhospitable. Identity construction has already emerged as an important factor here. What other factors can be considered? We are challenged to confront, either on the theological or on the practical level, those moments and intersections where our traditions become hostile and to address them in light of the broader spiritual vision of our tradition. Clearly, this undertaking requires more than a collection of chapters. It calls for sustained theological and educational attention to one of the most serious pitfalls that threatens our religions.

2. Our project suggests that hospitality is a virtue that must be cultivated. While precedents for it exist in the different traditions in different ways, it cannot be taken for granted. As we have suggested, hospitality means much more than the simple cessation of hostility. It implies a genuine openness to the Other, leading us from virtue to self-transformation and growth. This calls us to continue developing a theology of

hospitality, friendship and openness. As suggested above, such theologies need to be constructed and cannot be taken for granted. Having identified the need and made some preliminary suggestions in this direction, broad and consistent work is required to develop robust theologies of hospitality across our traditions.

3. Our project points to various ways in which our traditions are tainted by our humanity. All our traditions are caught in some fundamental tension between the reality of human life and the higher ideals of our traditions. The struggle for the achievement of the higher purpose of religion points to a process of purification. Such purification is carried out both on the level of the individual and his or her quest for higher awareness and in relation to the teachings of our traditions. Here purification takes the form of the intellectual examination of traditions, histories, precedents, ideals and more, in the attempt to bring forth the highest form of religion. Purification is broader than the purification of teaching and the retrieval of a higher spiritual message. It also concerns the educational and psychological work that relates to the lives of believers. Rabbi Sacks's fifth hypothesis, concerning letting go of pain, is a good example. Work must be undertaken with reference to our attitudes, memories and overall orientation if our hospitable theologies are to find a ground within which to flourish.

4. Our project has made us aware, time and again, of the interdependence of all traditions on one another. We have been struck by the echoing of various themes in our diverse presentations. Patterns of similarity and difference have presented themselves time and again, as both expected and unexpected relationships between the religions came within our sight. Our processes of growth are interdependent. This is a source of enrichment, but also a challenge for future work. Recognizing connections is important for strengthening bonds of common life. Such connections may be historical, phenomenological or theological. Realizing that we are connected, interconnected, is a foundation for a new way of being, mandated by today's circumstances. This kind of interconnectedness constitutes a contemporary social reality. But it is also a religious reality, and in some way or another our chapters have suggested it is also a metaphysical reality. Thus, the challenge emerges of how to bring home to our religious communities the sense of interconnectedness that we discover through a project such as ours. This is a significant educational and theological task that we hope can be carried forth.

5. Throughout our project, our awareness has been drawn, time and again, to the field of virtues as the testing ground for religious perfection and for inter-religious inspiration. We have repeatedly noted how core concepts, such as wisdom, compassion, mercy and more have

figured in our discussions. We have come to recognize that beyond theological differences lies a common aspiration for virtue and human excellence of which we can all partake and to which we can all inspire one another. This opens up important possibilities for future collaboration. The field of virtues is vast and provides one of the most important meeting grounds for the teachings of our religions. Recognizing our interconnectedness makes a joint comparative study of virtues an important task. This does not suppose agreement on all virtue-related issues. But it does assume that common appreciation of virtues will be enriching for the individual tradition and strengthening for today's society, as it seeks to move forward on a new platform, based on the commonality and collaboration of religions.

6. Our project is based upon the recognition of the significance of inter-religious dialogue. The importance of this dialogue is one of the points repeatedly argued by our authors. Dialogue, much like the spiritual life itself, must move forward, or it slips backwards. Recognizing the significance of interreligious dialogue is not a conclusion of a project, but an invitation for future work. The resources created by this project are helpful to dialogue. The substance of this project is an invitation to create further resources, in line with its vision. But perhaps even more importantly, if we seek to change the theological mood within our communities, we must extend our findings and recognitions to our communities. Good theological work must be grounded in and received by a community. A theology of hospitality must find its counterpart in the spread of hospitable attitudes — to people and to ideas—within the community. Thus, for our project to bear long-lasting fruit, its conclusions, its vision and its spirit must become the common legacy of all our religious communities. Herein lies our greatest challenge.[3]

NOTES

1. See most recently the comments of the Dalai Lama in *Toward a True Kinship of Faiths: How the World's Religions Can come Together*, Doubleday Religion, 2010, p. 57.

2. Might Hsin-Tao's reference to the care for all sentient beings provide an alternative means for incorporating a notion of creation in our attitude to all others?

3. In an effort to address this challenge, the chapters in this collection have been adapted to study units, designed for community use. These study units, titled "From Hostility to Hospitality" have been developed for the work of the Elijah Educational Network, that seeks to cultivate broad, community-based study and dialogue with the help of Elijah's scholars.

Afterword

Another Voice

Lord Rabbi Jonathan Sacks

Alon Goshen-Gottstein has written an eloquent statement—part analysis, part plea—of how Judaism has understood the Other and how it might do so in the future. To it and to the other contributions to this volume, I add the following footnote.

The Abrahamic monotheisms are distinctive in setting the religious life within the unfolding drama of history. As several historians of ideas have pointed out, the prophets of ancient Israel were the first to break free of cosmological time, time as it exists in the world of myth, in which nothing ultimately changes. There is birth, growth, decline, death and rebirth. There is order, the threat of chaos, defeat of the threat, and a return to order. There are, as Nietzsche put it, eternal recurrences. Time, for myth, is no more than a series of ruffles in the fabric of eternity. That is not how Israel's prophets saw it.

For them time was the essential arena of interaction between the free God and humanity—a humanity which, created in God's image, was thereby given a counterpart of that freedom. Because I always have the choice of how to respond to a situation, my tomorrow is not predestined to repeat my yesterday. The future need not be an endless recapitulation of the past. In this world-transforming insight, history was born, and with it choice, agency and moral responsibility. This may be the single greatest contribution of the Hebrew Bible to civilization (Thomas Cahill in his *The Gifts of the Jews* argued that it was) and from it flowed all the others. One in particular was decisive: the cluster of ideas linking remorse, repentance and forgiveness. If human freedom opened the door to a not-yet-written future, forgiveness broke the hold of a less-than-perfect past.

How does this work out in terms of the relationship between time-embedded humanity and the time-transcending God? The question is deep, the answer vast, but to put it at its simplest: God does not change, but we do. His covenant with us—with humanity, with Abraham's children and with the children of Israel—is unbreakable. But the drama unfolds as we are faithful or faithless to its terms. Hence the phenomenon of the prophet, one who hears within the word of God for all time, the word of God for this time. In the absence of prophecy we are left with what the rabbinic sages called the Oral tradition and its ongoing task of interpreting our sacred texts in the context of this time, this place, these circumstances. We call this activity Midrash, and it is essential to rabbinic Judaism. Between the eternal and the ephemeral, the timeless and the time-bound, lies the act of interpretation. Thus, new eras bring new perspectives to the unchanging Divine word. We hear new echoes that were always there but not heeded, perhaps not even heard, before. A new age is God's call to a new act of listening to His word.

Our own new age confronts world religions with potentially their greatest challenge of all time: making space for the Other, religiously, ethically, politically and existentially. For most of history, most of the adherents of the great faiths and civilizations lived closely and continuously with people who believed and acted as they did. Yes, there were minorities, and yes, there were conquered populations. How these were treated is not one of the more edifying strands in the human story. At best they were regarded as less than fully human; at worst they represented a dan*ger* to be held at a distance, or subjugated, or destroyed.

To be sure, cities, even in the ancient world, were places where people of different cultures came together to trade. From the Hellenistic words for cities—civis, polis, urbs—came the words we still use to describe living graciously with difference: civil, polite, cosmopolitan, urbane. Yet precisely for this reason, cities do not fare well in the monotheistic imagination. We think of Cain, the first murderer and the first builder of a city; of Babel, its Tower, and its hubristic builders; of ancient Egypt and its enslavement of the Hebrews. The word "Hebrew" itself, and its possible origin in the term habiru or apiru, suggests "outsider, stranger, alien." Abrahamic monotheism is born in a critique of cities and their many gods. Thus the question is real and now urgent: can Judaism and its close cousins, Christianity and Islam, embrace a world of instantaneous global communication in which the Other is constantly and immediately present—a world that eliminates distance from difference?

It is not too much to say that the future of humanity turns on this question. Thus far, the evidence is not good. Not only have communication and trade been globalized; so too have fear, hate, violence and terror, often in the name of religion itself. Yet though the challenge is new, the question is old, for it is implicit in the very first chapter of the Hebrew Bible. Can we recognize

God's image in one who is not in our image? If we fail to do so, there is a clear and present dan*ger* that religiously fuelled conflict may lead us into an escalating series of confrontations that will leave our planet as devastated as Easter Island, enduring monument of humanity's capacity for self-destruction. The time has come for a new act of listening to the Divine word.

That is what I propose to do now, briefly, schematically, no more than hinting at a way forward, in five simple acts of listening to the Hebrew Bible and what it has to tell us about the Other.

SCENE 1: THE FIRST OTHER

The opening chapters of Genesis are one of the great meta-narratives of Western civilization, and their literary form is designed to draw attention to fundamental features of the universe to which we are called on to respond. They use a repeated construction: "And God said, 'Let there be. . . .' And there was. . . . And God saw that it was good." The universe unfolds according to a plan and it is good. What breaks the mood is the sudden appearance, in the second chapter, of the phrase "not good." Nothing has prepared us for this expression. Thus far we have encountered only God, the natural world and its highest life-form, Homo sapiens, on whom the Creator has set His own image. Unlike mythic creation narratives, there is no resistance or struggle, since there is only one personality, the Artist who is not merely fashioning a work of art but also bringing into being the materials out of which it is made. What, in such a universe, can be "not good"? In a single phrase—five words in Hebrew—the origin of all love and conflict is set forth. "It is not good for man to be alone."

The Hebrew Bible thus sets out two propositions that frame its entire vision of humankind. The first is the sanctity of the human individual as individual. Every person is in "the image of God." The second asserts the incompleteness of the individual as individual. "It is not good for man to be alone." Hence the human need for relationship, association, and for stable structures within which these can grow and be sustained.

God then creates the first woman. The man responds with the first poem in the Bible:

> This is now
> bone of my bone,
> flesh of my flesh;
> she shall be called woman [ishah]
> because she was taken from man [ish]. (Genesis 2:23)

I have included two Hebrew words, because the Hebrew text contains a nuance often missed in translation. Until this point man has been called adam, man-as-part-of-nature (the word adam signifies "that which is taken from the earth"). Now for the first time man is called—indeed calls him-self—ish, which means man-as-person. Significantly, he does this only after he has named woman. The Bible is suggesting, with great subtlety, that the human person must first pronounce the name of the Other before he can know his own name. He or she must say "Thou" before he can say "I." Relationship precedes identity. Hypothesis 1: Until I know the Other, I do not know myself.

SCENE 2: CAIN, CONVERSATION
AND CONFLICT RESOLUTION

With the first human children comes the first act of fratricide. Cain's murder of Abel follows directly after the first human act of worship: "Cain brought some of his crops as an offering to God. Abel also offered some of the firstborn of his flock, from the fattest ones" (Genesis 4:3-4). The religious impulse is not always a force for good. It can lead to bloodshed in God's name. Religion is like fire. It warms, but it can also burn; and we are the guardians of the flame.

The narrative contains a remarkable literary device, often missed in trans-lation. We read: "Cain said to his brother Abel . . . then, when they were in the field, Cain rose up against his brother Abel and killed him." (Gen. 4:8)

The sentence is ungrammatical. It contains a lacuna: "Cain said to his brother Abel . . ." At this point the sentence breaks off. So jagged is the edge that the Greek and Syriac versions added the words "Cain said to Abel his brother, 'Let us go out to the field.'"

There are many traditional interpretations, each of which fills in the gap. Listening to the text, however, we hear the eloquence of its sudden lapse into silence. In the midst of speaking, Cain stops. When words end, violence begins. As long as people converse, there is hope that they will conquer hate. Confrontation is inevitable when two competing parties are unable to talk. "Violence," said Alan Brien, "is the repartee of the illiterate."[1]

Maimonides introduces this principle into Jewish law as an explanation of the command, "You shall surely rebuke your neighbour" (Lev. 19:17):

> When one person sins against another, the injured party should not hate the offender and keep silent, as it is written about the wicked, "Absolom never said a word to Amnon, either good or bad; he hated Amnon because he had disgraced his sister Tamar" (2 Samuel 13:22).
> Instead it is his duty to inform the offender and say to him, "Why did you do this to me? Why did you sin against me in this matter?" That is why it says, "You shall surely rebuke your neighbour." If the offender repents and asks for forgiveness, he should be forgiven. (Mishneh Torah, De'ot 6:6)

Speech is an essential element of reconciliation. Words heal. We find the same principle in another branch of Jewish law—the case of manslaughter. Someone who killed another without mens rea, criminal intent, was given protection under biblical law in one of the cities of refuge. This is not the case where the act of murder was an accident verging on the deliberate (shogeg karov le-mezid). One of the conditions the Torah lays down for accidental death is that the killer "did not previously hate" his victim (Deut. 19:6). The operative definition of hate in such a case is the fact that the two parties refused to speak to one another for three days (Sanhedrin 27b). Absence of speech testifies to the presence of hate.

It was the anthropologist Bronislaw Malinowski who, in his research into the Trobriand islanders in the early 1920s, first realized that conversation among the natives was not—as he had previously thought—to exchange information. It was to create and sustain fellowship. He inferred that this was true not only of the islanders of New Guinea but of society in general. "Our talk," he wrote, "serves to establish bonds of personal union between people brought together by the mere need of companionship." He called this phatic communion, "a type of speech in which ties of union are created by a mere exchange of words."[2]

Speech or violence; dialogue or war. These are the choices. When words fail, violence is waiting in the wings. Cain killed Abel when he could no lon*ger* speak to him. Hypothesis 2: Conversation, however difficult, is the alternative to conflict. Dialogue with the Other is necessary if we are to live peaceably with the Other.

SCENE 3: ABRAHAM'S OTHER TRIAL

We are familiar with the story of Genesis 22: the Binding of Isaac, Abraham's great trial. Yet we sometimes miss the significance of another trial, in the immediately previous chapter. Abraham had another son, Ishmael, born to Sarah's handmaid Hagar. God had told him that Ishmael would be blessed, but would not be the bearer of Abraham's specific covenant. After Isaac was born and weaned:

> Sarah saw that the son whom Hagar the Egyptian had borne to Abraham was mocking, and she said to Abraham, "Get rid of that slave woman and her son, for that slave woman's son will never share in the inheritance with my son Isaac." (Gen. 21: 8–9)

Abraham is greatly distressed, but God tells him to listen to Sarah and do as she says. The next morning he sends Hagar and Ishmael away with some food and water for the journey. Eventually the water runs out, and she realizes that, in the blazing sun of the desert, Ishmael will die. She places him under a bush for shade, and weeps. We then read:

> God heard the boy crying, and the angel of God called to Hagar and said to her, "What is the matter, Hagar? Do not be afraid. God has heard the boy crying as he lies there. Lift the boy up and take him by the hand, for I will make him into a great nation." . . . God was with the boy as he grew up. He lived in the desert and became an archer. (Gen. 21: 17–20)

They continue their journey. Ishmael lives.

Genesis 21 and 22 are parallel passages. In both, Abraham has to undergo a trial involving the potential loss of a son. Ishmael and Isaac, the two children, are both only dimly aware of what is happening. In both, they are about to die until heaven intervenes, in the first case by providing a well of water, in the second, a ram, to be offered as a sacrifice in place of Isaac. The similarities serve to highlight the differences.

The narrative of the binding of Isaac is notable for its complete absence of emotion. God commands, Abraham obeys, Isaac joins him on the journey, Abraham prepares the altar, binds his son and lifts his knife, at which point an angel says "Stop." Throughout the ordeal Abraham says nothing to God except one word at the beginning and the end: hineni, "Here I am" (22:1, 11).

By contrast, the episode involving Hagar and Ishmael is laden with emotion. Hagar weeps ("Then she went off and sat down nearby, about a bowshot away, for she said to herself, 'Let me not see the child die.' And, as she sat, she lifted up her voice and wept," 21: 16). Ishmael weeps ("God heard the boy crying," 21: 17). There is here a tenderness and pathos rare in biblical prose. There can be no doubt that the narrative seeks to enlist our sympathy in a way it does not in the case of Isaac. We identify with Hagar and Ishmael; we are awed by Abraham and Isaac. The latter is a religious drama, the former a human one, but its very humanity gives it power.

This is not what we expect. The hero of the narrative should be Isaac, the chosen patriarch's chosen son. But our sympathies are drawn to Ishmael. God "hears" him; indeed his very name means "God hears." He will be blessed. God is "with him" as he grows up. "Though my father and mother might reject me, the Lord will gather me in" (Psalm 27: 10). Ishmael is Isaac's Other. Hypothesis 3: God does not reject the Other.

SCENE 4: HOW ISRAEL ACQUIRED ITS NAME

The episode in which the Jewish people acquired its name—Israel—is among the most enigmatic in the Bible. Jacob is returning home after an absence of many years. He had left because his brother Esau was threatening to kill him. Esau was aggrieved—Jacob had taken his birthright and, in disguise, stolen his blessing. Now they are about to meet again, and Jacob is overcome by fear. He divides his family into two so that if there is a battle, at least some will survive. He prays to God. He sends Esau gifts in the hope that they may placate him. He avails himself of all the options. If the gifts fail, prayer will help. If prayer fails, he is prepared for war. But uneasiness still haunts him. He moves his family across the river. As he is coming back he meets a stranger:

> Jacob was left alone, and a man wrestled with him till daybreak. When the man saw that he could not overcome him, he touched the socket of Jacob's hip so that his hip was wrenched as he wrestled with the man. Then the man said, "Let me go, for it is daybreak." But Jacob replied, "I will not let you go unless you bless me." The man asked him, "What is your name?" "Jacob," he answered. Then the man said, "Your name will no longer be Jacob, but Israel, because you have struggled with God and with men and have overcome." (Gen. 32: 25–29)

With whom was Jacob struggling? A man? An angel? God? Why was it this moment that gave its name not only to Jacob but to his descendants? The encounter is clearly meant to be emblematic of Jewish destiny and identity. For Jews it is an intimation not only of who our ancestor was but also of who we are.

What clues does the Bible itself offer that might help us decipher the mystery? What else does it tell us about Jacob? It describes a series of events, all of which cast light on how Jacob saw himself. When he was younger, he bought Esau's birthright. Later he dressed in Esau's clothes, told his blind father that he was Esau, and took Esau's blessing. His very name Jacob was given to him because, when he was born, he was holding on to Esau's heel. Taken together they suggest that Jacob wanted to be Esau: the firstborn, the stronger, a hunter, the child whom his father loved.

Read the biblical text carefully and we make a remarkable discovery. The real blessing intended for Jacob was not the one he took while pretending to be Esau: "May God give you from the dew of the heavens and the fat of the earth" (Gen. 27: 28). That was a blessing of physical prosperity. The blessing meant for Jacob was the one given to him later as Jacob, when Isaac was distressed that Esau had married into the local Hittite tribes. It was then that Isaac blessed him with these words: "May God Almighty bless you and make you fruitful and increase your numbers until you become a community of peoples. May He give you and your descendants the blessing of Abraham, so that you may take possession of the land where you now live as a stranger, the land God gave to Abraham" (Gen. 28: 3–4). Children and a land: these throughout Genesis have been the covenantal promise. This blessing had all along been destined for Jacob. The irony is overwhelming. Jacob's striving to be Esau was unnecessary. To acquire the blessing, he needed to be not Esau, but himself.

Alone at night many years later, about to meet Esau again after long estrangement, Jacob faces the defining crisis of his life. Who is he? Is he still the man who wants to be Esau? Or is he ready to become himself? On this psychological drama the entire course of Jewish history will turn. Jacob cannot escape. The next day he was to stand face-to-face with his brother. Now or never he must decide who he is.

The simplest interpretation of Jacob's mysterious adversary is that it was himself. His greatest struggle was internal. Would he spend his life wishing he were someone else, or would he at last be content to be who he was? His struggle ended when he was able to let go of all the things he had clung to in the past. According to this reading, Jacob became Israel when he learned to be Jacob. No longer holding on to Esau's heel, his blessing, his identity, his name, Jacob conquered his sense of inadequacy and learned to be himself. For the first time he could meet his brother without envy, deception or fear. The next morning, the brothers meet and, instead of violence, they embrace, kiss, speak in friendship, and go their separate ways in peace. If Jacob has the courage to be Jacob, then he need not fight Esau.

Too often, the Abrahamic monotheisms have sought their brother's blessing: the mimetic rivalry that Rene Girard sees as the source of "violence and the sacred." Their followers have tended, in Shakespeare's words, to

> look upon myself, and curse my fate,
> Wishing me like to one more rich in hope,
> Featur'd like him, like him with friends possess'd,
> Desiring this man's art, and that man's scope,
> With what I most enjoy contented least. [3]

That is a feeling we must reject. The Torah commands Jacob's descendants: "Do not hate an Edomite [i.e., a descendant of Esau], for he is your brother" (Deut. 23: 8). Instead we must wrestle, as did Jacob, alone at night, in the depths of our soul, and discover the face, the name and the blessing that is ours. Before Jacob could be at peace with Esau he had to learn that he was not Esau but Israel—one who wrestles with G-d and never lets go. Seeking someone else's identity, someone else's covenantal promise, creates confusion, anxiety and insecurity. Hypothesis 4: When brothers, religions, faiths, are secure in their own identity, they can meet as equals and part as friends.

SCENE 5: LETTING GO OF PAIN

In the verse in Deuteronomy that commands the Israelites not to hate the descendants of Esau, there is a further clause, momentous in its implications, a command so counter-intuitive that we have to read it twice to make sure we have heard it correctly: "Do not hate an Egyptian, because you were a stranger in his land" (Deut. 23: 8).

What can this mean? The Egyptians of Moses's day had enslaved the Israelites, "embittered their lives," subjected them to a ruthless regime of hard labor and forced them to eat the bread of affliction. They had embarked on a program of attempted genocide, Pharaoh commanding his people to throw "every male [Israelite] child born, into the river" (Ex. 1: 22).

Now, forty years later, Moses speaks as if none of this had happened, as if the Israelites owed the Egyptians a debt of gratitude for their hospitality. Yet he and the people were where they were only because they were escaping from Egyptian persecution. Nor did he want the people to forget it. To the contrary, he told them to recite the story of the exodus every year, as we still do on Passover, re-enacting it with bitter herbs and unleavened bread so that the memory would be passed on to all future generations. If you want to preserve freedom, he implies, never forget what it feels like to lose it. Yet here, on the banks of the Jordan, addressing the next generation, he tells the people, "Do not hate an Egyptian." Why?

To be free, you have to let go of hate. That is what Moses is saying. If they continued to hate their erstwhile enemies, Moses would have taken the Israelites out of Egypt, but he would not have taken Egypt out of the Israelites. Mentally, they would still be there, slaves to the past. They would still be in chains, not of metal but of the mind—and who knows if chains of the mind are not the most constricting of all?

You cannot create a free society on the basis of pain. Resentment, rage, humiliation, a sense of injustice, the desire to restore honor by inflicting injury on your former persecutors—these are conditions of a profound lack of freedom. You must live with the past, implies Moses, but not in the past. Those who are held captive by *anger* against their former persecutors are captive still. Those who let their enemies define who they are have not yet achieved liberty.

The Mosaic books refer time and again to the exodus and the imperative of memory: "you shall remember that you were slaves in Egypt." Yet this is never invoked as a reason for retaliation or revenge. Instead it serves as the logic of the just and compassionate society the Israelites are commanded to create: the alternative order, the antithesis of Egypt. Don't enslave others, says Moses, or if that is too much to ask at this stage of history, treat slaves honorably. Don't subject them to hard labor. Give them rest and freedom every seventh day. Release them every seventh year. Recognise them as like you, not ontologically inferior. No one is born to be a slave.

Give generously to the poor. Let them eat from the leftovers of the harvest. Leave them a corner of the field. Share your blessings with others. Don't deprive people of their livelihood. The entire structure of biblical law is rooted in the experience of slavery in Egypt, as if to say, you know in your heart what it feels like to be the victim of persecution, therefore do not persecute others. Biblical ethics is based on repeated acts of role reversal. You cannot stay moral in hard times and toward strangers without something stronger than Kantian logic or Humean sympathy. That "something stronger" is memory. In Exodus and Deuteronomy, memory becomes a moral force: not a way of preserving hate but to the contrary, a way of conquering hate by recalling what it feels like to be its victim. "Remember"—not to live in the past but to prevent a repetition of the past.

Hatred and liberty cannot coexist. A free people does not hate its former enemies. If it does, it is not yet ready for freedom. To create a non-persecuting society out of people who have been persecuted, you have to break the chains of the past; rob memory of its sting; sublimate pain into constructive energy and the determination to build a different future. That is the profound insight in the paradigm-shifting words, "Do not hate an Egyptian, because you were strangers in his land." Hypothesis 5: Freedom begins when we let go of hate.

HUMAN OTHER, DIVINE OTHER

These are mere fragments of the larger interpretive task that needs to be undertaken by each of the Abrahamic faiths if they are to confront the "hard texts" each contains—words which, if understood literally and applied directly, lead to violence in the name of God.

Each faith contains the resources it needs to do so, for each understands that sacred texts need interpretation. Judaism, Christianity and Islam all have their hermeneutic principles and interpretive methodologies, their dynamic traditions that unfold as God's timeless word meets His timebound creatures and awakens in them the response appropriate to this time, this place, these circumstances.

One thing, however, is clear. Let me express it by way of four Hebrew words contained in the Babylonian Talmud (Berakhot 26b): Ein sichah elah tefillah. Their original context is not germane here, but I interpret their meaning as, "All conversation is a form of prayer." We meet the Divine Other to the extent that we are able to meet the human Other—respectfully, graciously, peaceably, unthreatened by our differences, knowing that they are part of the post-Babel world. We need the humility to accept that God is the One who defined Himself to Moses (Ex. 3: 14) as "I will be where I will be," meaning: even where you do not expect Me to be.

In my book, *The Dignity of Difference*, I tried to explain what such an Other-embracing faith would be like:

It would be like being secure in one's home, yet moved by the beauty of foreign places, knowing that they are someone else's home, not mine, but still part of the glory of the world that is ours. It would be like being fluent in English, yet thrilled by the rhythms and resonances of an Italian sonnet one only partially understands. It would be to know that I am a sentence in the story of my people and its faith, but that there are other stories, each written in the letters of lives bound together in community, each part of the story of stories that is the narrative of man's search for God and God's call to mankind. Those who are confident in their faith are not threatened but enlarged by the different faith of others. In the midst of our multiple insecurities, we need that confidence.[4]

NOTES

1. "From The Times November 20, 2008," *Alan Brien—In Memoriam*, November 21, 2008, alanbrien.blogspot.com/2008/11/from-times-november-20-2008.html.

2. Gunter Senft, "Bronislaw Kasper Malinowski," in *Culture and Language Use*, edited by Gunter Senft, Jan-Ola Östman, and Jef Verschueren (John Benjamins Publishing, 2009), 227.

3. William Shakespeare, "Sonnet 29," *The Oxford Library of English Poetry, Volume 1: Spenser to Dryden* (Oxford University Press, 1990), 162.

4. Jonathan Sacks, *The Dignity of Difference: How to Avoid the Clash of Civilizations*, rev. ed. (New York: Continuum, 2003).

Bibliography

al-Attas, S. M. N. (1995). *Prolegomena to the Metaphysics of Islam: An Exposition of the Fundamental Elements of the Worldview of Islam*. Kuala Lumpur Malaysia: International Institute of Islamic Thought and Civilization.

Algar, H. (2002). *Wahabbism: A Critical Essay*. Oneonta, New York.

Balslev, A. and Evers, D. (eds.). (2009). *Compassion in the World's Religions: Envisioning Human Solidarity (Religionswissenschaft: Forschung und Wissenschaft)*, Berlin: Littman.

Batchelor, S. (1997). *Buddhism Without Beliefs: A Contemporary Guide to Awakening* New York: Riverhead Books.

Besdin, A. (1984). *Perakim Bemachshevet Harav*, Jerusalem.

Biblical Archaeology Review, Issue 12,5 (1986). "The God-fearers—Did they Exist?"

Bindman,Y. (1995). *The Seven Colors of the Rainbow*. San Jose: Resource Publications.

Burge, G. M. (1993). *Who Are God's People in the Middle East?* Grand Rapids.

Chatterjee, B. C. (1966). *Aspects of Our Religion*. Bombay: Bhartiya Vidya.

Chittick, W. C. (1994). *Imaginal Worlds: Ibn al-'Arabi and the Problem of Religious Diversity* Albany, New York.

Cohen, S. J.D. (1999). *The Beginnings of Jewishness: Boundaries, Varieties, Uncertainties.* University of California Press.

Cornell,V. J. (2002). "Religion and Philosophy," in *World Eras, Volume 2: The Rise and Spread of Islam, 622-1500*. Susan L. Douglass, Ed. Michigan: Farmington Hills.

Crone, P and Cook, M. (1977). *Hagarism: The Making of the Islamic World*. Cambridge.

Dabashi, H. (1989). *Authority in Islam: From the Rise of Muhammad to the Establishment of the Umayyads*. New Brunswick, New Jersey.

Dominguez, V. (1989). *People as Subject, People as Object: Selfhood and Peoplehood in Contemporary Israel*. University of Wisconsin Press.

Dunn, J. D. G. (1988). *Romans 9-16, Word Biblical Commentary*, vol. 38b. Dallas: Word Books.

El Fadl, K. A. (2001). *Speaking in God's Name: Islamic Law, Authority and Women*. Oxford.

Eliade, M. (1974). *The Myth of the Eternal Return, or, Cosmos and History*. Princeton.

Esposito, J. L. (1992). *The Islamic Threat: Myth or Reality?* Oxford.

Finzsch, N. and Schirmer, D. (eds.), (1998). *Identity and Intolerance: Nationalism, Racism and Xenophobia in Germany and the United States*. Cambridge: Cambridge University Press.

"From The Times November 20, 2008." *Alan Brien—In Memoriam*. November 21, 2008. alanbrien.blogspot.com/2008/11/from-times-november-20-2008.html.

Goshen-Gottstein, A. (2003). "Speech, Silence, Song—Epistemology and Theodicy in a Teaching of R. Nahman of Breslav," *Philosophia*, 30, pp. 143–187.

————. (1994). "The Body as Image of God in Rabbinic Literature," *Harvard Theological Review* (87:2), pp. 171–95.

Groner, J. (1974–5) "Beyond Xenophobia: Jewish Fears and American Realities," *Response* 24, pp. 7–14

Gross, R. M. and Muck, T. C. (2000). *Buddhists Talk About Jesus; Christians Talk About the Buddha.* New York: Continuum.

Gutas, D. (1998). *Greek Thought, Arabic Culture: The Graeco-Arabic Translation Movement in Baghdad and Early 'Abbasid Society (2nd–4th/8th–10th Centuries).* London and New York.

Gyatso,Tenzin the Fourteenth Dalai Lama. (1996). *The Good Heart: A Buddhist Perspective on the Teachings of Jesus.* Boston: Wisdom Publications.

Halbfass, W. (1988). *India and Europe: An Essay in Understanding.* NY: State University of New York Press.

Hand, S. (ed.). (1989). *The Levinas Reader.* Cambridge.

Hayes, R. P. (2003). "Classical Buddhist Model of a Healthy Mind" in *Psychology and Buddhism: From Individual to Gobal Community,* edited by Kathleen H. Dockett et al. Kluwer: Plenum.

Herzog, Rabbi I. (1981). "Minority Rights According to the Halakhah," *Tehumin* 2, pp. 169–179. [Hebrew]

Ibrahim, M. (1990). *Merchant Capital and Islam.* Austin, Texas.

Izutsu, T. (1983). *Sufism and Taoism: A Comparative Study of Key Philosophical Concepts.* Berkeley.

Jackson, S. A. (2002). *On the Boundaries of Theological Tolerance in Islam: Abu Hamid al-Ghazali's Faysal al-Tafriqa bayna al-Islam wa al-Zandaqa.* Oxford.

Kamali, M. H. (1991). *Principles of Islamic Jurisprudence.* Cambridge.

Kant, I. (translated by Lewis White Beck) (1963). *On History.* Indianapolis: Bobbs-Merrill.

Kaufmann, Y. (1920). *A History of Israelite Faith vol. 8.* Jerusalem-Tel Aviv.

Kepel, G. (1993). *Muslim Extremism in Egypt: The Prophet and Pharaoh.* Berkeley.

Knysh, A. D. (1999). *Ibn 'Arabi in the Later Islamic Tradition: The Making of a Polemical Image in Medieval Islam.* Albany, New York.

Lorberbaum, Y. (2004). *Image of God, Halakhah and Aggadah.* Tel Aviv: Schocken Publishing House.

MacIntyre, A. (1990). *Three Rival Versions of Moral Enquiry: Encyclopedia, Genealogy, and Tradition.* Indiana: Notre Dame.

————. (1988). *Whose Justice, Which Rationality?* Indiana: Notre Dame.

————. (1984). *After Virtue: A Study in Moral Theory.* Indiana: Notre Dame.

Magonet, J. (1995). "Guest and Hosts." *Heythrop Journal* 36,4. p. 415

Mahadevan, T. M. P. (1971). *Outlines of Hinduism.* Bombay: Chetna Publications.

Makdisi, G. (1981). *The Rise of Colleges: Institutions of Learning in Islam and the West.* Edinburgh.

Malul, M. (2002). "The Origins of the Israelite People in its Self-Perception—the Motif of the Other and the Foundling," *Zion* 47,1. pp. 5–18 [Hebrew].

Marrus, M. (1994). "Antisemitism and Xenophobia in Historical Perspective." *Patterns of Prejudice* 28,3. pp. 77–81.

Moore, S.H. (2000). "Hospitality as an Alternative to Tolerance" *Communio* 27

Nasr, S. V. R. (1996). *Mawdudi and the Making of Islamic Revivalism.* New York: Oxford.

Novak, D. (1983). *The Image of the Non Jew in Judaism: An Historical and Constructive Study of the Noachide Laws.* New York: Mellen Press.

Pedahzur, A. and Yishai, Y. (1999). "Hatred by Hated People: Xenophobia in Israel." *Studies in Conflict and Terrorism* 22, 2, pp. 101–117.

Peli, P. (ed.). (1976). *In Aloneness, In Togetherness: A Selection of Hebrew Writings.* Jerusalem.

Pohl, C. D. (1999). "Welcoming the Stranger." *Sojourners* 28.

————. (1995). "Hospitality from the Edge." *The Annual of the Society of Christian Ethics.*

Popper, K. (2003 reprint of 1945 original). *The Open Society and Its Enemies.* London.

Porton, G. (1994). *The Stranger within Your Gates.* Chicago.

Radhakrishnan, (1963). *The Religion We Need*. Banaras Hindu University.

Rawls, J. (1999). *A Theory of Justice*. Cambridge, Massachusetts.

Reinhardt, A. K. (1995). *Before Revelation: The Boundaries of Muslim Moral Thought*. Albany, New York.

Reynolds, V. Falger, V. and Vine, I. (eds). (1986). *The Sociobiology of Ethnocentrism*. University of Georgia Press.

Sacks, J. (2002). *The Dignity of Difference: How to Avoid the Clash of Civilizations*. London: Continuum.

Sarma, D. (2003). "Viewpoint: Fostering Interreligious Dialogue and Conversation." *Hindu-Christian Studies Bulletin 16*.

Schiffman, L. (1985). *Who Was a Jew?* Hoboken: Ktav.

Searle-Chatterjee, M. and Sharma, U. (eds.). (1994). *Contextualising Caste*. Blackwell Publishers.

Senft, Gunter (2009). "Bronislaw Kasper Malinowski." In *Culture and Language Use*, edited by Gunter Senft, Jan-Ola Östman, and Jef Verschueren, 227. John Benjamins Publishing.

Shakespeare, William (1990). "Sonnet 29." *The Oxford Library of English Poetry, Volume 1: Spenser to Dryden*. Oxford University Press.

Silberstein, L. J. and Cohn, R. L. (eds). (1994). *The Other in Jewish Thought and History: Constructions of Jewish Culture and Identity*. New York: New York University Press.

Sontheimer, G. and Kulke, H. (eds.) (2001). *Hinduism Reconsidered*. Delhi: Manohar.

Stählin, G. (1967). "xenos, xenia, xenizō , xenodocheō , philoxenia, philoxenos" in *The Theological Dictionary of the New Testament vol. V*, ed. Gerhard Friedrich. Grand Rapids: Eerdmans.

Taha, M. M. (1987). *The Second Message of Islam*. Abdullahi Ahmad Naˊˆm trans. and ed. Syracuse, New York:

Taheri, A. (September 4, 2003). "Al-Qaeda's Agenda for Iraq," *New York Post Online Edition*.

Swami Vivekananda (edited by Swami Nikhilananda). (1953). *The Yogas and Other Works*. New York: Ramakrishna-Vivekananda Center.

Volf, M. (1996). *Exclusion and Embrace: A Theological Exploration of Identity, Otherness and Reconciliation*. Nashville: Abingdon.

Wansborough, J. (1978). *The Sectarian Milieu*. Oxford.

Wasserstrom, S. M. (1999). *Religion after Religion: Gershom Scholem, Mircea Eliade, and Henry Corbin at Eranos*. Princeton: Princeton University Press.

Weinsheimer, J. and Marshall, D. G. (trans.). (1994). *Truth and Method*. New York.

Wistrich, R. (ed.). (1999). *Demonizing the Other, Antisemitism, Racism and Xenophobia*. Harwood.

Yerushalmi, Y. H. (1982). *Zakhor: Jewish History and Jewish Memory*. Seattle and London: University of Washington Press.

Zarruq, A. (1992). The Principles of Sufism. Beirut: Amal.

Index of Sacred Texts

Jewish Sources

Torah:

Genesis 1:26, 54
Genesis 2:23, 165
Genesis 4:3–4, 166
Genesis 4:8, 166
Genesis 9:25, 56
Genesis 12: 1–3, 25
Genesis 15:13, 63
Genesis 18:1–8, 62
Genesis 21:8–9, 167
Genesis 21:16-17, 168
Genesis 21:17–20, 168
Genesis 22:1, 11, 168
Genesis 27:28, 169
Genesis 28:3–4, 169
Genesis 32:25–29, 169
Exodus 1:22, 171
Exodus 2:24, 62
Exodus 3: 14, 172
Exodus 17:14–16, 31
Exodus 23:9, 27, 63
Leviticus 19:17, 166
Leviticus 19:18, 27, 63
Leviticus 19:33–34, 27, 63
Leviticus 25:23, 43, 62
Deuteronomy 6:5, 63
Deuteronomy 14:29, 63
Deuteronomy 19:6, 167

Deuteronomy 23: 8, 170
Deuteronomy 26:5–9, 63

Prophets:

2 Samuel 13:22, 166
Isaiah 42:6, 35
Isaiah 49:6, 35
Ezekiel, 16, 22
Hoseah, 2, 22

Psalms:

Psalm 27:10, 168

Other Jewish Sources:

Passover Haggadah, 25, 26
Talmud: Berakhot 26b, 172; Sanhedrin
    27b, 167
Mishneh Torah, De'ot 6:6, 166
Zohar I, 83a, 26
Rabbi Nachman of Breslav "Likutey
    Moharan": Teaching 64, 39; Teaching,
    105, 40

Christian Sources

New Testament:

Matthew 6:10, 54

179

Other Christian Sources:

Muslim Sources

Qur'an:

Other Islamic Sources:

Hindu Sources

About the Contributors

Vincent J. Cornell is Asa Griggs Candler Professor of Middle East and Islamic Studies and Chair of the Department of Near Eastern and South Asian Studies at Emory University in Atlanta, Georgia. From 2000-2006, he was Director of the King Fahd Center for Middle East and Islamic Studies at the University of Arkansas. From 1991-2000, he taught at Duke University. His published works include over 40 articles, three books, and one book set, including *The Way of Abu Madyan* (Cambridge: The Islamic Texts Society, 1996) and *Realm of the Saint: Power and Authority in Moroccan Sufism* (Austin, Texas: University of Texas Press, 1998). His most recent publication is the five-volume set *Voices of Islam*, Vincent J. Cornell General Editor (Westport, Connecticut and London: Praeger, 2007). His academic interests cover the entire spectrum of Islamic thought from Sufism to theology and Islamic law. He is currently finishing *The Wiley-Blackwell Companion to Islamic Spirituality* with Bruce Lawrence of Duke University. He has often appeared on television and radio, including interviews on the National Public Radio show, "Speaking of Faith." From 2002-2012 he was a key participant in the Building Bridges seminars of Christian and Muslim scholars conducted by the Archbishop of Canterbury.

Alon Goshen-Gottstein is acknowledged as one of the world's leading figures in interreligious dialogue, specializing in bridging the theological and academic dimension with a variety of practical initiatives, especially involving world religious leadership. He is both a theoretician and activist, setting trends and precedents in the global interfaith arena. He is the founder and director of the Elijah Interfaith Institute (formerly the Elijah School for the Study of Wisdom in World Religions), and its rich website is testimony to his many and varied activities. A noted scholar of Jewish studies, he has held academic posts at Tel Aviv University and has served as director of the Center for the Study of Rabbinic Thought, Beit Morasha College, Jerusalem. Ordained a rabbi in 1977, he received his Ph.D. from Hebrew University of Jerusalem in 1986 in the area of Rabbinic thought. From 1989 to 1999, he was a member of the Shalom Hartman Institute for Advanced Studies, Jerusalem, where he also served as director for interreligious affairs. Stanford University Press published his *The Sinner and the Amnesiac: The Rabbinic Invention of Elisha ben Abuya and Eleazar ben Arach* in 2000, and the Littman Library published his co-edited volume *Jewish Theology and World Religions*. His *Beyond Idolatry—The Jewish Encounter with Hinduism* is to appear shortly. Several other collective research projects and edited volumes complement more than fifty articles, published in such scholarly journals as *Harvard Theological Review*, *Journal for the Study of Judaism*, *Journal of Literature and Theology*, *Journal of Jewish Thought and Philosophy*, *Ecumenism*, and *Studies in Interreligious Dialogue*.

Richard P. Hayes specialized in Indian philosophy in the Sanskrit and Indian Studies department of the University of Toronto. After earning his doctorate there, he taught religious studies at the University of Toronto and McGill University and Asian philosophy at the University of New Mexico. He was subject editor for the Indian philosophy entries of the *Routledge Encyclopedia of Philosophy* and for the entries on Buddhism in the Macmillan Encyclopedia of Philosophy and has published numerous articles and book chapters on Indian Buddhist scholasticism. He is now retired.

Rabbi Lord Jonathan Sacks is a global religious leader, philosopher, author of over 25 books, renowned speaker and moral voice for our time. He is currently the Ingeborg and Ira Rennert Global Distinguished Professor of Judaic Thought at New York University and the Kressel and Ephrat Family University Professor of Jewish Thought at Yeshiva University. He has also been appointed as Professor of Law, Ethics and the Bible at King's College London. Previously, Rabbi Sacks served as Chief Rabbi of the United Hebrew Congregations of the Commonwealth between September 1991 and September 2013. A frequent contributor to radio, television and the press both in Britain and around the world, Rabbi Sacks holds 16 honorary degrees and has been presented with several international awards in recognition of his work, including the Jerusalem Prize in 1995 for his contribution to diaspora Jewish life and the Ladislaus Laszt Ecumenical and Social Concern Award from Ben Gurion University in Israel in 2011. Rabbi Sacks has also recently been named as the Becket Fund's 2014 Canterbury Medalist for his role in the defence of religious liberty in the public square. He was knighted by Her Majesty the Queen in 2005 and made a Life Peer, taking his seat in the House of Lords in October 2009.

Deepak Sarma is professor of South Asian religions and philosophy at Case Western Reserve University, and the author of *Classical Indian Philosophy: A Reader* (2011), *Hinduism: A Reader* (2008), *Epistemologies and the Limitations of Philosophical Inquiry: Doctrine in Madhva Vedanta* (2005), and *An Introduction to Madhva Vedanta* (2003). He was a guest curator of *Indian Kalighat Paintings*, an exhibition at the Cleveland Museum of Art. He is a curatorial consultant for the Department of Asian Art of the Cleveland Museum of Art. After earning a BA in religion from Reed College, Sarma attended the University of Chicago Divinity School, where he received a PhD in the philosophy of religions. His current reflections concern cultural theory, racism, and post-colonialism.

Stephen W. Sykes studied at St. John's College, Cambridge, graduating in 1961. He was ordained deacon in 1964 and priest in 1965. After ordination he was appointed as a lecturer in divinity at Cambridge University and the dean (responsible for the chapel) of his alma mater, St. John's College, Cambridge. In 1974 he was appointed as the Van Mildert Professor of Divinity at the University of Durham and became a residentiary canon of Durham Cathedral. In 1985 he returned to Cambridge to take up the chair of Regius Professor of Divinity and was given a corresponding canonry at Ely Cathedral. He served as curate in St. John the Evangelist's Church, Cambridge, from 1985 to 1990. On 2 May 1990, he was consecrated as the Bishop of Ely. He stepped down from this position on 1 September 1999 and returned to education, becoming the principal of St. John's College, Durham, a position he held until his retirement in 2006. From 1991 he was a member of the Doctrine Commission of the Church of England and became its Chairman in 1996.

Dharma Master Hsin Tao is the founder of the Museum of World Religions, the President of the Global Family for Love and Peace, and the founder of the Ling Jiou Mountain Wu-Sheng Monastery on Taiwan's northeastern coast, which now houses nearly 100 nuns and monks. Master Hsin Tao also leads the Ling Jiou Mountain Prajna Cultural Education Foundation, the Ling Jiou Mountain Buddhist Foundation, the Social Welfare and Charity Foundation of Taipei County, and related projects in New York, Vancouver, Nepal, Burma, Thailand, Indonesia, and Hong Kong.

Ashok Vohra is professor of Philosophy at Delhi University and has published more than one hundred and seventy research papers and articles in national and international research journals, anthologies, and newspapers. He taught for over a decade (1975-1986) at St. Stephens College. He was the Member Secretary of the Indian Council of Philosophical Research from

1995 to 1998, and Director of Gandhi Bhawan, Delhi University from 1998 to 2000. He was the Vice-president of UNESCO's Asia Pacific Philosophy Education for Democracy (APPEND) for a term of two years from January 1999 to December 2000. He is the author of *Wittgenstein's Philosophy of Mind* (London, Sydney, 1986, reissued in the Routledge Revivals Series, Routledge London, New York, 2014) and is the co-author of *Radhakrishnan: His Life and Ideas* (New York, 1990). He has translated into Hindi Ludwig Wittgenstein's *Philosophical Investigations* (Delhi, 1996); *On Certainty* (Delhi, 1998); *Culture and Value* (Delhi, 1998); and *Radhakrishnan Memorial Lectures 1996 and 1997* (Shimla, 2000). He has co-edited *The Philosophy of K. Satchidananda Murty* (Delhi, 1996); *Dharma: The Categorial Imperative* (Delhi, 2005) and *Man, Morals and Self: A Philosophical Perspective,* Viva Books (Delhi 2014). He has delivered special lectures in various Universities in India, USA, UK, Austria, Japan, Thailand, Kenya, North Korea, South Korea, Lithuania, Greece, Czechoslovakia, and Canada. He is on the editorial board of *Humanitas Asiatica*; *Journal of the Indian Council of Philosophical Research (JICPR); Suvidya: Journal of Philosophy and Religion,* Bangalore; *Indian Journal of Analytic Philosophy*, and *Unmilan*. He is on the Advisory Board of *Dialalato Corde*. He writes regularly for the *Times of India, Hindustan Times, The Tribune,* and *The Pioneer* on philosophical themes with a view to popularize them.

CPSIA information can be obtained at www.ICGtesting.com
Printed in the USA
BVOW07*0946130814

362491BV00002B/2/P

9 780739 192566